Stuffocation

For Thiru, Indy-May, and Woody
And for Jack, Pam, Guy, and Elsie

Copyright © 2013 by James Wallman

Published in the United States by Spiegel & Grau, an imprint of
Random House, a division of Penguin Random House LLC, New York.

Spiegel & Grau and the House colophon are
registered trademarks of Penguin Random House LLC.

Originally published in the United Kingdom in a digital
edition by Crux Publishing in 2013 and subsequently in
paperback by Penguin Books Ltd. in 2015.

Grateful acknowledgment is made to the following for
permission to use preexisting material:
Grist Magazine, Inc.: Excerpt from "The Medium Chill"
by David Roberts, Grist.org, June 28, 2011, copyright © 2011.
Used by permission of *Grist* Magazine, Inc.
Python (Monty) Pictures Limited: Quotes from *Monty Python's
Life of Brian* by Graham Chapman, John Cleese, Terry Gilliam,
Eric Idle, Terry Jones, and Michael Palin. Copyright © 1979.
Used by permission of Python (Monty) Pictures Limited.

Wallman, James.
Stuffocation : why we've had enough of stuff and need experience
more than ever / James Wallman.
pages cm
Includes index.
ISBN 978-0-8129-9759-0
eBook ISBN 978-0-8129-9760-6
1. Consumption (Economics)—Psychological aspects. 2. Consumer
behavior. 3. Quality of life. 4. Well-being. 5. Simplicity. I. Title.
HC79.C6W35 2015
306.3—dc23
2014036553

Printed in the United States of America on acid-free paper

www.spiegelandgrau.com

2 4 6 8 9 7 5 3 1

First U.S. Edition

Book design by Liz Cosgrove

Stuffocation

Why We've Had Enough of Stuff
and Need Experience More Than Ever

....

James Wallman

SPIEGEL & GRAU NEW YORK

Contents

Introduction: We've Had Enough of Stuff   ix

PART I. The Problem: Stuffocation

1. The Anthropologist and the Clutter Crisis   3

2. The Dark Side of Materialism   22

PART II. How We Got Here: The Origins of Throwaway Culture

3. The Original Mad Men and the Job of Creating Desire   37

4. Barbra Streisand and the Law of Unintended Consequences   49

PART III. The Crossroads: Signposts to a Better Future

5. I Love to Count: The 33, 47, 69, and 100 Things of Minimalism   59

6. The Simple Life and the Cage-Free Family   75

7. The Medium Chill   88

PART IV. The Road Ahead: The Rise of the Experientialists

8. To Do or to Have? That Is No Longer a Question   103

9. The Experientialists   109

10. Facebook Changed How We Keep Up with the Joneses   126

11. We Love to Count Too: The New Way to Measure
    Progress   145

12. What About the Chinese?   160

13. The Gypsy, the Wasp, and the Experience Economy   167

14. Can You Be an Experientialist and Still Love Stuff?   174

Conclusion: Why You Need Experience More Than Ever   199

Acknowledgments   208

Appendix: The Way of the Experientialist   212

Notes   228

Index   265

Introduction

We've Had Enough of Stuff

One Monday morning in September 2010, a man by the name of Ryan Nicodemus woke up in a room that was bare except for a bed. Outside the sky was blue. There was a light breeze. People were starting the week, sipping coffee, getting in their cars, driving north for Dayton, south for Cincinnati. It was a day like any other.

Nicodemus, a square-jawed Irish American who could pass for the movie star Ben Affleck, sat up and squinted. There was no bed-side lamp or table, no pictures, nothing—except for the bed he'd slept on and the sheets he'd slept under.

He pulled the sheets back and padded across the carpeted floor, past the empty closets, into the hallway. The house was stripped bare. The only thing in it was an eerie sound. "It was really strange," Nicodemus recalls. "Like silence, but very echoey."

If you had been there, waking up alone in that house, you would have thought you'd woken up in some sort of surreal dream, in a strange house the day after the owners had moved out—and left all their things in boxes and trash bags at the foot of the stairs.

Nicodemus went down and picked up a box. He read the label—"Miscellaneous no. 7"—and put it to one side. He picked up another—"Kitchen junk no. 2"—and did the same. He kept going till he found "Bathroom no. 1." He rummaged inside. He pulled out shower gel, toothpaste, toothbrush. He started on the bags, till he found, and took out, one towel. He tied the bags closed, he shut the boxes, and he went upstairs to shower.

As water washed over him, Nicodemus wondered. How did it feel? Odd? Better? Was a home with no stuff better or worse? This wasn't a dream, you see. It was an experiment.

At the time Nicodemus was twenty-eight, and doing well. He had a girlfriend, a house, a job. He was making over $100,000 a year, managing stores for a telecom company called Cincinnati Bell. He liked what he did. He liked the people he worked with. He got a kick out of seeing his employees develop, and helping them sell one or two more things, so they could make their bonus or win that incentive trip to Hawaii. He wore Brooks Brothers suits, $300 shoes, and $100 ties. He had a hundred $100 ties. On the weekend, he went off-roading on an $8,000 four-wheeler with his buddies. He played Xbox and watched movies on his top-of-the-line, 53-inch Samsung TV. He drove a brand-new, metallic blue Toyota Tacoma, one of those big boy's toys that look like a life-size Tonka Truck.

"If you'd told my eighteen-year-old self what I was going to have at twenty-eight," Nicodemus says now, "I would've been the most excited eighteen-year-old there ever was. I would've been, 'Like, are you kidding me? This is gonna be the best life ever!'"

But ten years later, it did not feel like the best life ever. Nicodemus was not happy. Instead, he was confused. "I almost felt," he says, "ungrateful—'cause I had everything I'd always wanted."

At first, he kept plugging away, working, spending, hoping the feeling would go. But no matter how much he earned and how many things he bought, he could not shake it. Then a thought occurred to him. Maybe there had been a mistake. Maybe the happiness equation was wrong.

1. THE HAPPINESS EQUATION

Nicodemus grew up poor, in Lebanon, Ohio—population twenty thousand, average income $20,000. When his parents split he stayed in a run-down apartment with his mother. She was too busy with drink and drugs to notice the filth, the cockroaches, her son. So, at age twelve, he moved in with his father. Eric Nicodemus ran a small business called Nicodemus Fine Paint and Wallcovering. He was a devout Jehovah's Witness. He kept a clean house. Was it inevitable that Ryan ricocheted like a pinball between his father's God and his mother's demons? He took drugs. He went to church. He ate a lot.

During school holidays when Ryan worked for his father, he saw how the other half decorated their homes and how they seemed to have the sort of happiness he was looking for.

One day, father and son were in their overalls at a job. The house was nothing fancy. Everything was modern and new, apart from a grandfather clock in the hallway. As Ryan was setting things up, taking the family pictures off the walls, he noticed that the people in the pictures looked really happy. That morning, the owners had seemed pretty happy too. Maybe they were. Looking around he wondered: maybe this nice, middle-class house was the kind of home happy people lived in.

"Dad," he said. "How much would I have to make to own a house like this?"

"Son," Eric replied in his gruff, "Dad" voice. "About $50,000 a year."

It was that simple. Happiness had a look: the inside of that house. And it had a price tag: $50,000. Nicodemus shared this golden secret—"happiness = $50,000 a year"—with his best friend, Joshua Fields Millburn.

Today, Millburn is slim and good-looking. He looks like a younger version of the actor Christopher Walken. He has a wave of blond hair that rises straight up like Walken's. His smile is halfway between pleased-with-himself and please-listen-to-me. Back then though, he was just like Nicodemus: a fat teenager from a broken home.

After they left school, Millburn and Nicodemus worked their tails off to fulfill their side of the happiness equation. A few years later, they reached the magic number. That meant they should be happy, right? If only life was that simple. Millburn soon worked out the problem.

"The equation is wrong," he told Nicodemus one day. "We didn't adjust for inflation. Maybe it's not $50,000, maybe it's $80,000." Now, that made sense. After all, inflation meant things cost more, especially the things you wanted, the good stuff. And if the cost of the good stuff rose, that meant the cost of the good life would go up too.

So they kept on, working, spending, competing. Nicodemus bought a 1,700-square-foot house. Millburn got one that was 2,000 square feet. Nicodemus drove a Toyota. Millburn had a Lexus. Nicodemus owned a hundred ties. Millburn didn't have quite that many, but he did have seventy shirts by Brooks Brothers, and fifteen of their suits—three more than Nicodemus's twelve.

But it did not matter how much they earned or what they bought, whether they had more than before or than each other. Every time they hit the new inflation-adjusted target, the happiness equation did not work. It was like chasing the pot of gold at the end of the rainbow. Eventually, another thought occurred to Millburn: What if they didn't only need to adjust for inflation? What if the happiness equation was just plain wrong?

"All the things around me that were supposed to bring happiness weren't bringing me happiness at all," Millburn says now. "In fact, it was the opposite. Instead of happiness, I got debt, stress, discontent. I was overwhelmed. Eventually I got depressed."

Around that time, Millburn came across some people online who had a radically different idea of happiness. They were called "mini-malists," and they thought that the best route to happiness was not by getting *more*, but by having *less*. If it worked for them, could it work for him and Nicodemus too? It had to be worth a shot.

But what if it didn't work, and they only found that out after they had gotten rid of all their stuff? So they hatched a plan. To find out if they would be happier living with less stuff, they decided to run an experiment. They would put all Nicodemus's things in his house into bags and boxes, just like he was moving. Each time he wanted something, he would take it back out. The experiment would last twenty-one days. They had read it took that long for a new habit to stick. By the end of that time, Nicodemus would find out how much stuff he really needed, and if living with less made him happier.

It did. He never got around to unpacking all the things he had stuffed into bags and boxes. He took some things out, of course. After waking up that morning in echoey silence, he went looking for things like a toothbrush, toothpaste, and clothes to go to work in. And he took more things out—like a knife, a fork, a spoon, and a plate—as he needed them each day.

But after day ten, Nicodemus did not take anything else out. By then, he realized he had everything he needed. It wasn't the sound of the house that felt odd now. It was the waste. "It really opened my eyes to how little I used all the stuff I owned," he recalls. "Thinking about all the money I'd wasted on all that stuff—now, that was a really surreal feeling."

He had worried about what his girlfriend would think, but she thought the whole thing was funny. "She'd come into the living room grinning," recalls Nicodemus, "and say, 'Honey, have you seen *the spoon?*'"

Satisfied that he had enough and that less really was better, Nico-demus got rid of all the stuff still packed away. He sold some things on eBay and Craigslist. He gave others away. He filled a truck with stuff for his father to take to church. And then he started a new life with far fewer material possessions.

Many of us, at some point, have questioned whether we are really happy with our lives and our jobs, whether we're just working to make the payments on the things we own, and if we really need all that junk cluttering up our homes and our lives. So, every now and then, to keep that wondering voice quiet, we do a quick clear-out, spend less time working, and more time at home doing the things we enjoy—and we stop there. Nicodemus didn't. When he did a clear-out, he packed everything away, and most of it stayed boxed and bagged up till he gave it away. He stopped wanting and buying new things. He stopped working so many hours to pay for all those things he didn't really need. He started living with much less stuff. Instead of trying to reach materialistic targets, he started striving for other goals, like being healthy and having good relationships. And it worked. He is now, as he has told me many times, much happier. Why? Why did he find that living with fewer things meant more happiness? And is this new happiness equation good only for him, Millburn, and a handful like them, or will it work for the rest of us?

2. ARE YOU STUFFOCATING TOO?

Stuffocation is the story of one of today's most acute, till now unnamed, afflictions. It is about how you, me, and society in general, instead of feeling enriched by the things we own, are feeling stifled by them. Instead of thinking of *more* in positive terms, as we once did, we now think *more* means more hassle, more to manage, and more to think about. In our busy, cluttered lives *more* is no longer better. It is worse. Overwhelmed, and suffocating from stuff, we are suffering from an anxiety that I call Stuffocation.

Nicodemus, you see, is not the only one. There are millions, right now, all around the world, feeling like they have too much stuff. There are the two million, to begin with, who read the blog and books Nicodemus and Millburn write about living with less stuff each year. Then there are the twelve million—as many as live in

Greater London, or in New York and Los Angeles combined—who have seen a film online called *The Story of Stuff,* about the disastrous ecological impact of materialism. After watching the film and learning, for instance, that for every bag of rubbish they put out, another seventy bags of waste have been created to make the goods that filled that bag, most of them probably feel that they would like less stuff in their lives. And there are many more.

A political scientist by the name of Ronald Inglehart has been following people's attitudes toward material things—stuff—since 1970. When he began his research, he found, in the six countries he surveyed—the U.K., France, West Germany, Italy, the Netherlands, and Belgium—that four out of five people held materialist values. Most people were more concerned about how much money and how many things they had, and less bothered about quality of life issues.

Political scientists have been conducting similar surveys, at regular intervals, ever since in more than fifty countries. The message from the research is clear: we are becoming far less materialistic, as only around one in two now hold materialist values. "Almost half the people are now post-materialists," says Inglehart. It may even be more than that.

When one of the world's largest advertising agencies conducted a survey a few years back in countries like the U.K., France, and the United States, they found that "people in mature markets have had enough of excess," that they are "tired of the push to accumulate more," and that half have thrown out or thought about throwing out stuff in recent years. They also discovered that two in every three think they would be better off if they lived more simply—with less stuff, in other words.

When the same advertising agency repeated the survey in 2014, they reported that "many of us feel weighed down by our own excess," that "a majority of us could live happily without *most of the goods we own*" (their italics, not mine), and that "two-thirds of us make it a point to rid ourselves of unneeded possessions at least once a year."

If these numbers are right, that means there are around 240 million in the United States and 40 million in the U.K. who are actively "de-Stuffocating," and who would prefer a simpler life with fewer material things.

Maybe you feel it too. Have you had enough of excess? Are you tired of the push to accumulate more? Would you, truth be told, be happier if you had fewer things than you have right now? Take a trip through the cupboards, drawers, and shelves of your homes, in the quiz below, to find out if you—like Nicodemus and millions of others around the world—are also suffering from Stuffocation.

HAVE YOU HAD ENOUGH OF STUFF?

1. Do you feel like your possessions bring you (a) more joy or (b) more stress?

2. Is (a) everything well organized throughout your home, or (b) are there "clutter ghettos"—no-go zones you can't use and don't dare enter because of all the stuff that needs clearing out?

3. When someone you live with brings something home is your typical response (a) "why didn't we think of that before" or (b) "but where are we going to keep it"?

4. Do you (a) only have possessions you use regularly, or (b) do you keep things because they represent the person you would like to be—like the classic novels you really should read, the guitar you're definitely going to learn to play, or the clothes that *will* fit once you've reached your ideal size?

5. Do you (a) find it fairly easy to manage your belongings, or (b) do you wish that a "clutter fairy" would show up and organize everything for you, figuring out what you really need, and getting rid of the rest?

6. Do you (a) wear everything in your closet, or (b) do you have clothes you haven't worn for more than a year or more?

7. If you want to hang a new dress or shirt in your wardrobe,

is it (a) easy to pop it in there, or (b) do you have to heave the stuff that's already there left and right to make a gap, then jump in with the new thing before the gap closes up again?

8. Does (a) everything fit inside your drawers, or (b) when you open a drawer, do clothes pop out like they're trying to get some air?

9. When the kitchen looks clean and tidy, like a picture in an interiors magazine, is it (a) like that behind the doors too, or (b) are all those cupboard doors camouflage for the bedlam behind?

10. If you have a garage, do you (a) park your car in there, or (b) is it packed so full with stuff, there's no room for cars?

11. Do all your belongings (a) fit in your home, or (b) do you have so many you rent storage space?

12. Does "retail therapy" (a) pick you up or (b) leave you feeling deflated?

13. Are you (a) happy with our current materialistic culture, or (b) do you worry that it is, from an environmental point of view, like the proverbial frog in the saucepan as the water slowly comes to the boil?

14. Are you (a) happy with, or (b) do you feel like there's something wrong with, a society that places so much importance on the ownership of physical objects?

15. Think back to the last time someone gave you something in the last year. Perhaps it was at Christmas, when Auntie Doreen and Uncle Peter held out a gift-wrapped box. Maybe it was your birthday, when your mother really shouldn't have, but did, and handed over something, she said, was just the perfect thing for you. Was your gut reaction to think (a) "can't wait to see what it is" or (b) "not more stuff"?

If your answer was (b) to any of these questions, you too are suffering in some way from Stuffocation.

SHERLOCK HOLMES AND THE MYSTERY OF THE KRISPY KREMES

So why do we keep buying more and more, even though we already have more than we need and can cope with? The best way to throw light on this is through a story I think of as "The Mystery of the Krispy Kremes."

On Thursday, February 14, 2013, the Lothian and Borders police received what sounded, on the face of it, like a routine call. There was a traffic jam out on the ring road, by a shopping center called Hermiston Gait. Most other places wouldn't have mattered so much, but Hermiston Gait is by the start of the M8, one of the busiest motorways in the U.K. and the main artery connecting Scotland's two biggest cities, Edinburgh and Glasgow. Commanders at HQ soon decided to do what any police force anywhere around the world would have done, given the circumstances. They warned drivers to avoid the area, and sent a couple of squad cars over to check out the reason for the problem—the new Krispy Kreme doughnut store.

When it had opened for the first time at 7 A.M., an hour before sunrise, the previous day, three hundred people were lined up outside. Staff served coffee and the brand's doughnuts as quickly as they could. They served four hundred customers in the first hour of opening, setting a new Krispy Kreme record. But even that was not fast enough. No matter how hard they tried, the line of people outside kept growing and the line of cars for the store's drive-through kept building. First it jammed the retail park. Then it slowed down the cars and trucks on the roundabout. By the next day, it was clogging up the traffic for the M8. That was when the police came over to check on the queue, and the doughnuts.

Not everyone was as excited about the new store as all those people lining up. "I'm absolutely speechless," grumbled Tam Fry, a spokesman for Britain's National Obesity Forum. "If Edinburgh is overweight today, it will be obese tomorrow."

Krispy Kreme's Original Glazed contains 217 calories, including 22 grams of carbohydrate and 13 grams of fat. The calorie counts go up from there. Krispy Kreme doughnuts are, it's fair to say, not the world's healthiest snack.

The people standing outside knew this. The people sitting in their cars knew this. So why did they wait—for up to two hours—to get served, when they knew the thing they were queuing for was not even good for them?

Before you decide the answer is obvious—this is Scotland, home of the deep-fried Mars Bar, and therefore "case closed"—consider your own behavior for a moment. You know that Krispy Kremes, and all sorts of things, are not very good for you. Yet, every now and then, you eat them. Sometimes, you even queue up for them. Why?

There is no one better to solve this riddle than Brian Wansink, a food scientist sometimes introduced as the "Sherlock Holmes of food." Wansink has been working out why we eat what we eat for more than two decades. The answer to the Krispy Kreme question is in his book *Mindless Eating*. "We are hardwired to love the taste of fat, salt, and sugar," he wrote. "Fatty foods gave our ancestors the calorie reserves to weather food shortages. Salt helped them retain water and avoid dehydration. Sugar helped them distinguish sweet edible berries from sour poisonous ones. Through our taste for fat, salt, and sugar, we learned to prefer the foods that were most likely to keep us alive."

Wansink's explanation of why we like certain foods draws on a branch of the social sciences called evolutionary psychology. This not only makes sense of the sort of foods we are attracted to but also how much we eat. "We have millions of years of evolution and instinct telling us," Wansink wrote, "to eat as often as we can and as much as we can."

That wisdom made sense when food was scarce. But it made a lot less sense when, in the twentieth century, synthetic fertilizers and higher-yielding seeds and combine harvesters started to produce not only enough, but much more than enough.

This has given us an entirely new problem. Because although the automatic impulse to eat as much as possible is no longer appropriate, we haven't been able to simply turn it off like a light switch. Hardwired to eat, many of us have become fat. So many, in fact, that we now have a name for this problem: the obesity epidemic.

The idea that we are making decisions in an age of abundance using mental tools honed in an age of scarcity might seem obvious. But it is worth repeating at a time when many millions of us not only have enough, but way too much stuff. Evolutionary psychology is key to understanding why we keep wanting and buying more, even when we already have far more than enough.

We are now living in an age of material abundance. Before, material goods were expensive and scarce. Clothes, for instance, were so hard to come by that they were handed down from generation to generation. A shirt, before the Industrial Revolution, would have been ruinously expensive in terms of time, effort, and money: a historian called Eve Fisher has calculated that a shirt would have been worth around $3,500 in today's money. (See the third note on page 230 for how she added that up.) But now, things—shirts, shoes, cups, cars, glasses, books, toys, and a million other things—are ubiquitous and cheap. Once again, our inbuilt impulses have yet to catch up. As a result, many millions of us are filling our homes and lives with stuff. Overwhelmed and suffocated by stuff, we, as individuals, are suffering from Stuffocation. As a society, we are suffering from Stuffocation. Stuffocation is the material equivalent of the obesity epidemic.

STUFFOCATION IS A HEALTH HAZARD

Obesity is one of the most worrying problems we face, as individuals and as a society. Being overweight means you're more likely to have a heart attack or a stroke, or develop type 2 diabetes, an unpleasant condition that could take away your sight, arms, and legs. Being overweight means that you will probably die younger. If you are severely obese, you will die a full decade earlier than you would have. Despite all these nasty consequences, two thirds of people are now overweight or obese. Worryingly, not everyone agrees on the solution to this enormous problem, because no one knows for sure what is causing obesity—even though most scientists agree that it is some combination of what they call the "Big Two": eating too much and exercising too little. Even more worrying is the impact obesity could have on the next generation. So many children have weight issues today that they could be the first generation to live shorter lives than their parents. Given the seriousness of the obesity epidemic, saying that Stuffocation is similar is quite a statement.

Yet it is, I believe, a good comparison. Because both obesity and Stuffocation have similar numbers of sufferers. Because while there are many explanations for each—evolutionary, environmental, and work-related reasons, for instance—each has its Big Two factors. Moreover, just as obesity is bad for us, as individuals and as a society, so Stuffocation is bad for us as well. Just as eating too much and exercising too little is detrimental to a person's physical health and the health of society at large, so having too much and doing too little is damaging for an individual's mental health and the general well-being of our society.

Having too much, doing too little, and living a life focused on the accumulation of material things—according to a growing number of experts and studies, which I will introduce in this book—is making people anxious and causing them stress. It can, so new research suggests, lead to the sort of depression that makes people die before their time. In a few, extreme cases, it can even kill far more quickly. And since as many as two thirds of us feel like we have too much stuff, Stuffocation is clearly a very worrying problem.

What exactly are we going to do about it? Usually, in our modern societies, when we realize something, a product or an activity, say, is bad for people's health, we take steps to control it. In the name of making us healthier, the government passes legislation, runs ad campaigns, and nudges us to make better decisions. Take obesity, for instance, and the label information that encourages us to eat less of the wrong foods, like sugar and saturated fats, and more of the good ones, like vegetables. Or think about smoking. When the truth about the harms of smoking came to light, warning labels appeared on tobacco products with slogans like "Cigarette smoking may be hazardous to your health."

I wonder if, as the evidence grows about the damage that having too much stuff has on our psychological health, we will one day see Stuffocation-specific information and warning labels on other products as well. Perhaps the government, as it becomes more interested in our mental as well as physical well-being, will want labels on products that nudge us to buy the ones that are good for us, and avoid the ones that are bad. Maybe one day, products that cause clutter, and that bring more anxiety and stress than happiness, might carry warnings like "Having too much stuff may be hazardous to your health."

THE PERFECT STORM

If you consider the health hazards of Stuffocation, you can see in a split second why it is a problem we urgently need to solve. There are those who might talk about evolutionary psychology and the Big Two, and rush into a naïve tactical solution. But to have the best, most realistic chance of creating a strategy that will successfully solve Stuffocation in the long term, we need to know more about what is causing it.

The Mystery of the Krispy Kremes is useful. By illustrating how the decisions we make today have evolved over millennia, it makes sense of why we keep buying more and more things, even though we already have more than we need and more than we can cope with. It sheds light on how we got here. But if you think about it a little longer, you can see that while it explains why Stuffocation is happening, it does not make sense of why it is happening now. So the questions we need to ask are: Why have so many of us had enough of stuff now? And, why is it *now* that we are turning away from materialism?

As with anything as supersized and seismic as Stuffocation, there are many explanations. Ask a different expert, and you will hear a different emphasis.

A political scientist, like Ronald Inglehart, for instance, would say that because more of us have grown up in stable situations where we haven't had to worry about where our next meal was coming from, we have become less concerned about basic material needs like food and shelter, and more interested in post-materialist needs such as having the freedom to say what we want to say and do what we want to do.

A philosopher, like Alain de Botton, and psychologists, such as Oliver James and Darby Saxbe, would refer you to the health hazards we've just talked about. They would say we've had enough of stuff because our possessions, and the lifestyle and hassles that come with them, are causing us more stress than happiness. James calls this problem "affluenza." De Botton says keeping up with the Joneses is giving us "status anxiety." Saxbe would talk about the "clutter crisis."

An environmentalist will tell you we've had enough because of global warming, overstuffed landfills, our carbon footprint. We are worried that we are using up more resources than the planet can sustain.

A demographer might say that they can see that our stable upbringing, the stress of stuff, and the environment may all be valid, but there are four other, much more important reasons for Stuffocation: the aging population, the growing population, the rise of the global middle class, and the move to cities. As people get older they are less interested in having more things. As there are more people on our finite planet and more of them are becoming middle-class, there is ever more pressure on resources. And as more of us move to cities, we are buying fewer cars, and our homes are getting smaller, meaning less room to put things.

A social scientist, such as Ruth Milkman, would add that we are also increasingly tired of materialism because we simply don't believe in the system anymore. Milkman has pointed out that we are disillusioned with its inherent inequalities, that the protesters in the Occupy movement reflected the anger the rest of us felt.

Other social scientists might highlight the fact that we used to think that if we earned more and bought more things, it would make us happier. But new findings from a pioneering band of "happiness researchers," psychologists like Tim Kasser, Tom Gilovich, Elizabeth Dunn, and Ryan Howell, have shown that this is not the case, and as this truth reaches the mainstream it is encouraging people to shift their loyalty from possessions to experiences.

An economist might smile at all these explanations. Sure, she might say, our stable upbringing, the stress of stuff, the environment, the aging population, the growing population, the rise of the global middle class, the move to cities, a lack of belief in the system, and knowing that experiences are more likely to make us happier—all of these are important. But the real reason for Stuffocation is obvious: it's economics, stupid. In a world of rising costs and stagnating incomes, most people simply do not have the money to keep buying more stuff. So rather than "had enough," it may be more accurate to say that we cannot afford so much anymore.

A technologist might agree with all this, and then tell you the real reason why we are turning away from material goods is, actually, because we can. After all, what's the point in owning physical books and CDs when you can access them from the cloud?

And finally, what do I, a cultural forecaster, think? I have been analyzing trends and forecasting social change for more than a decade, helping clients such as Absolut, BMW, and Zurich Insurance prepare for the future. In the course of that work, it became increasingly clear to me that fundamental cracks are now appearing in the three key pillars of our society: the overarching structure of capitalism, the practice of consumerism, and the value system that underpins it all—materialism. When I looked around at solutions others were suggesting—like the anticapitalist and anticonsumerist movements, or the idea that technology will solve everything—none of them struck me as compelling or realistic alternatives. They all seemed too simplistic to me, like they were papering over the cracks rather than tackling the structural causes, or solving just one part of the problem and ignoring the rest. So I decided to strike out on my own, to see if I could use the human insights and analytical skills I had been practicing to find a better way forward. The result of that work is in this book.

When I write down this list of factors causing Stuffocation, a number of thoughts strike me. One is that they are more like waves than building blocks. Each has its own starting point, in other words, but does not rely on any of the others. So even if you disagree with the environmentalist, and you do not think people care enough about the environment to consume less stuff, that does not affect whether you agree or disagree with, say, the technologist or demographer. It is also perfectly possible to believe that each of the explanations is relevant and partly responsible for Stuffocation—and that is how I see them.

Even more important, the changes taking place are not minor blips that will be here one year, gone the next. The one exception is the economy and the fall in incomes. But as the economic situation improves and our incomes rise, and people have, and feel like they have, more money to buy stuff again, that will only exacerbate other factors, such as our concern for the environment.

All of the other factors causing Stuffocation—our stable upbringing, the stress of stuff, the environment, the aging population, the growing population, the rise of the middle class, the move to cities, a lack of belief in the system, knowing that experiences are more likely to make us happier, the rise in costs, and the switch to digital— are the result of well-documented, long-term trends. Taken singly, each of these would have the effect on our world of a wave as it swells and crashes against a sea wall. Since all are arriving at the same time, becoming more urgent, less avoidable, and more obvious, they are creating a perfect storm for our mixed-up materialist culture. That is why this will be one of the defining problems of this century. And it is why, right now, so many of us are disillusioned with material goods and materialism, and suffering from Stuffocation.

A NEW HAPPINESS EQUATION

There is a radical idea at the heart of Stuffocation, and it is one that is going to fundamentally alter our lives and upset a lot of apple carts—a lot of very big, very institutionalized apple carts, a lot of medium-size apple carts, and a lot of small personal apple carts. Perhaps even yours. Because an individual suffering from Stuffocation will make very different choices from the ones she or he made before, and a society responding to Stuffocation will look radically different from the one we have grown up in. How?

Until recently, the capitalist system we have been living in was largely based on a consumer who was materialistic. In that system, as in Nicodemus's original happiness equation, possessions and the pursuit of those possessions gave us status, identity, meaning, and happiness. In that world, greed was good, more was better, and material goods were the best way to keep up with the Joneses. They aren't anymore.

I don't want to bad-mouth all the stuff you've bought, though, or all the things I've accumulated over the years. And I don't want to bash materialism. Or, rather, not *just* bash it at any rate. I want, of course, to replace it. Materialism, and the consumer culture and capitalist system it underpinned, was the right idea for the right time. It meant that the masses, for the first time in human history, lived in abundance rather than scarcity. It gave us washing machines, TVs, and indoor toilets. It delivered clean water, the welfare state, and health care that has improved the length and quality of our lives. It has lifted living standards for those of us in the wealthy West. And while there are still many who do not have enough, let alone too much, materialism is now doing the same for billions of new consumers from Beijing to Bangalore, and from Lagos to São Paolo.

But materialism's success is catching up with us. All that abundance is, paradoxically, bringing scarcity once again. Now, for all the reasons causing Stuffocation, materialism is no longer such a great idea.

This book is about what I think should happen next. It is a call to arms. Because now that we know that materialism is bad for our health, bad for our happiness, bad for society, and bad for the planet, I think it is time to discard the old belief that more stuff equals more happiness, and, in its place, to create a new equation for happiness, and build a new manifesto for life.

This new manifesto should be informed by all the factors causing Stuffocation. It should be inspired by the realization, recently discovered by researchers like Gilovich and Howell, that experiences are more likely to lead to happiness. This idea should be the cornerstone of this new manifesto: the absolute imperative that happiness is more likely to come from the enjoyment of experiences rather than the accumulation of stuff.

This manifesto will serve as a new value system for a better, happier culture. Since the old value system, where people looked for status, identity, meaning, and happiness in material things, was called materialism, I think of this new way of living, where we find those in experiences instead, as "experientialism."

This book is more than simply a blueprint for better living. As well as being a prescription of what needs to change, it is also a description of what is going to happen in the future, and the changes happening right now.

As more people, like Nicodemus, question the system and decide that more is not better and that they will not find happiness in possessions, we will see nothing less than a cultural revolution. As more people realize that more stuff does not equal more happiness, but that the best place to find status, identity, meaning, and happiness is in experiences, we will witness the old age of materialism give way, I believe, to a new era of experientialism.

In this new era, we will buy fewer and different material goods.

What marketers call our buying motivators or consumption triggers will change, and they will change their business models. And the repercussions could be even more far-reaching. We will be more likely to choose our jobs based on what we want to do, rather than what we have to do to pay for possessions we don't really need. We will earn and judge status differently. Instead of projecting our own power through our material prowess, we will express our identities, and signify who we are—our character, our individuality—not through the purchase and ritual display of physical objects, however rare and valuable they may be, but through the activities, adventures, and encounters we experience. Government policy will shift as well, with less concern for the economy and gross domestic product, and more interest in new measures of progress.

I am not suggesting that this will all happen suddenly, that we will all wake up on the morning of, say, the New Year sales in 2016 or 2017, and our interest in material things will have vanished overnight. This cultural change, after all, is as significant as the shift our ancestors made when they gave up thrifty ways to become wasteful consumers in the twentieth century—and that took a good half century or so to really take hold. From the perspective of later historians, this will look like revolution, but from ours, it will feel much more like evolution.

And I am not claiming, even then, that we will get rid of all our things and become a bunch of possession-free ascetics. I do not think we will head for the hills and live naked in caves. We will still need and use shoes, bags, clothes, cars, and cell phones.

But it is my belief that, as we increasingly respond to Stuffocation, and more people join the experientialist revolution, we will accumulate far less, and we will do, feel, see, hear, touch, taste, smell, and experience far more.

Moreover, I think this is happening already, that the movement is already well under way. You may have felt the shift in your own outlook, or seen it in others. Where once you bought the people you care about material presents, perhaps you now think to yourself, "He has everything he needs," and you buy more experiential gifts. Where once you might have measured success in material terms, now you may be less bothered about quantity of stuff, and more concerned with experience and quality of life. After all, you have a big enough car, and more than enough stuff, so why earn more to buy a bigger car and more stuff, when you could take a trip or spend more time with your children or your friends? And perhaps you have noticed that a fancy car no longer signifies status the way it once did. Instead, you are now less likely to be impressed by what people *have* and more likely to be interested in what they *do*. To find out if you already think like an experientialist, or if you have it in you to become one, consider the questions in the quiz on the following page.

On the way to formulating the experientialist manifesto, we will cross continents and centuries—from sunrise over a Paleolithic tribe on the French Riviera forty thousand years ago, to the sun setting in New Mexico in the twenty-first century, as it turns the Sangre de Cristo Mountains scarlet red. On the way, we will walk the halls of the Élysée Palace with Nicolas Sarkozy, and we will witness the funniest superpower summit of the twentieth century, when Richard Nixon met Nikita Khrushchev. We will fly above Barbra Streisand's home on the California coast in a helicopter, and go back in time to the world of the original Mad Men.

The book is divided into five sections. In Part I, "The Problem: Stuffocation," you will read about detailed evidence—including video evidence gathered by scientifically sanctioned voyeurs in Los Angeles—that damns our current culture.

In Part II, "How We Got Here: The Origins of Throwaway Culture," you will find out how the original Mad Men and Women met the challenge of their era by architecting the materialistic system we have today.

In Part III, "The Crossroads: Signposts to a Better Future," I will introduce the innovators who are rejecting today's materialistic culture, and trying out new post-materialist ways of living. We will consider what they're doing, and why they're doing it, and find the signposts in the ways they are living today that point to a brighter future for us all.

In Part IV, "The Road Ahead: The Rise of the Experientialists," we will examine in detail—through rainy adventure weekends, squeaky shoes, and bus journeys that go horribly wrong—why experiences are better than material goods at making us happy. We will also meet some experientialists, and examine the ups, downs, and challenges of the experientialist revolution. We will ask: Is big business supporting it? Is the government? And, most important, will it work for you too?

The final section, "Appendix: The Way of the Experientialist," contains all you need to try out experientialism, and instructions on how to redesign your life and join the experientialist movement for the long haul.

And the point of all this—this book, this discussion, these sections—is not only to offer an opinion on one of the defining problems of our generation. It is to ask and answer the essential questions that we—as individuals, parents, and people who create the culture we live in—should be asking right now: Now that we know about the anxiety, stress, depression, and environmental destruction that comes with materialism, what is the best alternative? How can we solve the problems of Stuffocation? And how should we live in order to be happy in the twenty-first century?

COULD YOU BE AN EXPERIENTIALIST?

Answer the 20 questions in this quiz to find out if you think like an experientialist already, or if you have it in you to become one.

The best way to take this quiz is to take it twice. The first time, answer the questions as quickly as possible, to get your gut reaction. The second time around, give yourself a little more time to reflect, and notice whether you are happy with what you said the first time around. If you listen carefully to your reactions, you may note a difference between the person you are now and the person you would like to be. For some of us, these are the same. For many people, though, if we are honest, there is a gap between who we aspire to be and who we are now. That is not necessarily a bad thing. It is best to think of this as information you can use as a springboard for change.

1. Do you define yourself more (a) by objects you own, like your car, house, watch, or handbag, or (b) by experiences, like the sports, hobbies, and activities you take part in and the adventures you have?

2. Do you aspire to live (a) the rich life you see in reality television programs and celebrity magazines, or (b) a life rich in friendships, relationships, and experiences?

3. Are you more likely to catch yourself (a) comparing your life circumstances with others, or (b) wondering when you'll get a chance to go there, see this, or do that?

4. When you say someone is successful, do you mean (a) they have lots of expensive things, or (b) they enjoy life?

5. If you could pick a fantasy home, would it be (a) a huge house filled with rare, beautiful, expensive things, or (b) a tiny apartment in a great location with a wealth of things to do on the doorstep?

6. If you're feeling a bit low, are you more likely to (a) get some retail therapy—"buying new things always makes me feel great," or (b) see some friends—"seeing people always cheers me up"?

7. You're choosing your next job. Is your decision (a) based mostly on the money, or (b) are other factors equally important, like what the commute is like, how long the hours are, and whether you're interested in the work or not?

8. On a work trip to New York or London, your boss announces that you are not needed today and can have the day off. Which would you do: (a) hit the sales in shops like Macy's and Bloomingdale's, or Selfridges and Harvey Nichols, or (b) see

the city, doing things like go up the Empire State Building, bicycle through Central Park, and watch a basketball game in Harlem, or go on the London Eye and wander Portobello Road market?

9. Which gets top billing in your mind: (a) a shopping list of things to buy, or (b) a bucket list of things to do?

10. You have won a game show, and can choose either (a) $100,000 worth of physical goods, or (b) $100,000 of experiential goods. Which do you pick?

11. If you had to give up either (a) your car, or (b) the memory of a weekend away, which would you keep?

12. Which makes you feel more secure: (a) a bagful of things, or (b) a mind full of memories?

13. Which thought makes you want to jump up out of your seat and be there now: (a) the shops, or (b) the park?

14. Which would win your heart: (a) an amazing piece of jewelry, say a necklace or a watch, or (b) a weekend away?

15. Would you rather (a) get a bespoke dress by Diane von Furstenberg, or (b) attend the DVF runway show?

16. When you give presents, do you prefer to give (a) things, or (b) experiences?

17. Which would you prefer to curl up with: (a) a home shopping catalog, or (b) a novel?

18. Which impresses you more: (a) when someone tells you they have a Rolex, or (b) when they tell you they have walked up Kilimanjaro?

19. Which statement do you agree with more? (a) The problem with experiences is they don't last very long. You do it, and it's over. (b) The great thing about experiences is not only are they fun at the time, but you also get to think about them beforehand, and after.

20. Which statement do you agree with more? (a) When I go away, I always try to bring some souvenirs back, and take lots of photos, so it's more memorable, and so it's something I can

hold on to. (b) I'm not bothered about taking photos when I'm on vacation—I find they get in the way of enjoying the moment.

Give yourself zero points for every time you answered (a), one point for every (b), and add up your score.

If you scored 0 points, you are a committed materialist. You now have two options: put the book down, or be prepared to challenge many of the values you hold dear. If you're prepared to give it a try, you could well end up much happier—especially when you read the bit about how experiences are more likely to lead to happiness.

If you scored 5–10, you are quite materialistic at this point. But, as Luke Skywalker almost said to Darth Vader, there is experientialism in you, I can feel it.

If you scored 10–15, there are the beginnings of a fully fledged experientialist heart beating inside you. A few steps, and you could well be joining the experientialist revolution.

If you scored above 15—and especially if you chose (b) in the last two questions—great news. You are one of the lucky, enlightened few who already realize that experiences bring more joy, connection, and identity than objects. You might think this is all obvious, and to you it probably feels that way. But whether it is something you have thought about or not, you think like an experientialist.

If you're in a sharing mood, spread the news of the experientialist movement by taking the quiz online at www.stuffocation.org and using the buttons there to share your score.

PART I

The Problem:
Stuffocation

1

The Anthropologist and
the Clutter Crisis

Sometime in the summer of 2000, there was a knock on the door of Jeanne Arnold's office. It was most likely one of her doctoral candidates or grad students, come to ask her about methodology or whether an inference they were making about some evidence they had brought back from a dig sounded reasonable. In those days, Arnold's salt-and-pepper hair was swept up and back in a bouffant style that ended somewhere around her shoulders. The glasses she wore had oversized, 1980s-style metal frames. She looked up from her research, and smiled when she saw Elinor Ochs, one of her colleagues at the University of California, Los Angeles. "Got a minute, Jeanne?" Ochs asked—when what she really meant was, "Have you got ten years?"

Ochs was putting together a bid for a project, she explained. Would Arnold be interested in working with her on it? She was gathering a team to document life in the twenty-first century. They would use the same methods as anthropologists studying tribes in Africa, or archaeologists analyzing a dead civilization's remains, like Inca ruins in South America—except they would be doing the work right there in Los Angeles, with case studies who were very much still alive. The study would be the first of its kind. Well, there had been one or two studies a bit like it before, like one in New York that looked at the art people bought. But there had never been a study as ambitious as this. Instead of trying to understand people through one aspect of their lives, the plan was to record as much of their lives as possible, to create the definitive record of how people were living in the early part of the twenty-first century. The project, Ochs said, could really use a material culture expert like Jeanne. Arnold was not sure though. It sounded exciting, like it might be groundbreaking, but this wasn't really her field.

Arnold's specialty was the past, not the present. That had been her passion ever since she had gotten the bug as a little girl. Back then, she had spent her long summer holidays in the woods by her home near the Great Lakes, digging up crinoids and leaf fossils and arrowheads. "They were only little," Arnold recalls. "Nothing a real paleontologist or archaeologist would be interested in."

They were a start though. And as Arnold grew, so did her interest in the ancient past, especially archaeology, and its sister discipline, anthropology. She studied them at summer camp, at the local university, and then at the University of California. That is where, in 1980, she stumbled across her life's work—a native tribe called the Chumash and their old home on Santa Cruz, one of the Channel Islands off the coast of California.

When Arnold talks about the Chumash sites now, you can almost see her arriving on Santa Cruz those thirty-odd years ago. She would have just stepped off the navy supply boat. It was the only way to reach the island back then. It went once a week. The wind would have been blowing her brown hair around as she walked up the green hill to the site. There, she would have walked around wearing dark sunglasses, reading the landscape the way only an archaeologist could. Where you or I would have only seen dips in the ground, she saw the footprints of real people, and hints of where the Chumash had sited their pole and thatched huts. If you or I had ferreted around in the ground, we might have found some old fish bones. "A Chumash toss zone," Arnold would say. "They weren't bothered about mess. After they'd eaten, they just threw them on the ground." If we had kept looking we might have found, even up here, far from the sea, shell remains and the beginnings of beads. That is when Arnold would have asked us to stop. Those remains were for the professionals. With those, and many more like them, she could understand how the Chumash lived, what mattered to them, and how their society was structured.

After more than a decade of gathering and analyzing Chumash artifacts, Arnold realized she was not only excavating a site, she was building a case. Until the late twentieth century, the conventional wisdom had been that complex societies, in which there is an established hierarchy of a ruling elite and bureaucrats, had only emerged from agricultural communities—like Egypt under the pharaohs, for instance. But as the years went by and the evidence stacked up, Arnold became convinced that the Chumash—who hunted, gathered, and fished, but did not farm—had also lived in a complex society called a chiefdom. "That meant," Arnold will tell you now, "that a society didn't have to be agricultural for complex systems to emerge." In other words, as Arnold's work helped prove, the conventional wisdom was wrong, and it had to be replaced with a new theory that reflected the new evidence. "There are a few grumpy old men out there who still say they're not persuaded," Arnold admits. "But they're slowly disappearing."

Arnold was the sort of person who was not afraid of confronting the conventional wisdom when it no longer accurately reflected the evidence. No wonder Ochs wanted someone like her on the team.

After a few days, Arnold said she was in. Then she and the rest of Ochs's team at the Center on the Everyday Lives of Families (CELF)—

anthropologists, archaeologists, ethnographers, photographers, and psychologists—worked out a methodology, and got approval and the funds they needed. In 2000, the team set to work, and soon found themselves in the middle of a clutter crisis of epidemic proportions.

THE MIDDLE-CLASS CLUTTER CRISIS

With funding and methodology established, the CELF team began the next task: finding some families who were willing to open their lives to scientific inquiry—average, middle-class ones who were typical of households everywhere, and thirty-two of them. Once they had found them, explained what the commitment would mean to their lives, and what it would mean for social scientists who wanted to understand life at the turn of the twenty-first century, they began. They noted the makeup of their households, the size of their homes, what jobs they did. Each family had at least one child aged between seven and twelve. Their homes ranged from 980 to 3,000 square feet. The professions of the parents included teachers and lawyers, dentists and businesspeople, an airline pilot and a firefighter.

Ochs's team drew up plans of their homes. They photographed them—their bedrooms, bathrooms, kitchens, living rooms, playrooms, second bathrooms, garages, gardens. They came early. They stayed late. They asked questions. They stayed silent. But they never stopped taking notes—of where their case studies went, what they did, when they ate, what they ate. They were like flies on the wall or spy drones in the air, always there. They were the ultimate voyeurs, granted special permission to access all areas of their case studies' homes. And even when the scientists were not there, they found another way in. They gave the families video cameras to record their own home video diaries.

Sometimes it got to be too much—for the scientists at least. Once, when one family was having a heated argument, the researcher who was following them around could not cope and had to go outside.

But rather than stop recording what was happening, he carried on watching through the window of the family's bungalow. When the people inside—still arguing—moved to another room, he moved too. He stepped round the house and stood outside that room's window, still watching, still making notes.

As well as observing, Ochs's team did a lot of counting. Since they knew many counts would run to the thousands, they decided to use a set of counting rules devised especially for the project by someone who had gathered and counted and analyzed hundreds of thousands of artifacts for more than two decades—Jeanne Arnold. The aim of Arnold's rules was to help the counters all count the same way, and create verifiable, scientifically valid results. The first rule was that they would not look in cupboards or cabinets. They would only count what was visible. Arnold's second rule was to count not in the case studies' homes but only from photographs—in case someone asked a question and put the counter off, in case the counter just forgot what number she or he had reached, and so they could double-check the counting later. They would paste the photos together carefully to avoid double counting. Then they would begin: How many paintings? How many computers? How many chairs? And then they would tally up all the different categories.

CELF's researchers gathered a vast amount of data. They spent four years collecting it, and seven analyzing it. "It took that long to describe and digitize everything," Arnold will tell you, "and to work out what on earth was going on."

In all there were four terabytes of data, which is 4,000,000,000,000 pieces of information. The families made forty-seven hours of their own home video tours. Ochs's team shot 1,540 hours of videotape. They took 19,987 photos. And they counted a ton of stuff.

As the years went by and the mountains of evidence grew, some of the numbers and the observations, to tell the truth, shocked the researchers. They were amazed at how little time adults were spending outside in their gardens—less than fifteen minutes per week on average, even though they had often spent a lot of money on fancy barbecues and outdoor dining sets. They were surprised at how child-centric the houses were. Thirty-one of the thirty-two homes had things on display in the living room—like plaques, ribbons, trophies, certificates, and beauty contest tiaras—that showed off how well the kids were doing. They were, to be brutally honest, gobsmacked at what they saw some of the kids getting away with. One time, for instance, a mother told her little girl and little boy she had to make a conference call. It wouldn't take long, she said, but it was an important call with some important people at work. Could they keep it down for a few minutes? Then, moments after she had taken the call, as if on cue, her son started banging his drums and her daughter started playing her trumpet—both as loud as they could.

Above all, though, the researchers were astounded by how much stuff people had. The smallest home in the study, for instance, a house of 980 square feet, contained, in the two bedrooms and living room alone, 2,260 items. That count, remember, was only of the things that were visible. That did not include any of the stuff that was tucked into drawers or squeezed into cupboards.

The other homes were similarly packed. On average, each of the families had 39 pairs of shoes, 90 DVDs or videos, 139 toys, 212 CDs, and 438 books and magazines. Nine out of ten of them had so many things that they kept household stuff in the garage. Three quarters of them had so much stuff in there, there was no room left for the things that their garages were originally designed for—cars.

These families, these typical middle-class families, no doubt, have a lot of stuff. But when you think about it, a lot does not necessarily mean clutter. A lot of things could be a collection, like a set of books, records, CDs, clothes, or even toys that are tidily arranged, perhaps color-coded or neatly folded, or in height or alphabetical order. As well as being a lot of things, there are two further requirements, Arnold says, before you can call a group of objects clutter. Those are that the things should be messy, and they should be in the wrong place, like toys strewn all across the house, from the living room to the bathroom, and down the hallway and in the garage.

This—lots of stuff, in a mess, out of place—is what the CELF researchers found time and again in the homes of their case studies, and it is what they think is happening in middle-class homes today. Their research, the most extensive piece of work of its kind ever to be conducted, has led the CELF researchers to believe, as they wrote in the final report, *Life at Home in the Twenty-first Century,* that because of the "sheer numbers of artifacts" people today own, and because we are living in "the most materially rich society in global history, with light-years more possessions per average family than any preceding society," we are at a crunch point. We are at a point of "material saturation." We are coping with "extraordinary clutter." We, as individuals and as a society, are facing a "clutter crisis."

There are caveats, of course, to the study and these conclusions. Can we really take thirty-two case studies in Los Angeles, for instance, and generalize for all middle-class families in the United States? These case studies were chosen because they are average middle-class people, with typical jobs, incomes, home sizes, and family structures. They were picked because what goes on in their lives and homes reflects what others do. The CELF team spent months finding them and chose them for those reasons. So it is not only feasible but sensible to generalize for all middle-class families—in the United States, at least.

The clutter crises in other countries will be different, of course. But even if you think the Americans would "win" the clutter crisis, or at least elements of it, I am sure, as with the take-up of materialistic consumerism in the first place, the rest of the post-industrialized world is not far behind. Consider the homes and lives of people in Britain, France, Japan, Germany, Australia, Hong Kong, and Singapore, or any other developed country. Think of your own home and life, and those of the people you know. Is there lots of stuff? Spilling out? Messy? Are things in the wrong place? Would you ever call it "cluttered"? Do the kids have too many toys? What, would you say, are the average household counts for shoes, DVDs, and books and magazines? Is there any room left for cars in the garage?

Not everyone in the world, clearly, is at the mercy of this clutter crisis. There are hundreds of millions who do not have enough, and would love to have the problem of too much. But then, today, thanks to our materialistic culture, there are also many millions with far too much, who are running out of cupboards and cabinets and wardrobes and even space in the garage to store it all. The clutter crisis, when you think about it, is likely to be worst in the U.S., where materialistic consumption began and is more fully developed than most other places. But the problem of too much stuff is not only an American problem. There is a global, rich-world, middle-class clutter crisis.

Perhaps, as you read this, you are wondering if *crisis* is too dramatic, too harsh a label. Shouldn't we, after all, only call a problem a *crisis* if it is bad for the physical and psychological health of a significant number of people? That, as it turns out, is exactly the problem with having too much stuff, and why the word *crisis* is so appropriate. Because clutter, according to some groundbreaking and, until now, largely unnoticed research, has a number of specific, negative effects. The most worrying of those effects is that, as a psychologist would say, it increases your risk of mortality. There is another, less scientific way of saying this that would make a good health warning or headline: clutter kills.

CLUTTER KILLS

If you'd talked with Darby Saxbe in summer 2013, she might have slowed down long enough to tell you a bit about the clutter in her life and how it was, if not killing her, certainly getting to her. "We've got to get more space," she would have told you, most likely via her hands-free Bluetooth headset as she hurried from one side of the city to the other, driving her two kids to school as she juggled looking after them with her job and looking for a new home. "At the moment we live in an incredibly small house—it's 850 square feet—and we are literally drowning in clutter. Both my kids are constantly taking toys out of the box and moving stuff from one side of the house to the other. There are always little pieces of Play-Doh under my feet."

Saxbe is Ivy League–educated, with long brown hair, blue eyes, and bags of energy. She has the sort of enthusiasm for her subject, psychology, you would hope to hear in the voice of someone who has just started out—the sort of positive glow Jeanne Arnold felt when she started work on the Chumash all those years ago. Saxbe had, in the summer of 2013, just been given her first tenured appointment, as assistant professor at UCLA. No doubt her work as a psychologist on the CELF team, alongside Dr. Rena Repetti at UCLA, had helped. That work also means she, of all people, knows about the clutter problem. "There are so many people out there today just drowning in stuff, they feel totally overwhelmed by it," she says.

"Drowning" and "overwhelmed," Saxbe would be the first to recognize, are not objective scientific terms. But then, the problem of personal, at-home Stuffocation is not objective either. There is no objective number, no magic formula, that says, "If you have more than x items per square foot in your home, it is cluttered." Because some people can cope with more mess than others. Some do not mind mess at all. Some, of course, view having things all around them as comforting. There are only two ways to tell if someone has a clutter crisis. You either ask them how they feel or you measure their cortisol levels through the day. In the CELF study, Repetti and Saxbe did both.

They worked with thirty of the thirty-two families, and worked only with the adults. They gave each couple a camcorder and asked them to conduct a video tour of their home, describing their homes and talking about things that were important to them as they went.

They then gave each of the thirty men and thirty women a bagful of vials and asked them to spit in them at regular intervals over three days. The first spit was right after waking up. The next three were just before lunch, leaving work, and going to bed. What if you got nervous and your mouth went dry? "That's easy, we just tell them to think of something delicious to get their saliva flowing," says Darby. "Steak usually does it for most people, especially as it's a food you need to chew. But it could be strawberries or nectarines or chocolate—any food will do."

The idea was to compare the results from each experiment, to understand if how people felt about their homes—as indicated by what they said—could predict how well they were, or were not, coping with stress—the cortisol levels would show that. The results were startling. They were so surprising that Saxbe double-checked to make sure she had adjusted them, as is standard for psychological tests, for marital harmony, depression, and neuroticism. But even after double-checking, the results were the same.

Saxbe and Repetti collected the camcorders and had the home tours transcribed. Each was, on average, fifteen to twenty minutes long. After watching and analyzing the tapes, they realized there were four main subjects that people talked about. They talked about things associated with nature, using words like *outside, backyard, barbecue,* and *hedge.* They talked about their home as if was a restful, restorative place, using words like *relaxing, calming,* and *homey.* They moaned about all the unfinished jobs in the home, when they'd say things like *unfinished, repair, redo,* and *redecorate.* And they complained about the state of their homes, saying things like *messy, clutter, cluttered, unorganized, disorganized,* and *chaotic.* Repetti and Saxbe used a computer program to count the number of times the participants said words that fitted into these four categories.

Next, Saxbe gathered the vials. In the old days, they would have taken all 720 vials of spit and checked each one by hand for cortisol. There is a lab now that does that work for them, so they sent them there.

Why cortisol? What would that indicate? "Cortisol has a strong daily pattern that follows our circadian rhythm," our body's daily rhythm of hormones and functions, Saxbe explains. "The optimal, healthy pattern is where it starts out high, drops steeply over the course of the morning, and continues to drop over the day."

But if the fall in cortisol levels is shallow, it is considered to be a sign that the body is not managing stress very well. Shallow cortisol patterns are associated with people who have chronic fatigue, post-traumatic stress disorder, or a higher risk of mortality. In other words, if your cortisol declines slowly over the day you are more likely to feel tired and depressed and to die.

The starkest revelation, at first, was the difference between men and women. Men, so the results said, were not stressed by clutter. The more interesting, and far more worrying, result was the discovery that women who found their homes stressful—those women who, as they had carried the camcorder around their homes, had used words like *messy, disorganized, junk, unfinished,* and *chaos*—had a worrying cortisol pattern. Their cortisol levels followed the signature, less healthy, much flatter, slower fall across the day. These results raise a number of questions.

To begin with, why the difference between men and women? Are women fundamentally different? No one knows for sure at this stage, but the correct explanation is less likely to be biological and more likely to be cultural—because in our modern culture women are far more likely to take responsibility for the home, and therefore are more likely to get stressed out by a home full of clutter.

And then, does this mean clutter causes stress? It does not. "We haven't established a causal relationship," Saxbe explains. "But you don't need a causal relationship to get meaning. What the experiment has proven is this: that the more women feel stress and talk about their homes as being cluttered, the more likely they are to have a more depressed mood as the day wears on and at the end of the day."

So how does Saxbe explain the relationship between clutter and stress? There are, she says, three possibilities. The first is that clutter causes stress, because of something psychologists call "allostatic load." That is, the wear and tear clutter puts on your system from watching out for it, picking it up, and clearing it away—the sort Saxbe was struggling with in summer 2013 as she stepped around her children's toys and their Play-Doh. The second is that stress causes clutter, because it leaves the woman with less energy to clear up when she gets home. The third is that it is bidirectional: that clutter causes stress and stress causes clutter.

Whichever is the right explanation, this is clearly more than just a nagging problem. As we saw in the story about Ryan Nicodemus and Joshua Fields Millburn, too much stuff can bring stress and debt. As we have now seen in Saxbe and Repetti's scientific study, clutter can cause the sort of depression that leads to an earlier grave. And, as you are about to witness, in extreme cases, Stuffocation can kill far more quickly.

ONE MAN'S STUFF IS ANOTHER MAN'S FIRETRAP: CANADA'S KATRINA

Walk up to any firefighter in Toronto, ask him where he was on Friday, September 24, 2010, and he won't hesitate to tell you. Asking him this is like asking most people where they were on 9/11, or the day Kennedy or Diana died. Because that date is branded onto the collective memory of the Toronto Fire Services.

By midnight that Friday, Toronto's St. James Town Community Center looked like a refugee camp, albeit a First World one. People—men, women, children, babies, the elderly—were in the lobby, the halls, the gym, everywhere, mopped up and swept there by the emergency services. The human clutter that gets tossed aside in any disaster, they stood about and sat around, unsettled, disheveled, coughing. The Red Cross and a local politician handed out pieces of pizza, slices of orange, and bottles of water. Newshounds sought out anyone in the thousand-plus crowd who would talk. They asked questions and scribbled down answers. Some of the evacuees curled up on the temporary beds that had been wheeled in. Others, like John Ploeg, complained they couldn't sleep on those things. "This," he said, looking around, "is Toronto's Katrina."

That day, the sun had been shining in a clear blue sky. It had been hot, 86 degrees. There'd been a breeze blowing. Truth be told, it was more wind than breeze, blowing around thirty miles an hour, and gusting up to forty.

A call came through to Toronto Fire Services about a fire in an apartment just after 5 P.M. No one was too worried. These things usually took an hour or so to put out.

The first clue that this small domestic incident might be about to turn into a six-alarm fire—the highest level Toronto Fire Services assigns to a blaze—was when the first responders from Station 313 arrived at 200 Wellesley Street and went up the thirty-story, 713-apartment tower, searching for the fire. As they looked around the nineteenth floor, where the alarm had gone off, they soon realized there was no fire here. So if it wasn't here, where was it?

The fire had been started, so a weeklong official investigation would later determine, by a cigarette dropped onto the balcony of Unit 2424, on the twenty-fourth floor. Usually, a stray cigarette wouldn't have mattered so much, except this apartment, from the front door right through to the balcony, was piled high with possessions. Mostly the piles contained the legal papers and books that the inhabitant, Stephen Vassilev, had been using to fight a lawsuit over some town houses he had once owned. From a certain point of view, Unit 2424 was less an apartment, and more a 560-square-foot, one-bedroom tinderbox.

Walking five more levels up, from the nineteenth floor to the twenty-fourth, the first responders went to approach the door and were promptly beaten back by heat so intense that the door of the unit across the hall soon started burning. "It was like a tunnel of hell," one firefighter said later.

The men from Station 313 responded by calling in better weapons and more troops: eventually, more than three hundred firefighters and twenty-seven fire engines would get involved. The firefighters at the scene switched from the regular one-and-a-half-inch to the two-and-a-half-inch hoses, and started using a ground monitor. This is a device firemen use in extreme situations to create a single stream of water that can dump more than thirty bath-loads of water on a fire every minute. Struggling with the heat in that tunnel of hell, the first responders plugged their hoses into one side of the ground monitor, and started pumping a river of water out the other side onto the fire. At the same time, they sprayed water on themselves to keep their suits from melting, and their skin from burning.

The heat was horrific in that corridor, but the fire service also had to think about the smoke and fumes. Smoke inhalation, after all, is the most common killer in domestic fires. And the smoke was so thick and spreading so fast, it was forcing people back into their apartments as far away as the eleventh floor, thirteen floors below. So while some firefighters fought the fire, others set about getting the tower's residents to safety. They spread out across the tower, from the ground to the thirtieth floor, knocking on doors—and if there was no response, as happened in about two hundred cases, smashing them in—to make sure they got the people out of the burning building to safety.

Back on the twenty-fourth floor, the firefighters kept hosing more water into Unit 2424, but the fire kept raging. As day turned to night, orange flames were still licking up the outside of the building. The air in the tunnel of hell was still explosively hot. A divisional chief in the Toronto Fire Services who was on the scene, David Sheen, summed up the situation to a reporter from the *Toronto Star*. "The firefighters are taking a beating," he said.

By 11 P.M., though, the battle had turned. "We're winning the war," said Sheen. And soon after, the fire was under control. At 1 A.M.—a full eight hours after the fire crew had been called—the all-clear was given.

Seventeen people—three firefighters and fourteen residents, including a one-month-old baby—went to the hospital that night, suffering from burns, heat exhaustion, and smoke inhalation. Happily, all were released before morning, and, thanks to the unstinting efforts of the Toronto Fire Services, no one died.

Why had a fire that should have taken an hour and a few firemen to put out become a six-alarm fire that took twenty-seven fire engines and three hundred firefighters eight hours to put out, and endangered the lives of more than a thousand people? There were a variety of factors, like the high winds and the lack of sprinklers in the building. But the most straightforward answer can be summed up in three words: too much stuff.

THE SECRET HOARDER IN YOU

Before the fire, the resident of Unit 2424, Stephen Vassilev, and his cat, Fonzy, could have been stars in a genre of reality TV that has become popular in recent years: the hoarding show. There have been so many that you could say there's been a clutter of hoarding shows, from one-off documentaries like *Obsessive Compulsive Hoarder* and *Help! I'm a Hoarder*, to season-long series such as *Hoarding: Buried Alive, Extreme Clutter, The Hoarder Next Door,* and *Hoarders*—which was the most popular show in the American network A&E's history when it first aired in 2009.

If you're one of the millions who have seen a hoarding show, chances are you've been amused, shocked, and amazed—that a person can gather so many things, function despite the clutter, and find so many bottle tops, plastic bags, and broken fridges worth keeping. You have also probably felt pity that this person has drifted so far from normal living, and hoped that they will get better.

These reactions are a great stimulus for water-cooler conversation, and they keep audiences coming back (and networks airing more hoarding shows). But I think there is an even more important reason why so many of us keep watching hoarding programs: because they resonate with the hoarder lurking inside every one of us. The more I have discovered about hoarding, you see, the more I have realized there is a hoarder in me. As you find out more, I think you might recognize the secret hoarder in you too.

Till the 1990s, few experts thought much about hoarding. It was considered one of the nine telltale signs that someone had obsessive compulsive disorder (OCD), and even then a rare condition, limited to a few dilapidated minds and wealthy homes. This idea had come, principally, from an infamous story about two reclusive brothers, Langley and Homer Collyer.

When the brothers died in March 1947, and police entered their three-story, twelve-room brownstone in New York City, they found, piled from floor to within a foot or two of the ceilings, 120 tons of stuff: newspapers, tin cans, magazines, umbrellas, a gas chandelier, the top of a horse-drawn carriage, a rusty bicycle, fourteen grand pianos, an early X-ray machine, a Model T Ford, the remains of a two-headed fetus, a canoe—and, through it all, tunnels to move around, and booby traps that would drop rocks or bales of newspapers on anyone who dared try to enter. It was one of those newspaper traps that had killed Langley.

The story of these two eccentric hoarders has fascinated people ever since. At the time, thousands of New Yorkers turned out to see the stuff being hauled out of the old mansion. To this day, firefighters on the East Coast call hoarding homes "Collyer mansions." The story has been the subject of articles, books, and movies. And, in the early 1990s, it inspired a young psychology student by the name of Rachel Gross to conduct a study on hoarding with her professor, recognized OCD expert Randy Frost. When they published their findings in 1993, they changed the accepted wisdom on hoarding.

We now know, thanks to another two decades of studies, that hoarding is not a rare condition. Experts now believe that hoarding is twice as common as OCD, and that somewhere between 2 and 6 percent of people in developed countries suffer from it: there could be as many eighteen million hoarders in the United States, and three and a half million in the U.K. No wonder so many watch hoarding shows.

Hoarding, so researchers have concluded, happens principally because of three connected problems. One, hoarders have too much stuff coming in: some are compulsive shoppers, some can't say no to free stuff. Two, they have too little going out: they keep things because they think they are beautiful, or interesting, or important. They keep things "just in case" and because "you never know when they might come in handy." They keep things that were gifts or that have sentimental value. Three, hoarders are terrible at organizing. They can't work out what is important and what isn't. They can't decide how to categorize things or where to put them.

Consider these issues for a moment and you will begin to see what I mean about the secret hoarder inside every one of us. Because who hasn't confronted these problems and thought these thoughts at some point? Who hasn't, in the middle of a clear-out, kept something "just in case," even though they haven't used it for years? Who doesn't have clothes that they hope will fit or become fashionable again one day? Who doesn't keep do-it-yourself parts or sports gear they haven't used for years because you never know when they could come in handy? And who hasn't, when challenged, said, "But I like it!" out loud, as if that were enough to explain why something is worth keeping?

There is no material difference between you and a clinically diagnosed hoarder, you see. It is a difference of degree. "The features of hoarding are on a continuum," says Gail Steketee, author, with Randy Frost, of a book about hoarding called *Stuff*. "Hoarding is an extreme version, but in today's society we all face the same difficult decisions all the time: Do I buy this? Do I keep that? And we all save things for the same reasons: because it's pretty, because it reminds us of something, because it's useful. But some people go overboard on what they think is pretty or sentimental or useful—and they're the ones with hoarding issues."

Think about that continuum for a moment, because I think it explains why one in three households in the U.S. contains a collector, why one in ten Americans rents storage space, and why one in twenty is a hoarder.

Now, picture that continuum as a line, with zero at one end and ten at the other. If zero was an ascetic—a monk, say—with no physical possessions, and if ten was the hoarder whose home was so full there was stuff piled to the ceiling and you could only get about by crawling on all fours, what number are you?

I ask because where you sit on that continuum matters. It matters whether you're a two or a five or an eight because, as we saw in the case of Ryan Nicodemus and Joshua Fields Millburn, and in Repetti and Saxbe's studies, how much stuff you have can have a major impact on your psychological well-being. And it matters because, as we learned in the story of the fire in Apartment 2424, too much stuff can have an even more immediate and dangerous effect on your physical health—thanks to the role it plays in a phenomenon called flashover.

Flashover is the moment when so much heat has built up in a confined space that everything in it spontaneously combusts. Flashover is something firefighters think about a lot. Get to a room before flashover, and you may still be able to rescue anyone inside. Arrive after flashover, and you will be removing charred bodies—but only later, because the first thing you'll be doing is getting out of there. Even in full, heat-resistant firefighting gear, a fire that has flashed over will kill you in less than two seconds.

So, when flashover happens is vitally important. Thirty years ago, it tended to happen around twenty-eight or twenty-nine minutes after a fire had started. Now though—because of the increased amount of stuff in our homes, and because much of it contains plastic and synthetic materials—flashover comes much sooner. The moment from unfortunate spark to murderous explosion is now between three and four minutes.

That is bad news for all of us, especially firefighters, anyone who has a concentration of stuff anywhere in their home, and anyone who lives near someone who struggles with clutter. It is worst news of all, and deadliest, for hoarders and their neighbors.

So far, there has only been one scientific study on hoarding fires. It was commissioned in 2009 by the fire brigade in Melbourne, Australia, after three people had died in hoarding fires in the city that year. Based on a ten-year analysis, the report noted that hoarding, in the scientific language of the report, was a "feature" in only one in every four hundred fires. The report also found that, in the case of fire-related deaths that are considered preventable, hoarding was a feature of one in four. Consider those numbers together for a moment and you arrive at an alarming conclusion: if you get caught in a hoarding fire, rather than an ordinary fire, you are far more likely to die.

You don't have to be a hoarder with a nine or ten on the continuum to react to this fact. And you don't have to be an expert of any sort to realize what this means: that if you or someone who lives near you has too much stuff—especially the sort of flammable, man-made things so many of us have in our homes—that is not only hazardous for your general, long-term health. As the report on hoarding fires showed, and as the Toronto Fire Services found out that Friday, September 24, 2010, too much stuff is not only bad for individuals—it can be a very real, life-threatening menace to society as well.

2

The Dark Side of Materialism

In an infamous scene from the television series *Mad Men,* Don Draper goes on a picnic with his wife, Betty, and their children, Bobby and Sally. The grass is green. The sun is shining. The birds are singing. Don lies on a red-and-white-checked picnic blanket in the shade of a tree. Betty leans on him, her head on his chest. "We should do this more often," she says. "We should only do this," he replies. And they lie there, enjoying the simple joy of nature. Soon though, the world creeps in.

They should get going, Don says, to avoid the traffic. Hauling himself up, he drains the rest of his beer and, like a baseball pitcher pitching a ball, tosses the can into the parkland.

The camera pulls back to a wider shot. We can see the car in the background at the top of the frame. Betty gets up, and dusts herself off. She carefully takes one corner of the picnic rug in each hand and flicks it, tossing the remains of their picnic onto the grass. She folds the rug, and walks to the car as Don watches her.

The camera shot stays wide. We hear the sound of the ignition key, the first revs of the car. The car drives off. But no one in the audience is watching the car. We are still staring, open-mouthed, at the bottom of the frame, where Betty left all that trash without a second thought.

This scene sums up the attitude that earlier Mad Men and Women had bequeathed to people like Don and Betty Draper's generation: a casual disregard for the environment.

Yet even in the resounding economic boom of the postwar years, the environmental movement raised its hand and asked if there was another, not-so-idyllic side to materialism. The movement began in 1962 when Rachel Carson published a book called *Silent Spring* about a dystopian future where industrial practices had destroyed nature.

"The birds, for example—where had they gone?" she wrote. "Many people spoke of them, puzzled and disturbed. The feeding stations in the backyards were deserted. The few birds seen anywhere were moribund; they trembled violently and could not fly. It was a spring without voices. On the mornings that had once throbbed with the dawn chorus of robins, catbirds, doves, jays, wrens, and scores of other bird voices there was now no sound; only silence lay over the fields and woods and marsh."

Carson had first noticed silences like this just after the war. She had tried many times to publish articles about the problem. Magazines refused to print them, even though Carson was a celebrated author, in case they upset their advertisers. Eventually, she gave up and wrote the book. When it was published, the chemical companies causing the problems did all they could to suppress her message. For all their efforts though, all they did was create much needed media noise for *Silent Spring*. By doing so, they helped shine a light on what has turned out to be one of materialism's darkest sides: the senseless trashing of the planet we live on.

Despite occasional victories, like the banning of the CFCs that harmed the ozone layer, environmental damage has only gotten worse through the years. The runaway success of consumerism is now not only causing what may be irreversible climate change, for instance, but also, which is perhaps worse, the greatest extinction of plant and animal species since the dinosaurs died out. Materialism might mean that whole swaths of our planet could one day wake up, as Rachel Carson foretold, to spring mornings that are entirely silent. What would a picnic in that kind of countryside be like?

SNAKES AND LADDERS, AND THE DEPRESSING PROBLEM WITH MATERIALISM

There is another side of materialism that is just as dark as the many blots on the environment: its effect on our happiness. Now that it has provided so many millions of us with the basics of material well-being, materialism seems unable to also improve our overall well-being. Instead, it increasingly looks like it is doing the opposite. Rather than making us feel good, materialism is making millions of us feel joyless, anxious, and, even worse, depressed.

The first person to offer scientific proof of this was a researcher named Richard Easterlin in 1974. Easterlin wanted to determine whether having more makes people any happier. To find out, he compared data on economic growth and happiness since the end of the Second World War, from nineteen countries, both developed ones like the U.S. and the U.K. and less developed countries like India and Brazil. The results were startling: once people had enough to meet their basic needs, happiness did not vary much with national income. He also found that although people were earning ever more in the U.S. after the war, they were not becoming happier. In fact, they had become less happy since 1960.

Why? Perhaps the best way to answer that is over a hot drink and a cookie with a friendly philosopher. Each morning, the British philosopher Jeremy Bentham liked nothing more than munching some hot, spiced ginger nut cookies, and sipping a cup of strong coffee. But, as Bentham once observed, while he liked the first cup of coffee very much, the second was far less enjoyable. Economists and sociologists have a name for this: the law of diminishing marginal utility. But we do not need a technical term to understand Bentham's point. In that simple observation I think he has summed up the problem of Stuffocation and the paradox of materialism: a little is good, but you can have too much of a good thing.

A Hungarian American economist, Tibor Scitovsky, had another suggestion to explain why increasing prosperity was not leading to more happiness. In his 1976 book, *The Joyless Economy*, he wrote that it could be because of materialism's "dark side": all the unintended consequences of material progress such as the harm it does to our health, the environment, and future generations because of "our reckless brandishing of weapons, extermination of pests, squandering of resources, popping of pills, ingesting of food additives, and use or overuse of every mechanical aid to our comfort and safety."

"Could it not be," Scitovsky asked, "that we seek our satisfaction in the wrong things, or in the wrong way, and are then dissatisfied with the outcome?" The answer is "yes"—if those things are material goods.

Material goods, it must be said, can be useful for self-expression and signifying status—the type of shoes or shirt you wear says a lot about you, for instance. But in our consumer culture, we have come to rely on material goods too much, and they are letting us down.

Many of us believe material things can solve emotional problems. But this, as the psychologist Oliver James wrote, is a "false promise." Retail therapy does not work. Instead, it is more likely to make your problems worse—by putting you in debt, for instance.

In today's culture, material goods have become substitutes for deep and genuinely meaningful human desires and questions. Consumer culture has become a sort of pseudo-religion. Instead of pondering meaningful questions, like "Why am I here?," "What happens after death?," "How should I live?," it's easier to focus on questions like "The blue one or the red one?," "Will that go with the top I bought last week?," "What will she think if I buy that?" Instead of trying to understand who we really are, we reach for the "Real Thing." And, brainwashed by the system, when the goods we buy fail to match up to those deep desires, instead of giving up on material goods, we just keep banging our heads against the wall and buying more.

Mass-produced goods, which are the natural product of the system, are the worst of all. They are so stripped of meaning and novelty that they have little chance of genuinely exciting or inspiring us. "The monotony of mass production is fully matched," Scitovsky wrote, "by the monotony of its product." So we become quickly bored with the goods we have and, in the search for novelty, move on to the next thing, and begin the process again.

Even where material goods are helpful, by signifying status, they create more problems than they solve. Because in today's meritocratic society having goods signifies success and, equally, not having goods says failure. As a result, we are not only smugly or painfully aware of who is above or below us in the pecking order. We also know we can clamber up or slip down the rankings at any moment. It is like living in an immense, stomach-churning session of Snakes and Ladders, where the game never stops and where everybody is a competitor. To play this paranoia-inducing game—and it is a game we all play—millions of us spend our days and nights worrying about our place in the pecking order, and scheming to get up the ladders and avoid the snakes. The end result is millions suffering from material-focused status anxiety.

Even worse than giving us status anxiety, materialism is making people depressed, in record numbers and to a record extent. From the 1970s to the turn of the century, mental illness in children and adults in developed countries doubled. A quarter of Britons now suffer emotional distress. Americans are three times more likely to be depressed today than in the 1950s. Those statistics are so shocking that many try to explain them away by pointing out that people tended to suffer silently in the past, and that doctors are quicker to diagnose and prescribe antidepressants today. But those numbers are based on extensive and robust research, on anonymous survey reports from individuals and not from doctor diagnoses. So there is no doubt that depression is increasing, and at an alarming rate.

This becomes even more illuminating, and concerning, when you make comparisons between countries. Because, it turns out, emotional illness increases with income inequality, which also tends to be higher in English-speaking nations. In other words, as the psychologist Oliver James observed in *Affluenza,* the more a society resembles the United States, in that it becomes materialistic, the higher the rate of emotional distress. The logical conclusion is one of the darkest sides of materialism: mass production and mass consumption, ultimately, cause mass depression. That, surely, is not what anyone would call progress.

HOW DO YOU SOLVE A PROBLEM LIKE STUFFOCATION?

There is, of course, an obvious solution to the core problem of Stuffocation: buy, keep, and just have less stuff. And if only the world were that simple. If only we always did the sensible thing. Because if it was and we did, the solution could be reduced to a set of cartoon commandments from a late-night infomercial salesman:

"Don't want the stress of all those things in your home? Easy: just get rid of them!

"Don't want status anxiety? Simple: ignore what your neighbor has, or move to where the neighbors have less than you—and then hope none of them moves up in the world!

"Don't want the debt and depression that come from buying too much? No problem: cut up your credit cards and stop shopping!

"Don't want to harm the environment? Here's how: say 'No!' to all upgrades, don't use your car or your air-conditioning, don't buy new clothes till the old ones are completely worn out, and eat nothing but hand-reared, locally produced, no-pesticide, zero-packaging, guilt-free food.

"Take these four simple steps and you can solve Stuffocation!"

The problem is I don't think this supposedly simple approach would work. To understand why, think again about obesity—where the obvious starting point is to get people to eat less, and where knowing this has not helped. As Brian "Sherlock" Wansink has discovered, we can't help but keep eating, especially the things we now know are bad for us, because of how we've evolved. There are other factors, of course, like the complex relationship we have with food, the industrial revolutions that have made food abundant and cheap, and the cues in our environment, in particular those dreamed up by the food industry to keep us hungry for more. For all these reasons, eating less is easy to say, but hard to do. It is the same with stuff.

So instead of thinking a few snake-oil sound bites could cure Stuffocation, the approach I decided to take was not only to observe the symptoms, but to investigate its underlying causes. Once I had realized that the root cause of the problem was the value system that underpins our modern world—materialism—I tried to understand more clearly how it had come to pass, and I began searching for alternatives. In particular, I looked for people experimenting with new, post-materialist ways of living.

I found them all over the world, in Adelaide, Barcelona, and Stockholm, in California, New York, and Germany. Once I had made contact, I asked them why they were doing what they were doing, and I considered the outcomes of those choices. I also discussed their behaviors and beliefs, and the idea of Stuffocation, with academics and cultural commentators of all stripes: from sociologists, psychologists, and philosophers, to anthropologists, historians, and economists. Gradually, as the hours of interviews, and the days of search and discovery, added up, the way forward became clearer.

My inquiries have taken me down two distinct, but connected, paths. One path has evolved into a manifesto for a new way of being. The other has led to a vision of the future.

DRAWING A ROAD MAP TO THE FUTURE

You may well, at this point, be thinking something along these lines: "But no one knows what is going to happen tomorrow. The future is unknowable. How can you claim to know what the future holds?" And that would be a very good question.

To explain: I don't breathe in vapors or read tea leaves or gaze into a crystal ball. The method I use for forecasting is far less esoteric, and, I like to think, a fair bit more robust. It is inspired by something the essayist William Gibson once said: "The future is already here—it's just not very evenly distributed." And it is informed by a way of reading cultural change that, since it was first described in 1962, has been applied more than five thousand times.

Before I share this with you, a quick word on what forecasts are, and what they are not. We all make assumptions about the future every day. If we did not, how could we do our weekly shopping, arrange to meet someone, or know what time to turn up at the airport? Meal plans, departure times, and meeting arrangements are, if you think about it, nothing more than statements about the future. They are predictions of what you are going to eat, when your plane will take off, and when your friend will arrive.

So we should not, in truth, expect forecasts to be perfectly accurate—or friends and planes to always be on time. Instead of thinking of forecasts as facts, we should put them in the same category as timetables, plans, models, and maps. A good forecast, like a well-constructed model or an accurate road map, should provide us with enough information about the future so that we are able to plan. It may not mention every detail—every sight or traffic jam or bump in the road—but it will tell us when to turn left or right, it will give us ideas on how to get to our destination, and it will sketch out what it will look like when we get there.

The best way to draw a map of something as unknowable as the future is through detailed knowledge of two things that are far easier to know: the present and the past. There are two instances, in particular, when knowing the past can help. The more obvious is when there is a long-running trend that started many years ago and that looks likely, given certain circumstances, to continue in the future. Consider, for instance, the rise of the Chinese economy, or the growing acceptance of gay people in mainstream society. These changes are not smooth. They do not always fit convenient graphs. There is often plenty of noise around the signal. Sometimes they blip, make unexpected leaps, up, down, back, forward. Sometimes the Chinese economy surges. Sometimes it stalls. Every now and then, local laws make significant steps toward tolerance or intolerance, swiftly altering gay rights. But it is clear that these are both long-term trends from the past that are likely to continue in the future.

The second way the past can help is by showing how the world works. This is how weather and electricity and population forecasters do their jobs, for instance: they observe and analyze a set of circumstances from the past, and see what outcomes they led to. Using those insights, they create models that describe how the world works and how change happens. Then, by viewing the information they have about the present through those models, they work out how many people there will be, how much electricity will be needed, and whether it is going to be sunny tomorrow.

None of these is perfect—as you will know if you have ever been caught without an umbrella or wearing a sweater that's too warm—but they do work. They are accurate enough to be of use to energy companies that are planning for demand for electricity, and to help each of us work out what sort of shirt or shoes to put on.

Cultural forecasting works in the same way. Again, it is not a perfect, exact science. Cultural forecasters like me may not, in other words, know every bump, twist, rain cloud, and sunny spell along the way. But, by using information and insights from the past, we can read the present in order to plot a path to the future, and sketch out what it will look like when we get there. The best way to do this is by using a model called the "diffusion of innovations."

HOW TO FIND THE FUTURE IN THE PRESENT

Diffusion of Innovations, the book, is now in its fifth reprinting, and is read around the world. The first time its ideas were published was in the Midwest in the early 1960s, at the tail end of a rural sociology student's doctoral thesis. The student, at Iowa State University, a young man by the name of Everett Rogers, had been studying how farming innovations spread. In the course of his research, he had come across a paper that described how long it had taken for a drought-resistant corn seed to spread—or, in the technical language, to diffuse—through a farming community. In the appendix to his thesis, Rogers compared this study to diffusion studies in other fields like anthropology, geography, and public health. And he discovered something fascinating: it did not matter which field you looked at, ideas diffused in a strikingly similar way. They started off with a few "innovators." Next, they spread to a larger number of "early adopters." Then, from those early adopters, they reached a far larger number in the mainstream "majority." And, finally, the innovation would reach a few stragglers at the end that he termed "laggards."

Rogers also noted that if you plotted these adoptions on a graph, with time on the horizontal axis, and number of people who have adopted the innovation on the vertical axis, they made a smooth S curve.

The diffusion of innovations has been applied thousands of times since then, and, though there is often noise around the signal, the S

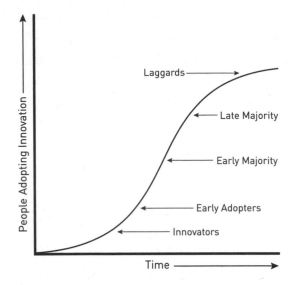

curve model that Rogers described always fits. It works if you are describing the diffusion of a new antibiotic like tetracycline, or the proliferation of a new technology like the fax machine or the cell phone. It works if you are looking at the adoption of new ideas like teaching children in kindergartens, or the use of IUDs in family planning. And it works if you want to describe the taking up of snowmobiles by the Skolt Lapps of northern Finland, or the dissemination of horses from Spanish explorers to American Indian tribes in the Southwest.

Rogers originally conceived the diffusion of innovations S curve as a way to describe how things have changed. It was a method for describing the past. But if you have enough insights about what is happening in the present, you can also use it to forecast the future.

If, for example, you look around the present and notice an innovation—like a new type of computer that has no need for an external keyboard, for instance—and then notice that certain types of people are adopting it, and then that more people are also adopting it, you can, with caution, make reasonable predictions of the future. This is what cultural forecasters like me do. They spot the future in the present. They work out which innovations—if any—

are going to catch on, and spread from the innovative few today to the many in the mainstream tomorrow.

To do this, there are a number of factors that will determine whether an innovation will be adopted or not. You need to know, for instance, how ideas, information, and inspiration pass through the community. This is an especially important consideration for us today, as in our hyper-connected world of the mobile Internet and social media, ideas spread, and change happens, very quickly. Until recently, for instance, new fashion ideas were disseminated by the select few at monthly glossy magazines. Today, they can be blogged, texted, tweeted, and Instagrammed in an instant by almost anyone.

You also need to consider how innovative the culture is. Is it the sort of culture that is open to new ideas? Compare London and Kabul in Afghanistan, for instance. In one of those cities, people are fairly open to change. They change their clothes, the foods and places they eat, and even the people they spend time with almost with the season. You are likely to come into contact with people from different cultures with different ideas every day. In the other, far more conservative system, people tend to eat the same food, and spend time with the same people, who hold the same views that they do. If you were launching an innovation—say a new exercise, toy, or TV show—in which of these two cities would you launch yours? The more innovative and connected a system is, the more quickly an innovation will spread.

In addition, you need to know who is implementing the change. Are there, for instance, any powerful people who might actively be trying to diffuse the innovation? Examples might be Krispy Kreme's marketers trying to get people to make more occasions for doughnuts, or the government trying to make people shop more, or stop smoking, or eat more vegetables and less sugar.

Finally, there is the innovation itself. To work out if it is the sort of innovation that will catch on, there are five key questions to consider. One, is it actually better? An improvement over the previous generation? Two, is it compatible with how we live today? Is it easy to use the innovation in everyday life? Three is about simplicity: is the innovation easy to understand? Four is about ease: is the innovation easy to try out and easily available? And five is about observability: if one person tries it, will other people notice? If the answer to each of these is a resounding "yes," the innovation is more likely to spread.

By considering these factors, and answering these five questions, it is possible to make a fairly accurate prediction about whether an innovation that is happening today will spread in the future. This is the method I will be using in this book to evaluate the most exciting, innovative post-materialist ways of living that are happening now. And it is the method I will be using to identify the movement that, I believe, is already catching on, that will replace materialism as our society's dominant value system in the future, and that will solve Stuffocation.

Before we examine the present though, we should begin with the past. We should investigate the last time the world faced a problem as significant as Stuffocation. The trouble then was not overconsumption. It was overproduction.

PART II

How We Got Here:
The Origins of Throwaway Culture

3

The Original Mad Men and the Job of Creating Desire

On Monday, May 11, 1925, just after 10 A.M., as sun streamed through the windows of a hall in Houston, Texas, a hush settled among a group of men and women from the advertising industry, as a tall, distinguished-looking gentleman walked in and took the stage. He was a man in his fifties. His brown hair, now graying at the sides, was slicked back and parted left of center. He was wearing a dark three-piece suit and a white shirt with a rounded collar. "Advertising was not always looked upon as a vital part of our economic system," said the future president of the United States, Herbert Hoover. It was now, though. "You have taken over," he told the assembled audience of Mad Men and Women, "the job of creating desire."

Advertising, Hoover believed, was one of the best ways of solving the most pressing problem the U.S. economy faced at the time— overproduction. Since the Civil War ended in 1865, peace and farming and factories had transformed the country. Millions of acres of prairie grass had been turned over and made productive, for raising pigs, growing wheat, and producing countless other things. Entire industries had sprung up. The nation was now littered with foundries producing iron, mills spinning textiles, and workshops making cars, tractors, and trains. Railroads crisscrossed the continent, bringing radios and razors and toasters, as well as magazines and influence from the skyscrapers in New York and Chicago to the north, south, east, and west. Even the First World War had helped, as it had destroyed crops and closed factories in Europe, and that meant more work for America's industries.

In the sixty years since the Civil War's end, the population had increased by a factor of three, from 35 million to 114 million. Over the same period, output had risen between twelve and fourteen times. So industry in the United States had grown four times faster than the population, and now, in the 1920s, America's manufacturing and agricultural industries were producing far more than they could sell. The Europeans were producing more of their own food and goods once again. And the American people had reached, so the U.S. secretary of labor, James J. Davis, told *The New York Times,* the point of "need saturation." By 1927, the country's textile mills could produce enough cloth for the whole year by operating only six months of the year. Less than a fifth of America's shoe factories could produce a year's supply of footwear.

As the 1920s progressed, the problem of overproduction loomed larger. Soon it threatened to blow the country and its folk off their happy, bumpy road to prosperity. As supply outstripped demand, the United States was coming to a fork in the road. The dilemma was simple: either the farmers and factories needed to produce less, or people had to consume more. If you had been in a position to choose the path the country took, which way would you have picked: produce less or consume more?

The seemingly obvious answer would have been to get the farmers and the factories to produce less. This was what men like the economist Arthur Dahlberg and the corn flake capitalist W. K. Kellogg proposed. This solution would be simple to achieve. Its outcome was more predictable. The people would work less. They would have more time off. They could use their spare time to indulge in what John Maynard Keynes called the "Age of Leisure." They could play in the park, sing in the choir, contribute to the community, take up a hobby, contemplate God, spend more time with their family and friends, even listen to the radio. Would you have chosen this option?

There were many others, though, who thought the other solution, to consume more, was better. These people—politicians like Hoover and industrialists like the General Motors CEO Alfred Sloan—did not even think of the problem in the same way. To them, the trouble was not overproduction. It was underconsumption. The solution, therefore, was to get people to consume more. The logic of this argument was really quite compelling.

It had first been made, in fact, hundreds of years before, by an Englishman, Bernard Mandeville, in a satire published in 1715 called *The Fable of the Bees: or, Private Vices, Public Benefits*. The satire was about a group of prosperous bees who lived, so the story went, a life of luxury and ease. But after grumblings that their way of living lacked virtue, they turned away from their fraud and greed and extravagance to a new life of simplicity and honesty and temperance. You might think that would be a good idea. But, as the fable showed, if the bees gave up their vices, especially their greedy, high-spending ways, that would be the end of their easy, luxurious life as well.

This was a revolutionary, counterintuitive idea. The conventional wisdom had been that the best way to become prosperous was by saving, not by spending. But Mandeville showed that things that were sins in the eyes of the Church—like being greedy and buying more than strictly necessary, or showing off by throwing extravagant parties—produced work, jobs, and wealth. In other words, the private vices of the rich led to public benefits for all.

The same logic that had worked for Mandeville's bees also made perfect sense for society in the twentieth century. If people bought more, they would create a virtuous circle where everyone benefited. They would create more jobs and more wages. The industrialists' profits would go up. The government would receive more tax revenue. Everyone would enjoy a higher standard of living. So if more people spent more, paradoxical though it might at first seem, they would have more. It all hinged, as you can see, on consumers acting like hardworking and, even more important, high-spending bees.

But before the leaders of industry and government, whom the New York academic Stuart Ewen has named the "captains of consciousness," could hurry everyone along into this sweet new future, there was one problem. The decision to produce less was clearly theirs to make. They could make it happen simply by reducing work hours. But getting people to consume more was far more complex. It was far *less* certain—that the outcome would be as they hoped—and far *from* certain—that they could make it happen in the first place. For that future to happen, they would have to get the good men and women of America to buy more things, more often—even though, at the point of "need saturation," they already had enough. To make the people buy more, they would have to change behaviors and attitudes that had evolved since the dawn of time, the sort that said: prize the possessions you have, then be careful with them and look after them, because they cost a lot of time and effort and energy to get. How could the captains of consciousness get the people of America to change the habits and customs not only of their own lifetime, but of all the lifetimes that had ever come before them?

THE NEW AND IMPROVED THROWAWAY CULTURE

Earnest Elmo Calkins's first break in advertising came in 1891. He won a competition, out of 1,433 other entries, to write the best advertisement for a household cleaner. His advertisement claimed the new cleaner "stays newer longer, and sweeps cleaner than a broom." He had, you could say, the gift of the ad. He wrote the kind of words that made people go out and buy things.

As his career progressed, Calkins's ads became more sophisticated. He pioneered the use of interesting typefaces and Modernist-style art, for instance, and he created one of the advertising industry's first art departments. In the early decades of the twentieth century that worked well, especially since many people were still buying their first of any product category—their first toaster, radio, or washing machine—and manufacturers often had some genuinely new and improved breakthrough to announce.

But as the U.S. economy slowed in the mid-1920s, and the signs became clearer that the twin problems of overproduction and underconsumption were looming, Calkins, and others, wondered if even that was enough. The question of how to stimulate consumption was the hot topic among all the Mad Men and Women of the 1920s and 1930s. It was discussed at meetings of the New York Advertising Club, for instance, and debated in the pages of leading trade publications like *Printer's Ink*.

Calkins and his contemporaries soon came up with two revolutionary ideas. The first was that industry should shift its focus from producing ever better products to creating products that would only last a short time. They should turn goods that people *used*, such as motor cars and safety razors, into goods people would *use up*, like toothpaste and cookies. Instead of selling products that were built to last, they should sell ones that were made to break.

The second idea was, in many ways, more radical: it was to take the happy, thrifty people of America and turn them into dissatisfied, wasteful, conspicuous consumers. Instead of just manufacturing products out of raw materials, industry should manufacture consumers. How could they do that?

To begin with, as Calkins reasoned, these new consumers would have to have enough money to buy products. Industry could make this happen either by paying them enough in their wage packets, or by giving them the financial means to buy now. This, of course, is consumer credit.

Calkins's next idea was more exciting, and certainly more colorful. The inspiration for this came from the art he had brought into the world of advertising. Just as advertising had evolved from those early, functional messages into works of art, so, he felt, products should do the same. This, it seemed to him, was the natural progress of any industry. At first, a person would be amazed that a new product even existed, and the industrialist would only need to make the product functional. Then, the consumer would want to see it beautified, through color, style, design. This was the evolutionary stage, he believed, industry had come to. "The appeal of efficiency alone is nearly ended," he wrote in an article for *The Atlantic Monthly* in August 1927. "Beauty is the next logical step."

If you think about this idea for a moment, it is clear that it is the statement both of an aesthete and of a businessman. The beauty of this concept, if you will, is that what is beautiful can also be engineered and manipulated according to a manufacturing cycle to keep people buying. In other words, Calkins was taking the idea that underpinned the success of the fashion business and transferring it to other industries. In this new vision, people would buy a new car, clock, carpet, or a new *anything*, as Calkins wrote, "not because the old one is worn out, but because it is no longer modern. It does not satisfy their pride . . . because it is out of date, out of style, no longer the thing."

And it worked. Retooled with these innovative ideas, America's industries started mass-producing products that were made to break, and engineering consumers who would use up what they had previously only used. Armed with these revolutionary ideas, Calkins and the captains of consciousness changed the habits and customs of ordinary Americans, and created a new throwaway culture.

THE EVOLUTION OF THROWAWAY CULTURE

This culture of "use and discard," it must be said, did not suddenly appear in the 1920s. Americans had been throwing things away for decades—disposable razors, for instance, and even, in an era when getting whites very white was difficult, shirt collars and cuffs. American men bought 70 million razor blades in 1915. They used and discarded 150 million disposable collars and cuffs in 1872.

To trace the idea back to its origins, though, you really have to go back to the 1830s, when a three-masted ship called *The Beagle* rounded the world carrying a gentleman naturalist by the name of Charles Darwin. With the evidence he found on that trip, Darwin was able to make a very strong case that all animals had evolved through a process of natural selection, where only the fittest survived, and those that did not adapt did not.

If you were a man of industry in the nineteenth century, Darwin's theory was both interesting and inspiring. If you thought about this idea for a moment, it sounded an awful lot like the industrial revolutions of recent years. When James Hargreaves had invented the spinning jenny in Lancashire in the 1760s, for instance, a spinner could now spin yarn twenty times more efficiently—and that meant the old spinning wheel was only useful as firewood. Then, just as Hargreaves's spinning jenny had replaced the wheel, so a few years later it was discarded—when the new spinning frame, which could produce much stronger yarn, was developed.

This process of natural selection, of use and discard, was a natural part of the progress of other industries as well. Once someone discovered that steel was better for building railways than iron, for instance, the iron tracks were cast aside. Actually, when you really stopped to think about it, this theory did not just sound like a number of industries—it sounded like the entire emerging system of capitalism. No wonder the waste that came with the throwaway culture resonated so strongly with the captains of consciousness. To them, discarding the old was more than simply a way to increase profits. It was proof that American industry, and society, was evolving.

Some industrialists fought the logic of this idea. Henry Ford, for instance, insisted that his cars were built to last, in terms of both build quality and aesthetic. "We want the man who buys one of our cars never to have to buy another," he said in 1922. But just over a decade later, as the economy and sales stalled, he changed his mind. And from 1933 Ford changed the styling of his company's cars every year.

Now that the leader of America's flagship industry was using beauty to make last year's model less attractive, and to encourage people to spend more often, all other industries, if they had not already, soon adopted the idea. As a result, the temporary, throwaway culture became standard practice, and it was soon recognized as the engine driving living standards in the United States to levels far above those anywhere else in the world. As one of the leading consumer experts of the day, Christine Frederick, observed: "We have more because we spend more, this is our American paradox."

Soon, companies, governments, and ordinary people around the world wanted to copy the U.S.'s success. And so, where once most businesses had made products to last as long as possible, now they built them to last a season. Where once most people had been careful with their money, they, gradually, over the course of the twentieth century, began to use up what they had previously only used, they learned to buy new things a little sooner than strictly necessary, and they became wasteful, conspicuous consumers. It worked for them as well: rising standards of living became a hallmark of the twentieth century. And so, the American paradox—to have more by spending more—became a universal paradox or, at least, a paradox for those of us in the wealthy West.

RICHARD NIXON IN THE KITCHEN AND THE
BEST IDEA OF THE TWENTIETH CENTURY

In 1959, Richard Nixon visited Nikita Khrushchev in Moscow, and had one of the oddest, and possibly funniest, superpower summits of the twentieth century—a rough-and-tumble, boyish debate in a kitchen. It was a time of some tension between the U.S. and the USSR. In the hope that a little more understanding would stop either country using the nuclear weapons each was then stockpiling, the two countries had agreed to a few cultural exchanges. The centerpiece of the Russian exhibit that landed in New York in June 1959 was a replica of the world's first successful satellite, Sputnik I. The intended message, which came through loud and clear to everyone in the U.S. administration, could not have been clearer even if a Russian politician had stood there thumbing his nose blurting: "Ner-ner-ner-ner-ner." The message was this: our communist system is better than your capitalist one, as proved by the fact that we Russians have superior space technology.

When the doors opened to their exhibition in Moscow a few months later, the Americans wanted to deliver an equally powerful, and perfectly opposite, message. How could they do that? What would show those pesky Russians that capitalism was better than communism? They decided to do so by creating a real-life suburban home, the sort of house the Cleavers lived in, in the television series *Leave It to Beaver.* It was in the kitchen of this home that Nixon met Khrushchev.

The CIA transcript of the meeting reads like a comedy sketch where the director has asked one actor to be reasonable, and the other to act the defensive, blustering ruddy-cheeked oaf. Can you tell who was given which directions?

The Kitchen Debate—transcript, July 24, 1959

[Both men enter kitchen in the American exhibit.]

NIXON: I want to show you this kitchen. It is like those of our houses in California.

[Nixon points to dishwasher.]

KHRUSHCHEV: We have such things.

NIXON: This is our newest model. This is the kind which is built in thousands of units for direct installations in the houses. In America, we like to make life easier for women . . .

KHRUSHCHEV: Your capitalistic attitude toward women does not occur under Communism.

NIXON: I think that this attitude towards women is universal. What we want to do, is make life more easy for our housewives . . .

NIXON: This house can be bought for $14,000, and most Americans can buy a home in the bracket of $10,000 to $15,000 . . .

KHRUSHCHEV: We have steel workers and peasants who can afford to spend $14,000 for a house. Your American houses are built to last only 20 years so builders could sell new houses at the end. We build firmly. We build for our children and grandchildren.

NIXON: American houses last for more than twenty years, but, even so, after twenty years, many Americans want a new house or a new kitchen. Their kitchen is obsolete by that time. . . . The American system is designed to take advantage of new inventions and new techniques.

KHRUSHCHEV: This theory does not hold water. Some things never get out of date—houses, for instance, and furniture. Furnishings—perhaps—but not houses. I have read much about America and American houses, and I do not think that this exhibit and what you say is strictly accurate. . . . You think the Russian people will be dumbfounded to see these things, but the fact is that newly built Russian houses have all this equipment right now.

But Russian houses had nothing like all that equipment. "There is no more truth in showing this as the typical home of the American worker," fumed the Soviet state news agency TASS, "than, say, in showing the Taj Mahal as the typical home of a Bombay textile worker."

Rather than expose the U.S. delegation as lying, though, this comment showed that the exhibit had done its job. It also highlighted the gulf that was opening up between the standards of living in a capitalist system and those under communism.

Moreover, what the entire episode—the exhibits, meeting, conversation, and reporting—demonstrates is that "keeping up with the Joneses" is not merely a petty concern for suburban housewives, city bankers, and those people who live next door. After all, while it is easy to laugh at people who compete too obviously, the desire to keep up is an essential human trait: in caveman terms, the slowest runners would not only miss out on lunch, they might become lunch. And, as Khrushchev and Nixon's conversation makes plain, keeping up is as fundamental for nations as it is for individuals.

That realization is key to understanding the history of the twentieth century, and why capitalism caught on as an idea. Because, as the century progressed and capitalism hauled millions out of poverty in the United States, the West, and Japan, it made the stagnating standards of living elsewhere, and the systems their leaders had chosen, look ever worse. It became progressively harder for official news agencies to deny that their countries were falling behind. And it became clearer that, when the captains of consciousness arrived at their crossroads in the 1920s and 1930s, they chose the right path. Because the capitalist system, driven by consumerism and underpinned by materialistic values, was not just different. It was better.

Eventually, especially after the fall of the Berlin Wall and the Iron Curtain, many communist, and other, countries started adopting elements of this system too, especially materialistic values, conspicuous consumption, and throwaway culture. Just as it did in much of the Western world in the twentieth century, so it is giving hundreds of millions around the world better lives today. The way is not entirely clear, but international trade, with materialistic consumerism at its heart, is pulling more people out of poverty around the world than ever before. Many, including the World Bank's president, Jim Yong Kim, even believe that we may have virtually wiped out poverty by 2030. For this reason, materialism, fueled by people and nations wanting to keep up with their neighbors, was unquestionably the best idea of the twentieth century. How ironic, then, that it has also given us one of the most pressing problems of the twenty-first century.

4

Barbra Streisand and the Law of Unintended Consequences

In February 2003, the entertainer Barbra Streisand was furious. A man had flown over her eight-bedroom, eleven-bathroom cliff-top mansion in Malibu, California, in a helicopter. He had used a tele-photo lens to take a photograph of Streisand's 10,485-square-foot home. Then he had put the picture on the Internet for anyone to see. If you really liked the shot, he was selling prints too.

Streisand was not in the photo, but that was hardly the point. Couldn't the entertainer at least get some privacy at home? Strei-sand's lawyers contacted the man. They asked him to take the photo down and stop selling it. In the letter, they invoked California Civil Code Sections 3344 and 1708:8—better known as the Anti-Paparazzi Laws. They also wrote: "Please be advised that no part of this letter may be published or disseminated without our prior written con-sent."

The man, who also lived in California and went by the name of Ken Adelman, did what any good, law-abiding citizen would have done. He scanned the letter and put it on his website—California Coastline.org, the place of record for the California Coastal Records Project. Adelman was not a paparazzo, you see. He was an environmentalist who had been trying to protect the California coast, by documenting its state from the air, since 1997. His aim was to shoot all 840 miles of the state's coastline—and it just so happened that Streisand lived on that coastline.

When Adelman refused to take the picture down, Streisand's lawyers sued for $10 million. They would have realized, of course, that filing papers would make the case public. But, in all likelihood, they would not have intended all the consequences that followed.

When the news became public, the reaction, at first, was mixed. A few thought Adelman had crossed the line. But most felt he was within his rights. They showed their support by clicking on the website and downloading the image.

If Streisand's attorneys' plan was to stop people from looking at her home, it backfired in the most spectacular fashion. Before the lawsuit, the image had been downloaded six times, including twice by Streisand's lawyers. After the case became public, though, the image was downloaded 420,000 times, and the story went global. It was reported, for instance, by the *Japan Times, Le Monde,* the *Sydney Morning Herald,* and the BBC.

Now, whenever someone tries to stop people from seeing something online—like when the French secret service wants Wikipedia to delete an article about a spy listening station, or Celine Dion does not want people looking at a site called Ridiculous Pictures of Celine Dion—but merely draws more attention to it, that is called, in honor of the great entertainer, the Streisand effect.

THE PRINCE AND THE RABBIT-PROOF FENCE

In October 1867, Thomas Austin was excited. Like the rest of his family in the village of Baltonsborough in Somerset, England, he had been poor. But in the tough times of the 1840s, like three dozen other Austins, he had emigrated to Australia.

Things had turned out well for him Down Under. He had occupied large sections of unclaimed land and raised lots of sheep. He was the first to bring over the Lincoln Longwool, which grew the most lustrous fleece of any sheep in the world. Now, three decades later, Austin was the local equivalent of a British aristocrat, a bona fide member of Australia's "squattocracy." To express his new status, he had bought a mansion called Barwon Park and renovated it in fashionable bluestone. Then he had imported twenty-four rabbits so that, just as King Henry III had done in England in the thirteenth century, he could found rabbit colonies by giving breeding pairs to his friends, and, just as the landed gentry still did back in Britain, he could hunt them.

This is why Austin was so excited in 1867, because Prince Alfred, the first British royal ever to visit Australia, had decided to come rabbit shooting at Barwon Park. Alfred enjoyed the hunt so much that he delayed an official engagement to spend another day shooting there, and he came again a few years later. By that time, though, the rabbits were turning from a source of pride for Austin to a cause for complaint. His neighbors had moaned that his rabbits were destroying their land, and he had put up a wire-cage fence to keep them in. But it was too late.

This part of Australia, it turned out, was ideal for the wild rabbits Austin had imported. There were no natural predators, and the winters were mild, so they could breed all year round. Like a biblical plague of locusts, there were soon so many they were nibbling everything in their path. As they ate all the native plants, they left the topsoil exposed, causing wholesale erosion and ruining what had once been great farmland. The price of an acre halved.

By 1869, there were so many bunnies running wild in Australia that even a cull of two million barely made a difference. In the 1880s, the New South Wales government offered a bounty for every rabbit killed, but when locals claimed the bounty on more than 25 million rabbit scalps, it withdrew the offer fearing it would bankrupt the state. In 1901, the federal government took decisive action, and began construction of a rabbit-proof fence that would stretch from the south to the north coast. When it was finished, seven years later, it was 2,000 miles long—about the distance from London to Cairo, or from San Diego, California, to Jacksonville, Florida. To make sure it was secure, the government appointed a Chief Inspector of Rabbits. He and his team did what they could, looking for holes, day after day, by car, bicycle, horse, and camel. But, like the fence around Barwon Park, it was too late. By 1950, Austin's original twenty-four had intermingled with other rabbits, crisscrossed the country, and multiplied to create a rabbit population of 600 million.

THE LAW OF UNINTENDED CONSEQUENCES

Although they are oceans apart, these two stories, about a man in Australia and a woman in California, have something in common. They are both archetypal examples of the law of unintended consequences. This law, which was codified by a sociologist named Robert Merton in 1936, states that for any action there will be results that were unexpected.

Streisand's aim had been to stop people from peeping at her home, not to get hundreds of thousands to take a look. All Austin had wanted was to have a few hundred rabbits to shoot on his estate, a few to give to friends, and to establish his social status. The last thing he wanted was to ruin the country that had treated him so well, slash land prices, and create a plague that would waste millions of man-hours and cost millions of dollars.

The law of unintended consequences is a helpful model, because it reminds us that people often play an unwitting part in how culture evolves. "Change," so the British historian Ian Morris believes, "is caused by lazy, greedy, frightened people looking for easier, more profitable and safer ways of doing things. And they rarely know what they are doing." In other words, as per the law of unintended consequences, no matter what people's intention when they do something, they rarely know what the ultimate outcome of their actions will be.

Consider the creators of the Industrial Revolution. Did they know, or even imagine, where their actions would lead? Did each of those men, working out easier, more profitable, and safer ways to weave, make metal, and move from one place to another realize how their inventions would, collectively, change the world? Of course not. It is unlikely that they were trying to create a revolution of any kind, except in their own area of expertise and fortunes. It is also unlikely that they would have anticipated the consequences of their actions and inventions, especially the widespread overproduction of the 1920s. They had been born and raised in a time when scarcity was the prevailing condition of society, when the greatest concern for the greatest number was that they did not have enough. It would have been hard for them to imagine that their inventions, collectively, would create such abundance that the greatest concern for the greatest number was that there was too much.

By the same token, it is unlikely that the captains of consciousness, those men and women who seized upon the idea that waste was good, who solved the problem of overproduction by creating a culture of materialistic consumption, would have realized that the throwaway system would lead to all the problems of Stuffocation today—and bring us, once more, to a crossroads.

FROM THE PYRAMID TO THE PANCAKE

As we stand at our crossroads, the choice we make is critical. It will change the course of history just as much as materialism did. The last time this happened, the debate was framed and discussed and decided by the elite, by the captains of consciousness of the day. The decisions they made, in the name of solving overproduction in the early part of the twentieth century, created materialistic consumer culture as we know it today. The industrialists and the government and the Mad Men and Women were, if you like, the puppet masters deciding what would happen. The people, in that era, were the puppets.

Back then, just as the industrialists had learned to mass-produce products by taking advantage of the new machines and systems of the Industrial Revolution, so the Mad Men and Women learned to mass-engineer consumers by leveraging the new tools of mass media that appeared in the nineteenth and twentieth centuries: magazines, newspapers, movies, radio, and television.

But then came the Internet, and everything changed. Suddenly the puppets had a chance to speak as well. Today, in our new Internet-enabled era, it is much easier for everyone and anyone to become successful, and influential.

The Internet has revolutionized publishing, for instance. *Fifty Shades of Grey* was rejected by professional agents. The author published the book herself via an online ebook and print-on-demand publisher, and then it was picked up by a mainstream publisher. It went on to become the fastest-selling paperback of all time.

The Internet has recast fame. When Jenna Mourey posted a video of herself getting ready to go to work as a dancer called "How to Trick People into Thinking You're Good-Looking," five million watched it in a weekend. Now she is Jenna Marbles, her video channel has nine million subscribers, and her videos have been watched more than a billion times.

The Internet has also transformed fashion. Once fashion's front rows were strictly reserved for Hollywood A-listers and VIPs. They still are—only the VIPs now include bloggers like Tavi Gevinson, who became one of fashion's key influencers at the age of twelve.

And the Internet has revolutionized politics: consider the impact of Facebook and Twitter on Egypt, Iran, and the Occupy movement.

Because of the Internet, the direction of influence and the structure of power have changed. Instead of the old system, where information and influence flowed from the top down, now they also flow in other ways, from the bottom upward, and also sideways. And before, the few at the top held sway over the many at the bottom. You could visualize this system as a pyramid. Today, because of the infinite connections enabled by the Web, many talk to many, those at the bottom are more powerful, and the system is far flatter. If you drew it now, the structure of power and influence would look much more like a pancake.

The world is not, it must be said, quite as flat as a pancake. There are still peaks of influence. The government is still far more influential than most individuals. And the world's big media and advertising companies, like Disney, Google, and News Corp, are certainly more likely to influence what you and I think and do, and especially when and how we spend our money.

At this new crossroads, though, it is clear that the world is not the same as before. This time around, it is not simply a matter of what the incumbent captains of consciousness, the government and big business, decide. They are not the only ones pulling the strings anymore. They no longer have the same control of what we read and watch and think and want. Now, more than ever before, we the people have a choice about what happens next.

One path that most governments and businesses do not want us to go down is minimalism. Why would they, when their economic and financial models are based on materialism, on us wanting and buying more? If the government, industrialists, and advertisers who rely on materialism had it their way, there would be no mention of minimalism. But partly because of the Internet, and blogging especially, the minimalist movement is a growing and powerful subculture. There is nothing the government or business can do to stop it. After all, if they tried to interfere with the *Minimalist Woman*, the *Minimalist Mom*, the *Minimalist Journey*, the *Minimalist Freak*, *The Minimalists*, or any of the hundreds of other antimaterialist websites, they might end up creating their own Streisand effect.

PART III

The Crossroads:
Signposts to a Better Future

5

I Love to Count: The 33, 47, 69, and 100 Things of Minimalism

A few years ago in Sacramento, California, a slim, tanned, immaculately dressed young woman named Cheryl stepped into her walk-in closet. She was followed by another woman, also smartly turned out, by the name of Tammy.

Tammy, whose last name was Strobel, had a cropped brown bob and a pixie nose. She had a singsong lilt to her voice: "Hi, I'm Tammy." Her eyes were green like a cat's. In those days, she would accent them with blue eye shadow and lashes curled so hard the tips stood straight up. Tammy inhaled the sweet smell of new closet and clean clothes. As she looked around, her eyes widened, her pupils dilated. You could shop in here. It all looked beautiful—the dresses, the sweaters, the pants, the shoes—and everything color-coded and neatly folded. No wonder Cheryl always looked like she had just stepped off the pages of a magazine.

It was a lunch break, Tammy recalls, like any other. The two friends from college had just been to the mall. That was their way, most days, of taking a break from the financial company they worked for, and thinking about more fun things, like clothes, fiancés, and engagement rings.

Tammy had spent ages finding her ring. Truth be told, she had become a little obsessed. She had devoured catalogues. She had made secret trips to the mall. "When she talked about that ring, her eyes sparkled," her sister-in-law, Tina Smith, remembers. "It was like, all of a sudden, she had purpose."

When Tammy's boyfriend, Logan Smith, proposed and put the ring she had chosen on her finger, life felt perfect—till she saw Cheryl's. Because while Tammy's had a single diamond, Cheryl's had three, and no matter how hard she tried, she could not get that thought out of her head. But how could she end up with a ring as good as Cheryl's, especially when, as she knew, that ring was all Logan could afford? Well, she soon figured, she could at least make a start by offering her current ring as down payment.

Logan is one of those men who look like a boy someone stretched and made taller. He grew up, the elder of two brothers, on a ranch in northern California. He has curly blond hair. He wears rimless glasses. He put a cartoon black handlebar mustache on his picture on Google+.

How did Logan feel when Tammy told him what she wanted to do? "I guess it hurt my feelings a little," he recalls now, "to know that all the ring I could afford still wasn't enough for her." But if a new ring was what Tammy wanted, so be it. He borrowed some more money from his brother and he bought it. Yet even that, after the initial, wide-eyed rush, did not keep Tammy happy for long. Nor, it seemed, did anything else.

That was odd, because she should have been, at the least, content. She was doing well at work. Her firm had picked her for its management-training program. She was with a great guy, and they lived in a pretty town near Sacramento called Davis, in a luxury apartment surrounded by manicured lawns and McMansions. "I felt like I had it made," Tammy recalls. "Like I had everything I could possibly want." From the outside looking in, to anyone who caught sight of her new three-diamond ring, or saw her and Logan out partying in town, or came over to their fancy home and saw the rooms full of stuff and closets full of clothes, she did.

Life was not so great on the inside, though. The two-hour drive to work and back was getting to her. So were the hours crunching numbers in her cubicle, and she began to wonder if she really believed in what she was doing. She started drinking more, and her weight ballooned. She had back pain, and it was getting worse. She was worrying about their bank loans, which always seemed to be growing. She began picking fights with Logan, even in public. "She'd say things, even in front of him, like 'If he was making better money I wouldn't have to go get money,'" Tina recalls.

In the midst of all that debt and stress and unhappiness, the singsong, happy-go-lucky Tammy had disappeared. Something had to give.

Logan had the idea first. It came to him in, of all places, the shower. He was in there when Tammy arrived home one night. He had had an idea, he called out, that could solve all their problems. "Oh, yeah?" was her muttered reply (which he did not hear). She could give up her job, he said. They would live on his income. To make that work, they would get rid of some of their stuff and move to a smaller apartment.

"Are you insane?" Tammy shot back. "Where the hell are my mom and dad going to stay when they visit? Where are we going to put all our things?"

"But your mom and dad hardly ever stay—" Logan began.

"We're not doing it," was Tammy's firm reply.

Logan heard *that*. He tried another tack.

"What if I get rid of my crap first?" he offered. "I'll get rid of that table you hate."

Now, that was an idea Tammy could agree with. So Logan got rid of the table. Then he sold his car and started cycling instead. "That's when Tammy got it," Logan remembers. "That's when she saw that getting rid of stuff wasn't wrong, that there was no shame in it. And without all the payments for my car, it meant we had a lot more money. That was when the lightbulb went on in her head." After that, they devised a safe, reversible way to find out if the reality of fewer possessions and less space would work for them. They would move everything out of their second bedroom. They would pretend they lived in a smaller apartment that had one bedroom rather than two. That way, if they did not like it, they could go back to their old life. Then, with their plan in place, they emptied the second bedroom and got rid of things they barely used or that just took up too much room, like Logan's guitars, a bookshelf Tammy's dad had made, and even their television.

Instead of being tough, as Tammy had worried, it was a revelation. After six months, they realized they were paying for a room they did not use anymore, and that having less did not feel worse, it felt better. They were spending less time managing, moving, and cleaning their things—and feeling guilty about not using them. They had more time, they were eating healthier, they were feeling less stressed, and getting along better.

Now that they had seen the upside of shedding their stuff, they got serious about it, giving some things away and selling the rest on Craigslist. They sold their other car. Tammy sold her wedding dress. They moved into a one-bedroom apartment.

Since they were paying less rent, Tammy was able to give up her job and her commute to do something that meant more to her— helping abused women. Even though she had taken a salary cut, from $40,000 to $24,000, their bills were much lower, so instead of building up more debts, they were able to start paying them off.

"All I wanted to do then," Tammy recalls, "was have fewer and fewer things and move into smaller and smaller apartments." Then she came across a woman online named Dee Williams. After being diagnosed with a heart condition, Williams realized that life was too short to spend wasting her energy and money on stuff, and so she moved out of her four-bedroom house and into a tiny home, which she had built for herself on a flatbed trailer. Along the way she had reduced the number of things she owned to fewer than three hundred, and got herself out of debt.

Tammy was transfixed. If she and Logan moved into a tiny home, she figured, that would mean even less room, less stuff, less debt, and, maybe, even more happiness. Now they had a goal, she and Logan kept downsizing their belongings. Tammy eventually slimmed her stuff down to only 69 possessions. That list included a camera, a toothbrush, a computer, three pairs of shoes, and four rings—including her wedding ring, though she was trying to sell it.

They kept moving into smaller and smaller apartments, paying off their debts and saving up, so they could buy a tiny home. Eventually, in September 2011, they moved into one. Designed by Williams, it includes a bedroom, a bathroom, a kitchen with the kind of cooker you use on a yacht, a pullout desk, and even a porch—and it measures 150 square feet. It could have fitted inside Cheryl's walk-in closet.

THE 39 SOCKS

If you think back to the bag-and-box experiment at the start of the book, you'll probably recall that Ryan Nicodemus pinpointed the things he owned as the root cause of his problems. With this approach, he exemplifies one minimalist response to Stuffocation. With Tammy Strobel's 69 things, she highlights another key aspect: the minimalists' obsession with numbers. Because this chapter is brought to you today not only by the number 69, but also by the numbers 33, 43, 47, 51, 100, and 288. You know how your more materialistic friends like to brag about how many, how much, and how great their possessions are? Minimalists do the same—but with how few things they have.

A Finnish man by the name of Henri Junttila and an American named Leo Babauta lived for some time with only 43 things. A woman called Nina Yau got by with 47 things. Colin Wright managed with 51. The counting all began in earnest when a blogger named Dave Bruno started the 100 Thing Challenge. In this, he asked his readers if they could reduce the number of their possessions to, you guessed it, 100.

The minimalist obsession with numbers is slightly absurd. Instead of showing off how many possessions they have, they are showing off how few they have. This is how they get status in their peer group. They have given up conspicuous consumption, if you like, for conspicuous anticonsumption. "It's a bit like a Buddhist running into a monastery," Colin Wright once admitted to me, "and shouting as loud as he can: 'I'm the humblest guy ever!'"

It is easy to laugh at the minimalists and their obsession with numbers. But think about those numbers for a moment, because there is something in them. How many things do you have? Count the things in your handbag, your wallet, or your wardrobe.

Wait a second, though: are you counting properly? How are you counting socks—does each sock count, does a pair count as one, or are socks one collective thing?

And here we have come across one of the thornier issues in the minimalist movement. Not everyone agrees on how you should count, and what counts when you are counting. Different people play by different rules. There is the Rule of Permanence, so perishable items are out. There is the Rule of Dependence, so the power cable to your MacBook does not count. And, crucially, there is the Rule of Ownership: if something is shared, like furniture everyone sits on, you do not count it. Or do you? Some do. Some don't, such as Dave Bruno. His 100 things do not include the dining room table, the family piano, and the plates everyone uses. Some start out saying they will count everything but soon realize how long that will take and give up. Some sound like they are really going to count everything, but then tail off when it becomes hard to keep track.

Here is Joshua Fields Millburn explaining how he totted up his 288 possessions:

"So, unlike many other people who count their stuff, I literally counted everything I own, including things like the clock on the wall, my toothbrush, photo frames, my solo oven mitt, the trash can under the sink, salt and pepper shakers, cooking utensils, and even that metal thing in the shower that holds shampoo. I even counted the items that other people leave off their lists—my couch, chairs, dining table, and other furniture—because they are considered 'shared items'; I live by myself so these things needed to be counted. I did group some things into groups (e.g., my underwear, clothes hangers, food, etc.), but I only grouped things when necessary (N.B. the only thing I struggled with grouping were my books. I don't own a ton of books/novels—I got rid of most of them this year—but I grouped the ones I still have because they all fit on my little coffee table, and I'm a fiction writer, so I use them as references quite often)."

So whose numbers can you trust, and how many things do you really own? This counting thing has become faintly ridiculous. But there is a serious point to be made here. Once you start your own counting, whichever rules you use, those 47, 69, or 100 things soon sound a lot more impressive. So, are you ready to count again? If that sounds like too much effort right now, let's take a trip to my sock drawer instead.

As I was writing this chapter, hoping you would play along and go and count your stuff before reading any further, I realized two things. The first is that I would not bother. I would keep on reading, just like you have. The second is that, actually, if I am going to ask you to do it, I ought to share how my counting went.

Since the importance of Stuffocation dawned on me and I started researching this book, I have read about and talked to some of the world's most compelling downsizers, minimalists, and postmaterialists. As I have found out more about how they are finding greater happiness and meaning in their lives, I have started following in their footsteps. I have cleared up and thrown out. I have stopped buying so much. I have started using what I already have. It turns out when I counted though—and this shocked me as much as it may surprise you—that I am still quite the Sock Guy.

I am far from a minimalist—as you are about to find out—so I knew counting everything I own would take forever. Socks, I thought, would be a good place to start. But before we delve into mine, picture your sock drawer for a moment. Is it tidy? Color-coded? Bursting out? Are all your pairs in there?

Okay, no more delays. Here is my sock confession: I have twenty-nine pairs of everyday socks, plus the bright blue pair I am wearing now. Then I have two pairs of sport socks, for the one time each year I play squash or go running. I have a pair of cycling socks. Who knew they existed? They were a gift from my stepdad. He loves cycling. I have three pairs of football socks, including a pair with so many holes I do not wear them anymore. They were my dad's. They are sentimental socks. Who knew that was possible? I also have three pairs of socks that are not in the drawer: ski socks, kept in a bag at the far end of the loft. So I have thirty-nine pairs of socks. I could go more than a month without washing any. And there I was thinking I had—excuse the pun—pared back. So where does that confessional count leave me? Easy. I would use the counting rules that best suit me. Socks? One item.

It is easy to laugh at how the minimalists count, and you can see why some people might look down their noses at the minimalists and say all they have done is swap one status game for another. There are two responses to that. First, expressing status—and displaying what evolutionary psychologists call "fitness markers"—is essential for all animals, including humans. To claim their position in the social hierarchy and get a mate, lions ruffle their thick, dark manes. Birds of paradise shake their tail feathers. Howler monkeys howl. And humans, in a materialistic consumer culture at least, wear big watches and diamond necklaces, and carry the latest mobile phone or handbag. And if all these other species have ways of telling others who they are and how fit they are, why shouldn't minimalists have a way to express status in their emerging culture as well? Besides, they tend to use the numbers as a target and a benchmark, and they often only count at the beginning of their journey to having less.

This is how counting helped a woman in Utah by the name of Courtney Carver, for instance. Carver had been a keen skier, a regular cyclist, a successful businesswoman, and a dedicated shopper. Whenever she went out of town, for example, she would buy a new pair of sunglasses. When, a few years back, she woke up to find all her energy had gone and she was diagnosed with multiple sclerosis, she blamed it on her materialistic way of life. "It was my body's way of rejecting my lifestyle of more," she says. To prove to herself that she could live with less, she began by reducing her wardrobe to 33 items. That count included her purse, one handbag, and a single pair of sunglasses. Then, to bring minimalism into all areas of her life, she and her husband, Mark Tuttle, invented a game where they would hide things from the other. "If you didn't notice it was gone, that meant you didn't need it," Tuttle says. "And that meant we could get rid of it."

By conducting Nicodemus's bag-and-box experiment, or by pretending to have less space like Strobel and Smith, or by playing Carver and Tuttle's "did you miss it?" game—trying minimalism on for size becomes far easier, more fun, and more engaging. That is useful, particularly when you bear in mind that it is not easy to get off the hamster wheel of materialism. It may even be essential, especially when you remember that minimalists are, after all, fighting impulses about acquiring and accumulating that have been ingrained over millennia.

And although it is easy to laugh at the counting, the results are far from laughable. The way Smith and Strobel's life has improved is compelling proof of that. By getting rid of their possessions, they reduced their spending and their debt and Strobel was able to take a job she found more fulfilling. That meant no more long commute, no more back pain, more time to make healthy food, and more time to exercise. As a result, her weight returned to normal, she felt healthier and happier, and she stopped fighting with Smith. That one decision—to have fewer things—set in motion a whole domino line of good effects.

It worked for them. It has worked for many others I have spoken with, like Nicodemus and Millburn, and Nina Yau, and Colin Wright. Minimalism clearly works for many people—though it is still easy, at first glance, to dismiss it as a lifestyle choice for single-tons in their twenties and thirties with minimal responsibilities.

But minimalism is also achievable for families. It has worked for Courtney Carver, who has a teenage daughter. Carver's sickness is now, as her doctors told her recently, "like it's in suspension." And minimalism works for many more people I have interviewed who have families, like Chris Wray in Cambridgeshire in the U.K., Rachel Jonat on the Isle of Man, and Joshua Becker in Peoria, Arizona. All of them juggle minimalism with family life and two children apiece. Minimalism makes sense for bigger families too. One of the leading lights of the minimalist blog community, Leo Babauta, lives in San Francisco with his wife and six children.

Minimalism clearly works for a lot of people, and it is beginning to catch on. It is hard to know exactly how many minimalists there are. There is no box, so far, on the census form marked "minimal-ist." But we can see the rise of minimalism in the hundreds, possibly thousands, of minimalist blogs all around the world—from Canada to Malaysia, via Texas, France, Australia, and the Netherlands—and the millions who read them. More than a million people read Leo Babauta's blog, for instance. And, as I mentioned before, more than two million have read about Ryan Nicodemus and Joshua Fields Millburn's minimalist journey: some of them met Nicodemus and Millburn in person, on the hundred-city tour of the United States, Canada, Ireland, and the U.K. they went on in 2014. So if minimal-ism is attracting all these people, does that mean it will work for you? If you want to be happier, should you get rid of most of your stuff?

IS GETTING RID OF STUFF ENOUGH?

It is clear, then, that de-cluttering is a good idea. As we have learned—from the stories of the minimalists and from the evidence gathered by the anthropologists and psychologists—too much stuff is a serious problem, and living with less can make people happier. Does that mean minimalism could solve Stuffocation? Does that mean you should become a minimalist? Does it mean that, under the mounting pressure of Stuffocation, we are all going to be minimalists in the future?

Consuming fewer things would solve many of the problems of Stuffocation. As minimalists, we would cause less environmental harm. Less burdened by things and the pursuit for more things, we would most likely be happier. We would be content in our downsized, smaller homes. We would happily shift away from material objects to technological solutions: from having a library of books or a collection of CDs to a hard drive of ebooks or songs, for example, or even not owning them at all, but only having access to them. Seen this way, it looks like minimalism offers an elegant, simple solution, and that the answer to the first two questions is clear. Yes, minimalism could solve Stuffocation. And yes, if you look at it like this, you should become a minimalist.

Does this also mean, then, that we will all be minimalists at some point in the future? To answer this question, to be able to confidently determine whether minimalism will replace materialism and become the dominant value system, requires, of course, close scrutiny. The first place to look is the past. Is there a precedent for this sort of thing, for wholesale cultural change?

This question is vitally important, because there are many who will say that all this talk of some enlightened new way of living is all well and good—but that materialistic consumerism is just too established, and that our culture will remain as it is. When you think about that point of view, you could see it as the typical, reactionary response from the sort of grumpy old men who are invested in the status quo. Or you could think it suggests a real lack of imagination. After all, thinking things will always remain the same requires far less mental agility than imagining how they could be different. But worse than that, thinking that things will remain the same in the future is, when you come to think about it, foolish.

Because things change. Technology changes. Our clothes and culture, what we eat and how we think, change. Or else how do you explain: cars, cameras, and camera phones, flared and skinny jeans, snacking, the changing structure of the family and the rise and fall of the family meal, and women getting the vote? Change is inevitable. Given this truth, the question shifts from "Will things change?" to "*How* will things change?"

To answer that question, we should begin by looking for another time when the majority of people changed their values, attitudes, and behaviors. Has that ever happened? As we saw in the story of how the captains of consciousness created a new throwaway culture in the twentieth century, it has. The attitudes, values, and behaviors of a rich, cultured, inquisitive, innovative few changed, and then the great mass of people in our societies followed. They sought happiness and status in material things. They found purpose and fulfillment by seeking better standards of living, for themselves and their children. So to answer the question, is a sea change in attitudes, values, and behaviors the sort of thing that happens? The answer is an unequivocal yes. It happened in the twentieth century.

That does not mean, of course, that the shift which is coming is necessarily from materialism to minimalism. Is there any evidence, from the past and the present, that suggests minimalism is a long-term, growing trend?

When you look at our behavior as consumers, it is actually quite the opposite. The British, for instance, consume far more than their ancestors did. The amount the average Briton spent on clothing almost doubled between 1990 and 2004. The average British woman now buys fifty-eight items of clothing each year. There are twice as many things in her wardrobe today as there were in 1980. There are twenty-two things in there she has never worn.

And Americans are similar, consuming three times as much as their ancestors did fifty years ago, and buying twice as many items of clothing today as twenty years ago. In 1991, the average American bought thirty-four items of clothing. By 2007, Americans were buying sixty-seven items every year. That's a lot of shirts, skirts, blouses, pants, and socks. It means Americans buy a new piece of clothing every four to five days. In 1994, they bought 1.4 billion bath towels. Today, it's 2 billion. In 1995, they bought 188 million toasters and toaster-like devices. Today, it's 279 million.

As these statistics clearly show, minimalism may be an innovative way of living for a few pioneers. But it is a million toasters and towels away from something you would call a long-term, mainstream trend.

Moreover, if you consider minimalism as an innovative lifestyle, and scrutinize it using the five key questions a forecaster would in order to work out if it is going to catch on, it starts to look far less likely that it will shift from the innovative few to the many in the mainstream.

In answer to questions one and two, minimalism, it is fair to say, does well: it is easy to understand, and also quite easy to try. Embracing total minimalism requires serious commitment, but there are many ways to give it a go, like Nicodemus and Millburn's bag-and-box experiment or Carver and Tuttle's "did you miss it?" game. The answer to question three—is it observable?—is both yes and no. It is observable online, in social networks and through blogging. Minimalists, remember, get a lot of kudos for their conspicuous anticonsumption. Why else would they announce how few things they have, and even post pictures of all their things online? But it is not observable in the real world. How could you tell that someone was a minimalist if they passed you on the street—unless you saw them every day and noticed they were wearing the same clothes?

Minimalism begins to stumble further when you consider question four: is it compatible with the way we live now? Since minimalism's central idea is to have less, rather than more, it is directly opposite to materialism. It is about as incompatible as it could be.

If minimalism faltered at question four, it falls flat at the last of the five questions: compared to the way we live now, is minimalism better? At first glance, the answer is a little unclear because while, as we've learned, excessive materialism is not good for us, it does not prove that the answer is to get rid of almost all of our possessions. Getting rid of your excess stuff is very different from getting rid of most of your stuff. But if you consider the question for just a moment longer, the answer will stop any movement to minimalism in its tracks. Because stuff, simply put, is good.

Stuff includes the tools that enable us to do more, go faster, and achieve things far beyond our natural capabilities. Consider: a stone chisel that opens a nut our bare hands couldn't break so we can access the food inside, or studded shoes so we can run faster or not fall over when we take our shot to get on the green, or cars that go faster than we can run, or airplanes that mean we can fly and go south not only for the winter but the weekend.

Stuff is good, because physical possessions can give us not only a sense of security, but actual protection from the elements to help us survive. Admittedly, your new fifty-inch OLED television may not ensure you make it through the night, but consider the difference between having a home and not having a home, or the coat that keeps you warm in winter.

Stuff is good, because it helps us express our identities and beliefs, and display our fitness indicators: as lions with their dark manes, and birds of paradise with their Day-Glo feathers, so human culture has evolved so that we indicate our suitability for mating through visible, physical objects. This is why some people wear aqua green Miami Dolphins shirts, others wear red Liverpool FC tops, and others wear gold lamé jackets. It's why one person drives a Prius and another a Mustang. It explains why one pedals a fixed-wheel bicycle and another rides a Harley. And it makes sense of why one sports a bead bracelet handwoven by the Amazon's Yawanawa tribespeople and another wears a fat gold chain.

And stuff is good, because it connects us to others, to events, and to our own pasts. This is why your friends have wooden statues from that time they went to Africa, and why you can't get rid of the vase your mother-in-law bought you, even if you only bring it out when she comes over for dinner.

Stuff is also good because it reflects our basic requirement for stimulus. Think of a baby with its first rattle, a child with a new bike, or you with a new phone or barbecue or piece of art for your living room wall.

And finally, stuff is good because it feels good, because we, as physical creatures, enjoy the sheer physicality of objects—the look and feel and smell, for instance, of an old wooden chair, a new leather bag, a cashmere scarf, or a 3D-printed mobile phone case.

Stuff, in short, is good because it is human, and useful, and social, and fun. It feels good, it makes us feel good. This is a serious problem for minimalism. Because if stuff is so good, why would anyone join a movement that says you should have as little of it as possible? This list of reasons why stuff is good looks, to me at least, like a set of very difficult hurdles for minimalism to get over.

And I don't think it will clear them, so I do not believe the answer to Stuffocation is minimalism. I do not think you should give up most of your stuff and become a minimalist. I cannot see minimalism replacing materialism as our defining value system.

Perhaps the problem with minimalism stems from where the idea comes from. It is, if you think about it, defined more by what it is not—that is, materialism—than by what it is. This almost knee-jerk negativity makes it less its own idea and more of a reactive response. If materialism was a love affair that was breaking up, minimalism, sadly, is nothing but the rebound.

Or if you were to think of today's capitalist system—underpinned by a consumer culture that, in turn, is upheld by materialistic values—

as a car driving along a road, and Stuffocation is the name of the crossroads at which it has just arrived, then minimalism would be like going straight ahead, along the same road, but pushing the brake pedal as hard as you can, and most likely with both feet. If that is the case—and that seems to sum it up to me—minimalism is not very aspirational. Who, after all, drives a car with the brakes on all the time? That is hardly the type of lifestyle that the masses will aspire to and buy into and fall in love with. It is unlikely to be the sort of message that will spark a revolution in attitudes, values, and behaviors. Minimalism has many merits. But I do not think it will appeal to enough people to replace materialism. The solution to Stuffocation will not simply involve pushing on the brakes, throwing out the stuff, and slowing down the materialistic machine. The answer, I am sure, will be far more aspirational and positive.

Perhaps the ultimate problem with minimalism, though, is not that it is negative, but that it is not extreme enough: while it rails against the current system, it is still defined and bound by that system. The people choosing it remain within the system. So perhaps what we need is not to reject the rules of the game as it stands, but to play a different game altogether. Maybe, instead of just dragging our feet and slowing the system down, what we should do at this crossroads is take a sharp turn off the path we are currently on, onto a route much less traveled, one that will take us even further away from today's throwaway culture.

6

The Simple Life and the
Cage-Free Family

When Aimée LeVally decided that today's system was not for her, she slammed on the brakes and hauled her family—husband, children, dogs—from their smart suburban home in Texas across the country to the side of a rugged mountain in New Mexico, miles from their nearest neighbors.

LeVally is tiny. She is five feet tall. She has porcelain skin that is flecked with freckles. She wears her fiery red hair in a shoulder-length bob or wrapped in a head scarf. She looks, from a distance, a little like a pixie doll.

It was July 2008, the wettest July anyone could remember in that part of Texas. Rain fell morning, afternoon, evening. All day, every day, gray sheets came crashing down. Eighty inches fell in all. It turned the grass in LeVally's garden a green so bright and shiny it looked fake. She was staring out through the floor-to-ceiling windows of her suburban home, sitting in a big leather easy chair in the living room, with her legs tucked under her. She felt like her life had shattered like a vase thrown hard at a stone floor.

LeVally did not dare move. She had suffered for years from fibromyalgia, a debilitating condition that causes pain all over the body, and sometimes hurt her so much she couldn't walk and couldn't stand anyone touching her. It was often so bad LeVally thought she might go mad. She was desperate to scream, to let out some of the pressure inside. But she was afraid that if she started she might never stop. She couldn't share the pain—not even with her husband, Jeff Harris, or her father, Ren LeVally, who was living with them to help out. Telling other people about it made them squirm. Whatever she did, she dared not move: any movement would invite in more pain.

Days before, doctors had told her they had given up. They had tried everything, they said, even the latest treatments. But there was nothing more they could do. "When I heard that, something snapped," LeVally says now. "And I just screamed, right there, as loud as my lungs would scream. And I kept crying for days."

Eventually, the crying stopped and she sat, in silence, in that easy chair, desperately trying to come to terms with the shattered fragments of her life and to get used to the idea that she might spend every single day feeling that level of pain. She had slipped deeper and deeper into despair, until she finally hit rock-bottom. In that moment, at the lowest ebb of what life could offer, as she sat staring out of the window, she came across a glimmer of hope.

"Suddenly I realized that nothing could be worse than that moment," she says. "And as that thought came to me, I felt this very odd, very strange sense of peace. In that moment, I realized, if no one could help, the only person who could do something about it was me."

From then on, whenever her energy levels would allow, LeVally was researching—reading this, clicking that, connecting with people who had similar issues, looking for clues to solve her problem. "I looked around for what I could change, and the first thing I saw was food," she says. "If I changed what I put in, would that change what came out?"

She experimented. She cut out meat. She drank raw milk. She brought back meat, but only meat from farmers' markets. She avoided preservatives. She made stock out of bones—it helps heal the lining of the stomach. She bought chickens and roosters and big bags of chicken's feet—they contain gelatin, which is good for cartilage, bones, and joints—and made more stock. She stopped eating anything that, she decided, was not food.

"The more I looked at most things that come in a box or a bag or a can, the more I realized they contain things that are known to cause serious health problems," she says. "Most food that's available is covered in chemicals of all kinds. Once I discovered all that, it was obvious why I was sick."

Her new diet worked—not perfectly, but it was at least a start. Most of her symptoms eased. Her strength returned. She got her life back. She could be a mother to her kids, Quinn and Nichola, again. She reveled in every moment, playing with her children, cooking for them, going for walks with Harris and their fluffy white Great Pyrenees dogs. She sucked as much pleasure as she could out of everything she did—because she knew that the fibromyalgia and its agonizing pain were never far away.

Then LeVally got to thinking. If the system she'd been taught to trust produced the food that had been poisoning her, what else was wrong with it? So she started to change more than just the food she and her family ate. She started purging every aspect of their lives. She canceled the cable television subscription. She threw out the kids' plastic toys. She got rid of all the spare spatulas, spoons, dishes, pots, and pans that were cluttering up the kitchen. "I kept going and going," she will tell you now. "I went around the house like a crazy person with a sledgehammer."

The more stuff she shed, the better she felt. Then she wondered, if modern culture had made her sick, what if she lived outside it? What if she lived in a different time and place?

That's when she realized that everything else—all the things that her husband's career as a $120,000-a-year IT consultant brought them—had to go too, including the house. Her father suggested they put some of their possessions in storage "while they figure things out," but, to Aimée LeVally, all that stuff was exactly what was holding them back. Harris was right behind her.

They gave a few things to Ren, mostly family heirlooms, like a silver sugar bowl and a bone china cream pitcher, and a few bits of furniture. They donated the rest—vases, wood carvings, their oval, eight-seater dining table, the chairs and cabinet that matched it, their spare computers—to charity.

They kept only enough to keep them going, and what they could fit in a motor home that Harris had found. It was thirty feet long, the size of a small bus, painted brown and white, with aluminum panels.

The day the family left town is seared into Ren LeVally's memory. That day, he and Harris had filled up a truck with the last of their stuff and taken it to a charity shop, and Harris had helped Ren move into a new place in the city. The parking lot outside his apartment building was their last stop before they took off. After hugs and see-you-soons, the dogs jumped, the kids were carried, and Aimée LeVally and Harris clambered into everybody's new home on wheels.

"I think the sun was setting but I wasn't really paying attention," Ren LeVally says now. "It was pretty emotional. Everybody was waving. Aimée and Jeff were waving. The kids were waving. I was waving. The dogs were barking. It was quite a send-off. I watched them go out of the parking lot, down the driveway, onto the street, and waved till they were gone. Then I went upstairs, opened a beer, and sat down on that big leather easy chair in the dark."

For the next year or so, Aimée LeVally and Harris, the kids and the dogs toured the country. They visited twenty-six states. They went to LeVally's sister's graduation in Wisconsin. They went to a festival called the Rainbow Gathering in Wyoming. Finally they stayed at the edge of a mountain community called Taos in New Mexico. "We stayed on top of a mountain that first night," LeVally will tell you. "We watched the sun go down and the Sangre de Cristo Mountains turn scarlet red, and then we saw the Milky Way."

When LeVally woke the next morning, she knew she had found the place she wanted to live. So they went out that day and found the home where they live now. It is a cabin, about a thousand feet above and a ten-minute drive from the main town of Taos. It sits in three hundred acres of woodland—ideal for Harris to chop logs for their fire, for their kids to play, their goats to graze, their dogs to roam, and for growing as many potatoes, tomatoes, chickpeas, black beans, green beans, and jalapeños as they can. It is about as far, in terms of lifestyle, as they could get from their old home and life. "Back there, everything is so prescribed," says LeVally. "You get up in the morning, you go to work, you come home. If you're lucky and the traffic wasn't bad, you spend a couple of hours with the kids. Then you do the same thing the next day. You do that for five days and then you have two days to go out and spend the money you made. And the big reward for all that is a vacation once a year, when you get to buy things. And that's it. That's life. A lot of people can't see a problem with that. But some of us aren't happy with it. Some of us need more from our time on this planet. I do. I don't think I would even know how to live that way anymore. Everything here, all of it, it's all so much more intense. Everything feels so real, and so much more rewarding and healthier and free and fulfilling."

And LeVally's fibromyalgia? The threat of its return will never leave her, but she does not have the symptoms anymore. She no longer spends her days curled up on a sofa, screaming inside. She is far too busy—with the kids, the kid goats, the vegetables, and her life outside the cage of the modern world.

IS THE SIMPLE LIFE THE EASY ANSWER?

LeVally and her family are not the first to reject the modern world and prefer a simpler life closer to nature, of course. People have been turning their backs on civilization ever since it began. One of the first documented examples is of the Greek philosopher Diogenes of Sinope. In the fourth century B.C., he got rid of all his possessions and lived in a barrel in the Athenian marketplace.

The most famous person to reject the modern world and advocate simple living was the nineteenth-century American author Henry David Thoreau. In 1845, frustrated by modern life—especially at the way people were no longer self-sufficient and spent so much time worrying about what was going on in far-off places—he escaped it and went back to nature. He did not go a long way, only to the woods at the edge of his hometown. There he lived a simple life in a wood cabin, ten feet wide by fifteen long, with a window on either side. He grew vegetables. He gathered wild apples and chestnuts. He swam in the nearby Walden Pond. He watched the sun come up and set. He listened to squirrels scuttling across his roof, foxes barking in the woods, and trains whistling along the far shore. He counted his belongings. They included one bed and one desk, one cup and one spoon, one jug for oil and one for molasses, two knives and two forks, three plates and three chairs—"one for solitude, two for friendship, three for society." Thoreau had escaped modern life less to count though, like today's minimalists, and more to question what life was all about.

Thoreau is arguably the most influential advocate for simple living. His influence has been so strong that when a man named Duane Elgin set out to write what is now considered the bible of the modern simple living movement, Elgin felt he had to explain that, to live simply, you did not have to follow Thoreau's example and go live in the woods.

Published in 1981 and again in 1993, Elgin's book, *Voluntary Simplicity: Toward a Way of Life That Is Outwardly Simple, Inwardly Rich,* struck a nerve with many of the overworked and overspent Americans of the era. In a 1989 article in *Fortune* magazine called "Is Greed Dead?," three quarters of working Americans aged twenty-five to forty-nine said they would like "to see our country return to a simpler lifestyle, with less emphasis on material success." And a cover feature in *Time* magazine in 1991 called "The Simple Life" reported that 69 percent of Americans said they would like to "slow down and live a more relaxed life," and that only 7 percent of them thought it was "worth bothering to shop for status-symbol products."

These statistics remind me of the more recent surveys that I quoted at the beginning of this book, which, you may recall, noted: that "people in mature markets have had enough of excess," that "a majority of us could live happily without *most of the goods we own*," and that two thirds of us—almost exactly the same proportion as in the *Time* survey from 1991—would prefer a simpler life.

Simple living, it is clear, is the sort of thing that has appealed to people in the past, and appeals to people now. It also, so research has shown, makes people happier. Could it be the answer to Stuffocation?

IS SIMPLE LIVING PLAIN BORING?

Thoreau lavished the highest praise he could muster on simple living. The answer to life, he wrote, was "Simplicity, simplicity, simplicity!" His readers, he thought, should "Simplify, simplify." But, a little after two years, he did not. Two years, two months, and two days after he went into the woods to live frugally, simply, and close to nature, Thoreau reemerged and reentered modern life. He had, as he wrote, "several more lives to live, and could not spare any more time for that one." He had had enough, in other words, of the simple life. He spent seven years living in the comfort of a friend's home, writing up his notes, and then published his hymn to the simple life, *Walden; or, Life in the Woods*. Later, he moved into his own regular home. He even ran the family pencil business, John Thoreau & Co., for a time.

Think about that for a moment. Isn't it odd that the man most famous for advocating voluntary simplicity gave it up after only two years? If he thought it was so great, why didn't he stay? More important, what does that tell us about simple living as a lifestyle choice? I think it is a bit like someone telling you they love a restaurant and that you really should go there, but, actually, they've been there a couple of times and they're not going back: if you heard that, would you eat there?

And contrast Thoreau's ultimate comment on voluntary simplicity with what Samuel Johnson said about England's capital: "When a man is tired of London, he is tired of life." Isn't Thoreau, by saying he wanted to do other things, and by leaving after such a short time, effectively saying the opposite—that "When a man is tired of simplicity, fair enough, there are other, more interesting things to do"? With that, Thoreau has damned simple living, especially for anyone today. Because if simple living could not keep someone in the nineteenth century interested, how much duller will it seem to someone in the twenty-first, when there are so many more exciting distractions and possibilities?

What Thoreau tells us, ultimately, is that escaping the comfortable cage of modern life is fun for a limited period of time, and it can help us put things into perspective. But voluntary simplicity is not stimulating enough to be a serious, long-term life choice.

And there is another side to simple living, even more curious than the fact that it is not very stimulating: it is actually quite complicated.

THE COMPLICATED SIDE OF SIMPLE LIVING

Most years, there are three hundred days of sunshine in Taos. In summer, the temperatures are balmy too. But they are not in winter, when, on average, 305 inches of snow falls. For a family from a wealthy suburb in Texas, unused to chopping down trees and preparing firewood, who did not know how much wood they would need, or how often they would get snowed in, that first winter was really tough. The second one was as well. And the third. Those winters in Taos, they are all tough. If you had talked to Aimée LeVally one of those winters, she would have told you.

"We're in survival mode at this point," she'd say. "We're always learning new rules to get by. It's hard to reflect on what we're trying to do here. All we can hope for is that, at the end of the day, we're still afloat. It's really hard right now. On a hierarchy of life, we're dealing with the foundation. It's almost impossible for us to consider higher levels. We're living on a day-to-day basis. When we've survived another day, when we've tackled another new problem, all I can think is, 'Now I need to go to sleep.'"

Their first problem was Harris collecting enough firewood to keep them warm, and doing it in a way that did not get him killed. "It takes weeks of extremely hard physical labor to go out in the snow to bring the amount of wood we need, to turn into firewood. And Jeff had to learn how to do it—how to take a tree down without killing himself," LeVally would say. "In cartoons, they just shout *timber* and then stand and watch the tree arc towards the ground. But it isn't like that. It's incredibly dangerous. They can fall in any direction. That's why they call them widow-makers."

Sometimes LeVally even thought about going back to their old life. "When the rent's about to be due and we have to buy groceries because the garden didn't produce enough to get us through winter, I wonder, I really do," she would admit.

Here we have come across one of the thornier, and unintended, consequences of simple living. When you first think about it, especially when you're daydreaming from your armchair or bed or sun lounger, picturing what a rose-tinted simple life would look like for you, it looks something like this: the sun is shining, the vegetables are growing, your kids are playing safely nearby, and your partner looks rosy-cheek-healthy and rather sexy in that country get-up. But, as you can see in LeVally and Harris's case, simple living just is not that, well, simple. While it may seem, from a distance, simple because it is unencumbered with the stuff of modern life, close up that simplicity is complicated by the necessities that come with staying alive—which are precisely the sort of pressures that modern life is supposed to shield us from.

There are some exhilarating benefits that come with the simple life LeVally and Harris lead: like fewer chemicals and additives in your food, a greater sense of self-sufficiency, and more time to spend together as a family.

But there are also some tough downsides, because the odd truth of simple living is that LeVally and Harris have swapped the stresses and cage of the modern material world for the problems of life before the Industrial Revolution. Okay, so it isn't exactly seventeenth-century living. LeVally and her family have electricity, after all, and a pickup truck. But like people in the seventeenth century, they spend most of their energy, as LeVally said, "dealing with the foundation." So they tend vegetables, not for a school project or for fun, but to keep the family alive. And they heat their home and their water through the heavy work of felling trees, then chopping, hauling, hoarding, and burning logs.

Survival, in their way of living, is not something that happens at the flick of a switch and thanks to a monthly direct debit. Instead, it happens as a direct result of the hard work they do each day with their own bare hands. So, in this respect, they are living far closer to how people lived before the Industrial Revolution. At least people had far lower expectations of life back then, and the legacy of generations who knew how to live on the land. Those skills have largely been forgotten by most of us. Who today knows how to milk a cow, kill a chicken, make yarn, or plow a field?

So there are some serious problems with simple living as a lifestyle, and with any notion that it might become mainstream, replace materialism as society's defining value system, and solve Stuffocation.

If simple living is actually quite tough, how do we make sense of the idea that so many people would like a simpler life? Consider again those statistics that Elgin reported, that 75 percent of twenty-five- to forty-nine-year-old working Americans wanted to live more simply in 1989, and that 69 percent of the population said the same in 1991. How do those statements fit with the fact that, in the years since then, Americans have consumed so much more—that in the decades directly after, for instance, the amount of clothes they bought doubled?

The way to make sense of this is, as behavioral psychologists have shown time and again, to realize people do not necessarily behave in a rational, logical way. It is perfectly possible to say we want one thing and then do something entirely different. We want to avoid Krispy Kremes, for example. But when someone opens up a box and offers us one, it is hard to say no. And we like the sound of a less stressful, simpler life. But we are not prepared to give up all the benefits of the modern world, like Wi-Fi and smartphones and central heating and dishwashers, to get it. Besides, many of us are stuck in the deep ruts of materialism. We still believe that to be considered successful, by our peers and by ourselves, we need material badges of success—and that still means a lot of stuff.

The reason why so many of us think we want a simpler life with fewer possessions, while at the same time leading a more complex lifestyle with more stuff, can be found by taking a close look at the system the captains of consciousness engineered. That system has provided us with a great many things that are enjoyable to wear, watch, drive, and play with—like J Brand jeans, HD televisions, the MINI Cooper, and the iPad. But as much as the system provides these thrills, it also undermines them, by deliberately making us feel like we are behind the times and missing out. It does this by creating an endless cycle of new and improved things—like J Brand's new skinny jeans, 3D televisions, the MINI Cooper Coupe, and the next-generation iPad.

No wonder, when you think about it this way, the system makes us wish for one thing but do another. It leaves us pining for the older, simpler version that did the job perfectly well yesterday and still works fine today. But, at the same time, it tells us about the next, new and improved, better thing now available, and makes us think about it, lust after it, and buy it.

NOT SIMPLE, BUT SIMPLER LIVING

LeVally and Harris did not give up. They made it through their first winters. They learned fast. He learned to cut trees safely and to prepare enough firewood. She has gotten better at growing vegetables and raising animals. But it was still not enough.

In February 2013, they came down from the mountain, recrossed the country, and went back to Texas, where Harris had taken a job. They moved into a complex with two swimming pools, huge flat-screen televisions, a dishwasher, central heating, air-conditioning, and maid service. Had they given up? Not entirely. They only stayed two months. The job is an IT role, so Harris can do it remotely, from their mountainside cabin. The money from that job will ensure the future of their simple life. They plan to spend it on a long list of things LeVally has drawn up, including: a new car, new fences, a barn, a woodshed, a cellar, an underground greenhouse, and to fix their wood-carrying truck. With all these new things, winter will be much easier to manage. Life will not be so hard, nor will it be so simple.

But they have not given up on their dream. They are just trying again, treading a fine line between the simplicity of plain living and the complications of modern life. Rather than blindly following the road ahead of modern life or stumbling along the much rockier path of simple living, they have found a compromise route somewhere in the middle. They do not have television. But they still have Wi-Fi. She writes a blog from her MacBook, called the *Cage Free Family*. He does his work from home. They have helped pay for their escape from materialism by going back in, if only remotely. This may be the only practical way that simple living might work in the future. A better name for this more realistic version of voluntary simplicity might then be *simpler* living.

This, I believe, holds the clue to understanding how voluntary simplicity will impact on society and the world we live in. Just as most people saying they wanted simpler lives at the end of the 1980s and beginning of the 1990s did not lead to a mass exodus from materialism, so the studies showing that most of us feel "weighed down by our own excess" today will not lead to a simple living revolution this time around. While simple living sounds like a good idea in theory, in practice it is too dull, and it involves too much of the sort of hard manual labor people did in the seventeenth century. But its appeal is likely to affect mainstream values. In fact, it already has. You can see it in the trend for people to grow their own and buy organic food. But while people in mainstream society have embraced many of the values of simple living, they have co-opted them into ever more complex, consumption-based ways of living. Growing your own has spawned an industry, for instance, in seeds and gardening equipment. Organic has become another marketing category. The impact of simple living, clearly, will not be large enough to solve Stuffocation.

And so, if we are not going to find the answer to Stuffocation by taking a sharp turn off the path we are currently on, maybe it would be better to look for a solution inside the system.

7

The Medium Chill

You may, by now, have thought about the way you currently live your life. You may have wondered about the attitudes and ambitions you have long embraced, about whether they really are ideal for your long-term happiness. You may have toyed with the idea of getting rid of some of your things or adopting a slightly simpler life.

But even as your imagination went down that path, it probably wandered back to that bigger house, better car, or this season's handbag, and, deep down, you wondered if you really have the stomach for all the changes these new lifestyles require. And then you might have realized, as you read, that even though you would, genuinely, like to be happier and live a more meaningful existence, each of these ways of living sounded too much like hard work.

If that is the case, I have the perfect solution for you, the ideal easy-access pioneer lifestyle—the sort you could try at home today, without much fuss, without doing too much. In fact, the less you do the more you'll be doing it. To live this next lifestyle, you do not need to pull up stakes and head for the mountains or the countryside. You do not have to give up all the conveniences of modern life and start living like it's 1700. And you do not have to bag up all your shoes, shirts, and socks, and make each possession justify its existence in your home.

This easygoing way of living is less an angry struggle against the rat race of modern life, the way that minimalism or voluntary simplicity is. Instead, this lifestyle is more like a "No thanks, I don't think I'll bother with that" shrug. Instead of an energetic battle against the one-way system of materialism, this innovative way of living is happy to chug along the same path. Instead of getting all het up about the bothersome parts of today's culture, it ignores them. Rather than fret about the competitive arms race that is conspicuous consumption, it consumes as and when it needs. This lifestyle has an unlikely, and slightly reluctant, hero. He is a tall man with a bushy, black beard who goes by the name of Dave.

Most days, you'll find Dave—full name David Roberts—in regular blue jeans and a dark red plaid shirt. He grew up lower-middle-class, in backwater Tennessee. It was the sort of monotonous town that is the inevitable result of mass production. It was based, if you can call it that, on the modern world's signpost to materialism: a suburban row of big-box stores. "It was very dull," Dave will tell you. "The sort of place where kids would drive up and down the strip and the parking lot for fun, and where you'd bump into people you knew in Walmart."

Dave now lives a regular, low-key life, in a nondescript neighborhood in a smallish house, in Seattle, with his two children and wife, Jennifer Roberts. He calls her Jen. She has long, dark hair. Friends say she looks like a taller version of the comedian Tina Fey. Jen works for a local coffee importer. She has been there more than fourteen years. Dave writes for a website called Grist.org that covers environmental issues. He has been there nine years. They take regular vacations, to see family or spend time with old friends and their kids. They go with them to the three-day Pickathon roots music festival in summer, for instance, and they ski with them in winter. They spend their free time hanging out, watching television, teaching their boys to read. They are very happy, and they had never really thought much about how they lived, till Dave got talking a while back with a friend from college named Teyo. He wrote about that conversation in an article on Grist:

"I was visiting with an old friend of mine who lives in Portland now. He's helping to run a tech startup, working 80-hour weeks, half that on the road, with barely enough time at home to maintain a relationship with his dog, much less a romance. The goal, he said, is to grow like crazy, get bought out by Google, and retire at 40. 'It's the big chill, man!'"

That set Dave thinking. How come his old friend Teyo had turned out so hardworking and ambitious—and he hadn't? Jen and he talked about it a fair bit. "Teyo had all this money, he'd just bought a house for cash," Jen remembers. "He was going for the big chill—to burn hot and fast and get to a place where he could just relax and rest. We just didn't have that sort of energy, the sort of drive to put it all out there. I guess we just wondered: How come we didn't have that much money? And what did that say about our values?"

Dave answered that question in the article.

"If we wanted, we could both do the 'next thing' on our respective career paths. She could move to a bigger company. I could freelance more, angle to write for a bigger publication, write a book, hire a publicist, whatever. We could try to make more money. Then we could fix the water pressure in our shower, redo the back patio, get a second car, or hell, buy a bigger house closer in to town. Maybe get the kids in private schools. All that stuff people with more money than us do.

"But . . . meh. It's not that we don't think about those things. The water pressure thing drives me batty. Fact is, we just don't want to work that hard! We already work harder than we feel like working.

We enjoy having time to lay around in the living room with the kids, reading. We like to watch a little TV after the kids are in bed. We like going to the park and visits with friends and low-key vacations and generally relaxing. Going further down our respective career paths would likely mean more work, greater responsibilities, higher stress, and less time to lay around the living room with the kids."

In other words, when Dave and Jen thought about their life, in the context of a successful friend who was sacrificing so much to chase the all-American materialistic dream, they realized that they were happy as they were. Since Teyo called his way of living the "big chill," it gave Dave a good title for his lifestyle. He called it the "medium chill."

WHY THE MEDIUM CHILL MATTERS

The medium chill may seem, at first glance, like a throwaway idea, or maybe even a manifesto for slackers. Its message, after all, goes something like this: "Don't worry, be happy. Let other people speed past you on the highway to success, if that is what they want. Just because they are hurrying about, it doesn't mean you have to. You can just chill." If this, or some other version of "take it easy," is all there is to the medium chill, is it really worth bothering with?

The funny thing about the medium chill is that it is that simple. But just because it is easy to grasp, that does not mean that the medium chill is anything less than a radical and very important idea. And just because it might seem, at first glance, like a statement from a layabout, that does not mean it is. Rather than an apathetic, can't-be-bothered sort of outlook on life, the medium chill, as you will soon see, is a far more ambitious and active idea.

Imagine, for a moment, that you go into work, and your boss takes you into a conference room, closes the door, sits you down, and offers you a bigger salary and a better title. What do you say? What do you do? Who is your first phone call to, to share the news of your promotion? Now run the movie again, but this time, instead of ac-cepting, you say, "Thanks, but no thanks." You explain that while you appreciate the offer, you are actually quite happy with where you are, what you are doing and, as it happens, what you are earning. Think about the look on your boss's face, and what goes through her or his mind. Consider, when you tell your partner, parents, friends about what had happened—the offer of promotion, you turning it down—how they would react. Wouldn't they think you were just a little bit mad? Wouldn't they think that, for some odd reason they had yet to figure out, you had lost sight of the system that we are all part of? Wouldn't they worry that you'd forgotten the point of work in the modern world: to get on and get up, to go out there and get more?

This is precisely why the medium chill is such a radical idea, and why it is worth thinking about. Because, at its heart, the medium chill can protect you from one of the least pleasant aspects of our current system: the bullying sense that you have no choice and there is no way out. It is not, to be clear, the sort of go-on-strike, do-nothing protest you might hear from a slacker. It offers a real alter-native to the highway of materialism. It is a signpost, if you like, to another way of living, one that is slower and gentler and more human.

The ever-faster pace is an essential aspect of the system that the captains of consciousness set up in the twentieth century. In that sys-tem, where more is always better, you can never have enough. You can never fulfill your side of the happiness equation. Instead, as Ni-codemus and Millburn found out, you are always scrambling to get more, to keep up, to catch up, to overtake. But no matter how hard you try and how much you gather, you can never feel like you've truly made it.

One consequence of this is that people sacrifice too much life to get more stuff. Another is that anyone who deliberately turns down the opportunity to get more success is frowned on. "When you have big life decisions," Dave will tell you, "it's weird how you're not allowed to say: 'Yeah, I could do that but I don't want to work harder. I don't want to sacrifice more time to achieve that. I would rather, say, lay around and read.' It's just not socially acceptable to do that."

In today's system you are supposed to always say yes to material success, no matter what. But in a system where medium-chill values hold sway, you can make another choice. In the world of the medium chill, you can measure your achievements a different way, you can turn off the supercharged road of materialism, and take a slower, more laid-back route, and not worry what people will say. You can say, "Thanks, but no thanks," to a promotion, and no one will look down on you for doing so.

This is one of the reasons Dave has become—unwittingly, it must be said—something of a torchbearer for the idea. "I want it to be okay to say no," he says. "I want it to be a positive good. I want it to be encouraged. So if you make that decision—to not work harder— you don't get called lazy."

Dave is not the first person to take it easy, of course, and he is not the only person who likes the idea of the medium chill. By giving this lifestyle a name, though, Dave has touched a nerve. His post on the medium chill was shared thousands of times. The idea was picked up by publications and media outlets like *The Economist*, MSNBC, *National Review*, and *The Atlantic*. And he has had a greater reaction to the idea than anything else he has written in his nine years at Grist.

By giving the idea a name, Dave has created a rallying point, and made many realize that they are not alone: that they, like Dave, are not happy with the current definition of success. By talking about the idea in public, he may have already made the idea of openly saying "No, thanks, I have enough already" more socially acceptable, and at the same time made it easier to try out.

You already know how, of course. And you no longer have to be embarrassed about not being one of the go-getters on life's fast track if someone asks why you've stopped getting up for the 6:23 express and started taking the later, more leisurely train that gets you to the office just in time, or why you no longer work late but head home to spend more time with your kids or see friends. This isn't laziness, you can tell them. You are taking part in a lifestyle experiment. You are involved in an emerging twenty-first-century trend, and it is called the medium chill.

CAN DAVE SAVE US FROM STUFFOCATION?

The idea of Dave as a workaday, reluctant, modern-day hero—swooping down in his blue jeans and red plaid shirt to save us from the perils of working too hard and spending too often—is an arresting image. But will the masses really follow his example? Can Dave and his medium-chill lifestyle save us from Stuffocation?

To answer, as before, we will ask the same questions any good cultural forecaster would ask of any new, innovative lifestyle. Is it the sort of thing that happens? Is there a long-term trend? And then, is it observable, easy to try and to understand, compatible with how we live now and better than materialism?

The idea at the heart of the medium chill has been around for a very long time. It has probably been a way of living since modern humans emerged. Take, for instance, the life of your average Paleolithic woman, about forty thousand years ago, as envisioned by the anthropologist Geoffrey Miller. She is a healthy mother of three in her early thirties. She lives in southern France. (There is a reason for putting her in this picturesque setting: the first discoveries of early modern humans in Europe were made there.) "Every morning," Miller wrote, "she wakes gently to the sun rising over the six thousand acres of verdant French Riviera coast that her clan holds." She spends most of her day gossiping with friends, breast-feeding, watching over her children. She flirts with hunters to get free-range meat. She works, according to Miller's calculations, around twenty hours a week, gathering organic fruits and vegetables. Life in the Paleo-

lithic era, when you put it that way, sounds very much like the medium chill.

The idea of taking it easy has been with us ever since. From the
birth of agriculture around twelve thousand years ago until the Industrial Revolution, work was generally whatever was needed to
keep everyone in the tribe alive. That meant, certainly, that there
were times of hard work, especially during the spring planting season and autumn harvest when the entire community would come
together to sow seeds, gather crops, and do whatever had to be done.
Alongside those periods of hard work there was plenty of time to do
what we now call chilling. In summer, when the crops were planted
and the sun was shining, and in winter, when the days were shorter
and it was better to stay in, there was a lot less to do—except take it
easy.

The Industrial Revolution brought an end to what you might call
the medium-chill era. The industrialists, with their machines and
factories and clock-time, began the onslaught against anyone who
was content to take it easy. They made people work long hours,
meaning there was less time to chill. They paid them handsomely for
their work—relatively speaking, at least—making anyone who chose
less well paid work look bad, even if that did entail a more easygoing
life. Then, with the help of the captains of consciousness, they ex-
ploited the masses' natural inclinations to keep up and do well, and
conditioned them into believing that their ultimate goal should be
ever-higher standards of living. Since that could only be achieved
through hard work and constant consumption, anyone not working
hard and consuming eagerly was letting everyone else down. The result was a society where people thought of quantity of stuff first, and
quality of life only as an afterthought. That brought many benefits.
But as the appeal of more stuff wanes, we have once again become
concerned with our quality of life.

The medium chill, despite the hiatus created by the architects of
our current system, is clearly the sort of thing that happens and ap-

peals to people. Anyone who has ever lain out in the sun, who has put their feet up at the end of the day, or ever stayed in bed wishing they could remain there another ten minutes, or even an hour, can understand its appeal. It is interesting to think, given the eons-long history of the medium chill, that those feelings are not just natural, but actually *more* natural than the get-up and hurry-up of the go-getting materialistic capitalist.

The medium chill has many more positives on its side. It is simple to understand and easy to try. It is almost perfectly compatible with how we already live. You simply work a bit less than you do now.

But although other commentators besides Dave have written about the idea, referring to it with terms like "enoughism," "satisfic-ing," and "threshold earners," there is no convincing quantitative evidence that the medium chill is on the rise. There is no sign of the tipping point which would suggest that it is set to make the leap along the adoption curve, from risk-taking, free-thinking innovator types like Dave and Jen to all the other, more risk-averse later adopt-ers who prefer to wait and see, and only try something if they hear about it from people they know well.

This also brings to light another problem for the medium chill: if we only have a few pieces of circumstantial evidence, this suggests that the medium chill is, by its nature, not a very visible innovation. By talking about it openly, and by giving the lifestyle of taking it easy a new name, Dave has gone some way to resolving this. He has no doubt struck a chord. But there is a chasm between a lifestyle being socially acceptable and a viable alternative, and being aspirational and dominant.

If a large-scale shift to voluntary simplicity is like hauling society off the current way of living to a new path, and minimalism is like going along the same road but with the brakes jammed on almost to a standstill—then the medium chill is like going along the same road but taking your foot off the accelerator and cruising along in second gear. It is a far more pleasant pace of life. It is laid-back and relax-ing. There is plenty of time to look out the window, watch television, play with your kids. But who really wants to drive along in second gear? Isn't that like saying: "Okay, I'll play along, but I'm not going to try too hard"?

This, in the final analysis, is the problem with the medium chill. Although it sounds nice, and although it resonates with almost everyone, it does not feel aspirational, and it does not provide a way for people to indicate their status. After all, "Look at me, I'm in second gear" does not have much of a ring to it. So I do not think that it will appeal to most people. It will not become a mainstream alternative to materialism.

WHAT THE MEDIUM CHILL, MINIMALISM, AND SIMPLE LIVING HAVE IN COMMON

The medium chill, minimalism, and voluntary simplicity—none of them is about to replace materialism as society's dominant value system. But if you consider them closely, they each hold clues to the answer to Stuffocation.

The point of the medium chill, for Dave and Jen, is not merely to live life in second gear. Their aim is not simply to avoid getting caught in the work-hard, play-hard, spend-a-lot trap of consumerism. It is to step out of that race so that they can put life first—before money and material things. When you think of it like this, the medium chill is a liberating philosophy. It frees you up so that rather than always thinking about tomorrow, the future, and what might be, your focus is on today, the present, and what actually is.

That is a simple statement, but it changes everything. It changes how you view life. It changes what matters, and how you measure success. "What matters are kindness and being good to people, and having good friends and love in your life," Dave says. "Life is not about having things. It's about having good experiences."

Compare that idea with the life choices Aimée LeVally and her family made. Just as Dave and Jen have chosen to forgo material success for experiences, so LeVally, by swapping the material goods of modern life for the intense experiences of scraping a simple living, has too. Now compare this perspective with that of the minimalists, and you will soon see a common thread.

Tammy Strobel, for instance, says that "It's not about the tiny house. If we weren't here we'd be in a tiny apartment, but it isn't about that. Instead of buying more things now, we invest in things that matter—like experiences and community and family. We get to do things we couldn't do if we had a regular home with traditional jobs and the debt that comes with all that. If we want to hang out with our parents for a week, we do it. That was really useful when my dad died. We were able to give my mom a lot of real support. We could really be there for her."

Minimalism, then, for most minimalists, is more like a starting point, or, as Joshua Fields Millburn puts it, the "first bite of the apple." It is, when you think of it like this, really only a practice, rather than an all-encompassing philosophy. It is a reaction to materialism. It is, first, a way of doing things that is not materialistic. As such, it is only the first step that many people take on a new route to happiness.

When you look a little closer at these innovative ways of living, then, it is clear they each have something in common. They are, to begin with, reactions to the dominant value system. They are anti-materialism. But they are more than this. In a world that has buried the idea of a healthy, fulfilling, intense life under a pile of material things, they are statements of defiance. Each one rejects the idea that life should be measured in terms of material possessions, and thinks, instead, that it should be evaluated in terms of experiences. Each believes, in other words, that quantity of stuff comes second to quality of experience.

And what exactly is "experience"? It is, in contrast to a physical good, not something you can hold and touch. Rather, it is intangible, something you do, observe, or encounter, like running, going to the beach, having a barbecue, or simply, as Tammy Strobel said, spending time with people you love. It could mean learning something new, helping a friend, or teaching your kids to read—which, Dave told me, has been one of the best experiences of his life.

By putting experience first, it makes anyone who lives a life of minimalism, simple living, or medium chill a lot closer to the final and most important innovative lifestyle in this book.

Until now in Stuffocation, we have met the lifestyle pioneers who are actively conscious of the fact they have had enough of material-ism and the lifestyle that comes with it, and are rebelling energeti-cally against the system. There is one more trailblazing movement I want to explore. Like the others, the pioneers of this movement are no longer inspired by, or excited about, material things. Instead of spending their energy on what they do not want, though, they are positively engaged with finding status, meaning, identity, and happi-ness elsewhere.

Since that elsewhere is experience, I call these people experien-tialists.

PART IV

The Road Ahead:
The Rise of the Experientialists

8

To Do or to Have?
That Is No Longer a Question

There was a time, not so long ago, when you couldn't say categorically whether it was better to choose experiences or material possessions, whether one or the other would be more likely to lead to happiness. Some thought it was obvious that experiences—like relationships, or cycling, or dancing—were more meaningful and made you happier. Others believed that if you felt this way, you were buying the wrong things. New clothes or shoes or a handbag or a car always made them feel great. The skeptical observer could have considered the opinions of one or two or even dozens of people from either side—and dismissed them as anecdotal evidence. Perhaps one or the other was better, but, without scientific proof, you could not say for sure whether experiences or material possessions were better.

What you could say, though, was that the virtuous circle of materialism was not as great as it had first seemed. Richard Easterlin made that clear in 1974 when he argued that higher income, above a certain point, did not lead to higher happiness. In the decades after, researchers noticed another truth: that more materialistic people tended to be less happy. That was interesting but it created a new riddle, because no one knew which way the relationship worked. Did being materialistic cause people to be less happy? Or was it the other way round, that unhappiness made people more materialistic? Or could it be, as Darby Saxbe suggested for the relationship between stress and clutter, bidirectional? Or, lastly, did neither cause the other, and were the two only loosely connected, in what scientists call a correlation? Understanding this relationship is not just an academic question. It is key, if you care about people's happiness.

Then, in 2003, two psychologists, Tom Gilovich and Leaf Van Boven, collaborated on a landmark study that answered this question. In their paper, "To Do or to Have? That Is the Question," Gilovich and Van Boven began with a simple query: "Do experiences make people happier than material possessions?"

To find out, the first thing they did was establish the difference between the two concepts. The simplest way to think about this is that an experience is something you do and a material possession is something you have. In some cases, the difference is black and white: hosting friends for a barbecue, for instance, as opposed to a chair. But, as you may have already realized, there is also a lot of gray area. Most objects provide some sort of experience. Even a chair provides you with, hopefully, a comfortable experience of sitting. Then there are objects that are even more closely associated with the experiences they provide. How do you count those? Is, for instance, a pair of skis or a 3D television or a Porsche a material possession or an experiential one?

The solution, Gilovich and Van Boven decided, lies in the intention of the individual. If you buy something with the aim of acquiring experience, that is, for the event or events it will provide, it is an experiential good. But if you buy something with the primary intention of having a physical, tangible object that you keep in your possession, it is a material purchase. This may sound complicated when you first consider it, but it has been shown, by Gilovich and Van Boven and by other psychologists, to work. It also allows for people to choose. Some people, when they think about their television, for instance, think about the big thing on the wall in their living room that looks good with the furniture and impresses their friends. Others think first about the movies or sports they will watch on it.

Now that they had clearly defined the two key concepts, Gilovich and Van Boven conducted a series of experiments where they asked people to think of experiential and material purchases they had made. Then they asked questions like: When you think about this purchase, how happy does it make you? How much does this purchase contribute to your happiness in life? To what extent would you say this purchase is money well spent? To what extent do you think the money spent on this purchase would have been better spent on something else that would have made you happier?

The results were clear, the conclusion simple: experiences *do* make people happier than material possessions. That meant that Van Boven and Gilovich were able to answer the other question that had vexed researchers for so long, and confirm how the relationship between happiness and materialism worked. By showing that experiences—things we do—make people happier than material possessions—things we have—they were able to solve the riddle of the relationship between materialism and unhappiness. Materialism, they concluded, causes unhappiness.

To do or to have, in other words, is no longer a question. The answer is unequivocal. If you want to be happy, you should spend your money, time, and energy on experiences rather than material possessions. They are more likely to help you be happy.

Why? Why is it that experiences are better than material goods at making us happy? A small band of pioneering psychologists—people like Ryan Howell, Travis Carter, Elizabeth Dunn, as well as Van Boven and Gilovich—have been trying to work that out ever since. So far, they have found five principal reasons.

Experiences, for one thing, are more prone to what psychologists call "positive reinterpretation," and what you or I might call "looking through rose-tinted glasses." So if you make a mistake and buy a bad material good, like shoes that hurt or pants that make you look fat, it is a bad choice. You are stuck with it.

But with experiences it is different. Even when experiences go badly wrong, our rose-tinted reinterpretations tend to give them a positive spin. That camping vacation when all it did was rain, the bus trip when someone in the seat behind you threw up the whole journey, the time you got laid off—somehow, those experiences, so awful at the time, never seem quite so horrific in the retelling, do they? Somewhere inside each of us we already know this. That's why we sometimes say, "We'll look back and laugh about this one day." And then, however unpleasant, painful, stomach-churning, or embarrassing something was at the time, one day we do.

Second, material possessions don't hold up as well as experiences because they are subject to something psychologists call "hedonic adaptation." Think of a new game or toy or mobile phone. When you first walk out of the shop or when the delivery man has just left, you are excited to have your shiny new thing. You play with it constantly, press buttons, learn how to use it, show it to friends. But as the days, weeks, and months pass you get used to it, until eventually you do not even notice it anymore. You adapt to having it and, as you do, you get less and less pleasure from it.

Third, experiences are better, psychologists say, because it is harder to compare them than material goods. This is not to say that you cannot compare experiences—we all do, of course—but that experiences are less directly comparable than material goods. Think of it like this. Judging material goods is far more objective. Comparing cars or houses is not so far from comparing apples with apples. Weighing up experiences is far more subjective. It is like saying rock or hip-hop or classical music is better. Or like comparing skydiving with reading a book, or gardening, or singing, or going to a costume party.

This fact—that experiences are harder to compare—matters. Because if it is harder to say which experience is better or worse, so psychologists have found, you are less likely to worry whether you are making the best choice or not, less likely to regret your choice afterward, and less likely to think about the status implications of your choice. For these reasons experiences are more conducive for well-being than material goods.

Fourth, experiences are better because we are more likely to view them as contributing to, and part of, our identities. That is, we are more likely to think of experiences as part of what makes us who we are. Think of the last time you went to a costume party or climbed to the top of a hill or went to a sporting event. Hasn't each one contributed to who you are in some way? More than the last things you bought? And if you had to give up a thing or an experience, which would you be more likely to let go—would you rather wipe the memory of a bachelor party or a wedding you went to, or would you prefer to give away the clothes you wore to the bachelor party, or the dress you wore to the wedding?

And, last, the fifth key reason experiences are more likely to make us happy is that they bring us closer to other people. And, since we humans are social animals, that makes us happy. There are three dimensions to this. To begin with, by doing something, rather than having something, you are more likely to be doing that thing with other people.

Also, psychologists have found that while material purchases tend to keep people apart, experiences are more likely to make them feel part of a group. Think of cars and camping, and compare a Nissan owner and a Porsche owner as they get out of their cars in a parking lot, with two neighboring campers coming out of their tents at the same time. The car owners are far less likely to feel connected, and far less likely to strike up a conversation, than the campers. Their material good, you see, is far less likely to make them feel part of a social group than an activity like camping. Even if the two car owners both owned Porsches—so they had the same material good—

they would still feel more alienated from each other than the campers. And even if the campers were from completely different camping sets, they would still talk. Even if the person you met on your way out of the tent had camped halfway up Mont Blanc or Mount McKinley, and it was only your second time and you were in a glamping tent with curtains and a fridge, you would still feel more of a connection. Since you are both in the "camping club," you have things in common—stories to share, experiences that are similar.

This idea, of having something in common with others, makes sense of another reason why experiences bring people closer—because, quite simply, they make better conversation. If you *do* something rather than *have* something, you are more likely to end up with something interesting to say. Research has even shown that people prefer others who talk about experiences rather than material goods. After all, would you rather listen to someone talk about their new car or their recent camping trip?

Psychologists, then, have found five main ways to explain why experiences make us happier than material goods: they are more prone to positive reinterpretation, they are less likely to be dulled by hedonic adaptation, they are harder to compare, we are more likely to view them as contributing to our identities, and they bring us closer to others. I would add a sixth reason. The unintended consequence of being materialistic is that you are more likely to have a cluttered home, which is likely to bring you and those around you stress and unhappiness. And the unintended consequence for a society where having is rated more highly than doing is the same: stress, unhappiness, and Stuffocation.

That problem can be solved by a shift in our values. If more people put experiences before possessions, if more preferred doing rather than having, we would have less clutter, less stress, and a happier society. If we want to solve all the problems of Stuffocation, we should all start living life like the experientialists.

9

The Experientialists

By the 1950s, when you could see the Jet Age and the Space Race reflected in so many cars' chrome tail fins, the work-hard, buy-now, throwaway consumer culture was in full swing. Toward the end of the decade, a man named Dirk Jan De Pree, better known as D.J., set out to solve a problem. He wanted to see if he could do for offices what Henry Ford had done for factories a generation or so before. He wanted to design offices so that people could work more efficiently in them. Or, at least, that was his stated aim. Truth be told, he also hoped to see if his company, the office furniture maker Herman Miller, could sell more of its products.

After many years of research and one false start, his solution was a flexible, three-sided cube—called the "Action Office II," but which you and I know better as a typical office cubicle. The aim of this new cubicle was to make office workers happier and more productive. In these new cubicles, they would be shielded from sights and sounds that might put them off. They would have a private space of their own they could personalize. They would have territory they could call their own. That, at least, was one point of view. Another, as voiced by Herman Miller's director of design, George Nelson, who had stayed away from the project, was that office cubicles were the ideal way to cram as many "corporate zombies" into an office as possible.

In a typical cubicle in Silicon Valley, California, many years later, a telephone rang. A young man in a suit and a tie, with blond surf streaks in his hair, picked up the receiver. He had just come from one meeting. He had another to go to. It was a workday like any other.

Cliff Hodges, then twenty-four years old, was an entry-level manager in a technology firm, a subsidiary of the chip maker AMD. This was his first proper job after five years at MIT, the Massachusetts Institute of Technology, in Cambridge. It was his first step toward the sort of success that seemed to grow, like so many magic beanstalks, out of the rich soil of Silicon Valley.

Hodges had always had two loves. One was computers. "Clifford was a natural," his father, Don Hodges, would say. "Ever since he got his first machine, an Apple IIe, when he was only four years old, he just seemed to get it." The other was the outdoors. "Some days," an old roommate of Hodges's from MIT, Kai McDonald, recalls, "I'd come back to the house expecting to see him working on his thesis. But he'd be out back trying to start a fire with nothing but sticks."

When his studies were complete, Hodges did what millions of other graduates do. He sent out some CVs, got a job, and knuckled down.

"Hello, Cliff Hodges speaking," he said, in his best business voice.

"Clifford?" said a shaky voice at the other end.

It was his father, no doubt about it. But his voice didn't sound right. He didn't want Clifford to worry, he said. He was fine. But something weird was happening. He was trying to write but couldn't hold his pen.

Concerned, Hodges explained to his boss what was going on and left the office right away. As it turned out, he never went back. When he arrived at the hospital his father was in a medical gown, slumped in a bed. There were tubes dripping things into him and taking things out. There were pads on his chest with wires coming out of them.

Cliff spent the next weeks in the hospital, watching his father gradually recover from the stroke. As the wires came off and Don got better, they got to talking about what he was going to do next. He could not go back to work, to his practice as a doctor, full time. He had to take it easy from now on. Life was precious.

The more they discussed it, the more Cliff realized that while they were talking about his father's life, he was also thinking about his own. "Seeing that happen to my dad," he says now, "made me think: life is short. If you don't love what you're doing you need to figure out another way."

And Cliff did not love what he was doing. "My job was going to meetings all day," he says. "Meetings with the engineers to understand what they were doing. Meetings with the businesspeople to explain what the engineers were doing. Then, more meetings with the engineers to tell them what the businesspeople were doing."

He was working Saturdays, staying late for conference calls with the company's office in Japan. "I felt like I was dead inside," he recalls. "I was getting up in the dark, getting home in the dark, driving three hours a day."

Yet the commute was one of the highlights of the job. "I always prayed for traffic," he recalls. "I had too much of a conscience to leave late. But if I left early enough and there was a bunch of traffic, it wasn't my fault. I always prayed there'd be traffic so I could stay longer in my car."

Those conversations with his father made Cliff realize he had to quit. His parents weren't sure if that was a good idea. "Why did you go to MIT if it wasn't what you wanted to do?" his mother asked. "Why don't you build up a career and some money, so you've got something to fall back on?" Don suggested.

But it was too late to worry about any of that. "You can't measure your life by money—or at least I realized I couldn't anyway," he decided. "You measure your life by the experiences you have."

For Cliff, he wanted those experiences to be outdoors, as far from those conference calls and that cubicle, and as close to wildlife, as possible. He started working outdoors, taking people on wildlife adventures, and he now runs his own adventure company, teaching surfing, climbing, and Stone Age survival skills. His "office," if you like, is the wilderness where he runs his courses. He shows people how to survive in nature, how to light a fire without matches, how to make your own bow and arrow, how to catch and skin a wild animal.

You have probably heard a story like Cliff's before. They usually go like this: Someone goes through a traumatic experience, an illness, say, or the death of a loved one. Then, as a result, they realize that life isn't about working hard and having lots of money and possessions. Enlightened, they throw it all in and start a new life that is more meaningful.

From that point of view, Cliff Hodges's tale is a cliché. But it is also a true story. And, more important, I chose Hodges as I chose Tammy Strobel or the way the CELF researchers selected the families in their study. He is a typical example of this emerging group of people I call experientialists. His story represents what many other experientialist innovators have been through: they have realized, for whatever reason, that they no longer believe in the system, that they are not motivated by materialistic values, and that they find the idea of experiences more meaningful and exciting.

There are similarities between the experientialists, the minimalists, and all the other case studies in this book. But there are also important distinctions. Compare Ryan Nicodemus with Cliff Hodges. As a case study minimalist, Nicodemus experienced Stuffocation from the material objects he had gathered. He gave up his job as well.

But the principal way he rejected materialism was by getting rid of most of his stuff.

As a typical experientialist, Hodges, on the other hand, felt Stuffocation because of the life he was leading, the one that came with the current system. The primary way he rejected materialism was not by getting rid of his possessions: he didn't have that many in any case. It was by trading in the job and life that the materialist value system necessitated, and upgrading to a new, liberated lifestyle that measures success in experiential rather than material terms. There are many more making that choice today—like, for example, a thirty-something Australian in London named Marianne Cantwell.

MARIANNE AND THE FREE-RANGE LIFESTYLE

Stuffocation exploded into Marianne Cantwell's life, not far from the Houses of Parliament in London, about two hundred feet below ground.

It was a London morning like any other. Outside, gray clouds. Inside, in her apartment in North London, the alarm on her Black-Berry went off. She stopped the noise, checked her email.

She had, as she will tell you now, her dream job. In her late twenties, she revered her boss. She loved her work. She was a gung ho marketing consultant, thinking up smart ideas for blue-chip clients with big problems. She was well respected. In the office she was hailed as a member of the Heroic Boys Club. "That meant you were so busy," she says, "you wrote the presentation in the car on the way to the meeting and presented it without any preparation."

Cantwell got up, stroked her tabby cat, Elvis, and opened the wardrobe to survey the things success had bought her. "Working in the city, you're always buying new shoes and handbags," she says. "They're a reward for all the hard work. Working as hard as I was, I deserved them too."

She picked out clothes that said smart-but-not-too-sexy. With her blue eyes and blond bob—"She looks like Gwyneth Paltrow," says her friend Katherine Tickle—Cantwell always made an effort not to look like a secretary. She paired a gray shift dress by a hip Australian brand called Cue with a black leather belt and black patent heels by the British fashion brand Ted Baker, and added her designer accessories: a fawn-colored Longchamp handbag and a pair of tortoiseshell Prada glasses that, when she deliberately, delicately removed them in a meeting, helped her hold a room.

That morning, she took the slow route to the tube, ambling past Victorian-era houses and the green parkland of Highbury Fields. At the station, she took the escalator down into the ground and the busy tube south, changing, along a tunnel packed with commuters at Green Park, from the Piccadilly to the Jubilee line.

Since the Jubilee line heads to one of the world's most important financial centers, it is crowded with two types at this time of day. "The bankers and corporate lawyers wear blue-and-white-checked shirts, too-wide ties, and iPods turned up so everyone else can listen too," Cantwell remembers. "The secretaries carry designer bags and wear too much makeup, their nails manicured in the French style: natural to the end of the finger, and then white to the sharp ends." Everyone herds at the points on the platform where the train doors open.

"It feels really aggressive," recalls Cantwell. "Everyone's over-hyped on adrenaline already. It's like they're already in the office."

The pack Cantwell squashed herself into couldn't squeeze into the first train that stopped. When the next one screeched into the station, the pack surged forward again. She heaved herself forward, shuffled her shoes, shimmied her shoulders, and got on—and hoped her body would not press too intimately onto whoever was in front, behind, and beside her. Her face was in a man's sweaty-but-not-smelly armpit. Someone else's was in hers. Had she put deodorant on? She couldn't remember.

She held her breath and closed her eyes, trying to push current reality from her mind. She daydreamed about being outdoors, walking in the park at Highbury Fields or, better yet, in the Hunter Valley where she had grown up. Then she opened her eyes again, to take in her surroundings: the suits, the secretaries, all doing their best to ignore everyone else, engrossed in their mission-critical emails and news. Shoved up against one another, they looked like animals in a pen.

"That's when it hit me," she says. "We were supposed to be the best and brightest people of our age, we were meant to have it all. And we were standing in each other's armpits, trapped in a metal tube hurtling hundreds of feet beneath the street. We couldn't even breathe. We were just like caged animals. And if we had actually been livestock, this would not be allowed. There'd be animal rights protesters protesting. And in that moment, I just suddenly realized I couldn't be in that cage any longer. I had to get out. I had to live a cage-free life."

Cantwell started plotting her exit that moment. A few months later, she walked out of her career, and started living as far from her animal-cage commute as possible. She still travels, but not every day as a commuter. Instead, she moves every few months, switching between her favorite places around the world, like Thailand, Italy, Australia, and the U.K. She still likes possessions, though she has fewer than before. "I don't collect material possessions, but I don't avoid them either," she says. "I like nice things around me—and that could mean a fun experience, a countryside view, or a beautiful dress." She still works, but not in a nine-to-five, Monday-to-Friday job that, with a smartphone and a demanding boss, had felt more like a five-to-nine, Monday-to-Sunday sentence. Now, as a career and life coach, she thinks up smart ideas for everyday people with real problems. She helps others escape to what she calls a free-range life. And she still, when in London, takes the tube. But not, ever, at rush hour.

We have all, at some point in our lives, taken public transportation in rush hour. Who hasn't wondered if there's a better way? After moaning about it all, though—the heat, the sweating, the smell, the dirt, the delays, and, worst of all, the other people—most of us accept that this is simply part of life, and just get on with it. Cantwell didn't. After one close encounter with a stranger's armpit too many, she vowed that enough was enough. She didn't walk away that day. But the seed was planted that morning. In the weeks and months after that, her escape plan became the only thing she thought about. She suddenly looked at the people above her in the system in a whole new light. Before, she had envied their bigger homes and more expensive handbags. But now she realized all those things had not made them any happier. So, like Cliff Hodges, she chose to put life experiences before the traditional, material markers of success. And it has worked. Like Hodges, Cantwell has told me many times she is now far happier than before.

Making the choice may seem easy when you're still single, in your twenties or thirties, with minimal commitments when you decide to drop everything and try something else. But what if you are not young, free, and single—can you still, even then, become an experientialist?

THE EXPERIENTIALIST FAMILY

Not long ago, on a typical Saturday morning, Sue and Bertrand Lenet, who are now both in their early fifties, woke up in their three-story Victorian home in Clapham, London, and wondered aloud what life was all about.

Sue and Bertrand are a classic Anglo-French couple. Sue is pretty and prim and wears her dark hair short. There is something of the schoolteacher, or perhaps Maggie Thatcher, about her. Though she is the sort who says "thank goodness," she has a steeliness that suggests that once she has made a decision she is unlikely to change her mind. Bertrand is from a seven-sibling family in Brittany. He keeps his gray hair cropped, right down to his wide sideburns, and he looks like he could be a soldier in the Foreign Legion. But talk to him for a moment, and you will instantly recognize the bon viveur's appreciation of good food, fine wine, and company. He is as friendly as Yogi Bear and has a smile to match.

That morning, they were propped up in bed, sipping coffee as the sun shone through the open window. Their daughter, Solen, ten, and two boys, Anton, nine, and Jude, three, were bounding in and out. It felt, as Sue says now, "like one of those bright mornings when anything is possible." They had a great life. She ran her own textile business. Bertrand had his own restaurant, a French bistro by the name of Gastro. Their kids were in private school. But what was the point of it all? Not much, they decided. So they started picturing what an alternative life would look like. That weekend, they started planning and saving, and they kept on, even when Bertrand was diagnosed with cancer. As soon as the cancer went into remission, and five years after the idea had first come to them, they put their plans into action. Sue closed her business. Bertrand handed the running of Gastro over to his managers. They rented out their house. They divided their stuff into two piles: junk and things worth keeping. They threw the junk out. They gave their eight favorite paintings to friends to hang on their walls. They put a few other bits in storage. They gave it all up to live with nothing but the things that fit in their backpacks, to travel the world as a family, and to see where that took them. Who knew? Perhaps they would end up living somewhere else. At least, with any luck, they would have the kind of experiences that made life worth living—even the sort that happen when things don't go according to plan, like the time they got stranded in a snowstorm in Peru for two days, wearing nothing but T-shirts, shorts, and flip-flops.

On that trip, they had decided to go to Machu Picchu by taxi—Jude was too young to walk the Inca Trail. When they set off, it had been warm and sunny, a typically tropical day. But as they climbed into the mountains, the weather rolled in. Before they knew it, as they neared a high mountain pass, the air and then the road and everything around them was thick with snow. The busy road now clogged up in both directions. Trucks got stuck trying to turn around.

They were stranded. The taxi driver shrugged his shoulders, turned to look at them, and said there was nothing to do but wait. "You're in Peru!" he said. The Lenets were not sure if he was trying to explain the situation or cheer them up. As day turned to night, they continued to wait it out in the taxi and passed around the only food they had—a few Snickers bars. They huddled like penguins to keep warm. They shivered through that first night. Sitting upright in the dark, Bertrand resolved that as soon as it was light, he would go down the mountain and get help. At daybreak, Bertrand went out looking. He found a village, and asked some locals where the nearest town was: three hours down the road, on a good day. On a bad day, they shrugged, who knew? There was a shortcut, though, they said, pointing. He wandered for a few hours, but snow had covered the way and it was far too steep and dangerous—especially in flip-flops. He gave up and trudged back to the cab. There, things were getting worse. "The cold had got into their bodies, into their bones," Bertrand recalls. "Solen and then Anton started to be really cold. Then Sue couldn't move her jaw. It was like she was paralyzed. That's when I thought we were in big trouble." As night came in, there was nothing to do but sit and shiver through. And at first light, Bertrand rallied his troops. "We walked for three, maybe four hours, until we got out of the traffic jam, and till a bus came along. We squeezed in, got to a town, got a taxi back to our hotel and went straight to bed."

They have had other bad journeys, like the twenty-four-hour bus ride across Bolivia when the toilet was out of order, the air-conditioning was broken, it was ninety-five degrees outside, the road was really a dirt track, and the journey took twice as long as advertised: two whole days. Just as the nightmare was coming to an end and they arrived in the Bolivian capital, La Paz, nearly twelve thousand feet above sea level, the temperature plummeted, they all started shivering with cold, got altitude sickness and stomach cramps, and started vomiting. It took them a week to recover.

The Lenets would not, of course, swap any of it. "We'd worked so hard all those years to build our businesses," Bertrand will tell you now. "I'd worked eighteen-hour days. The kids had grown up in the restaurant, those years went by so quickly. But that wasn't life. Life is about spending time with the family. That is what matters: our family having experiences all together."

Sue agrees. "Modern children grow up too quickly, they're ever more materialistic, and we weren't seeing enough of them," she'll say. "Now we are sharing this adventure together. What we see and what we experience together is definitely what life is all about."

When they originally went, the plan was to go for a few years, and "see what happened." Last I heard, they had settled semipermanently near a beach on the island of Bali, in Indonesia. They surf. Friends visit them. Their children go to the local French lycée. They cannot remember what they put in storage, and, even if they come back to see family and friends and check on the restaurant every now and then, they do not know if they will ever return to their old lives in London.

Many of us have daydreamed about leaving it all behind to go off traveling. But most of us accept that gung ho trips are a thing of the past, something we did during a golden period of our youth, before mortgages, commitments, children, work, and all the other excuses that come with growing up. So we accept the few weeks of vacation we get each year, and take that as our lot. The Lenets didn't. They had plenty of stuff, they had all they wanted, and they had worked hard for it. But once they had it all, they realized that the rewards for success in the consumerist system weren't enough for them.

So Sue and Bertrand meticulously planned their exit, got rid of most of their things, rented their house, and escaped the system, as an intact family unit, to travel the world and do something that meant more to them. By doing so, they prove that you do not have to be young or free and single to be experientialist. They show that experientialism is also possible for people who have commitments and children.

WHY DON'T YOU JUST CALL THEM HIPPIES?

Maybe you are thinking, "I'm really happy for these so-called experientialists, but there's nothing new going on here. Didn't the hippies do all this back in the 1960s?" And you would have a point. The hippies did reject the establishment. They did criticize the more-is-better values of mainstream materialistic society. They did look for meaning elsewhere, and especially in experiences. They passed up lucrative careers, like Hodges. They rejected the commute, like Cantwell. They went to live on beaches, like the Lenets. But when they turned on and tuned in, they also dropped out. They turned their backs on society.

The people I call experientialists are not doing that. Their focus is less about rejecting the materialistic values of modern life than it is about evolving beyond those old values. They are quite happy to have things, if they need them, but they are not hoping to find meaning, status, or happiness in material things. The experientialists' minds may be focused on a new set of values, but their feet are firmly planted in mainstream culture. They have not given up or dropped out of society. Instead, they are very much participating in it.

Cliff Hodges did not give up his big-money Silicon Valley career to wear a flower in his hair. Just because he wanted to spend his time outdoors does not mean he wants to reject society completely. Leaving the tech world to start his own business was not a purely financial decision, of course. He does still make money and he still wants to make money. But he also gives free classes to children whose parents cannot afford to send them. "I give one percent of my profits away," he says. "But I also save a lot. My goal is to buy a large piece of land so I can have my own wilderness that I can use and protect." He is also, last I heard, getting married and is planning to buy a house.

Sue and Bertrand Lenet have given up their straight life of working long hours and living in a big house. But although it was impractical for Sue to keep her textile business going, Bertrand still runs his restaurant. During their travels, when they arrived somewhere with an Internet connection, he would log on to see how things were going—to check the stock, look at the webcams, and speak with his managers. Now he does the same from their home in Bali. And in March 2013 he came back to London and spent a month with his staff, overseeing the running of his restaurant.

And Marianne Cantwell still works. She has simply exchanged the hemmed-in, buttoned-down experience of commuting, an office job, and the caged hopes and dreams that come with those, for a life that is on her own terms.

Like the hippies and the counterculture movement before them, Cantwell, the Lenets, and Hodges have rejected the mainstream model. Unlike the hippies, even though they have dropped out of conventional materialistic society, they are still turning on their computers and tuning their minds in to running functioning businesses. They are still making money. They may prefer doing things to accumulating stuff, but they still have their computers and their calculators, their spreadsheets and their profit and loss accounts at hand. I call them experientialists, but you could, if you wanted, think of them as "hippies with calculators."

Although each of the hippies with calculators we have met so far still earns money like the rest of us, every one has also, it must be said, made big, brave decisions—the sort that most of us, locked into mortgages and comfortable routines that, for the most part, work, would not make. Does this mean that experientialism is still a closed shop to the rest of us? Does it mean that if you want to get the sort of happiness that researchers say this life promises, you have to give up your job and your home, and abandon the life you live now?

PART-TIME HIPPIE, FULL-TIME PROFESSIONAL

You wouldn't say Stuffocation really ever quite hit Jim Whyte. It was more like something he had always felt. He grew up with plenty of stuff, in a big house that was listed as a building of historical interest, in the green southeast of England. He slept in a four-poster bed that, so he told his friends, Anne Boleyn had once slept in. At school, he used to carry a rabbit's foot, called Oscar, with him. "For luck," he used to say.

Now in his forties, he has a ready smile, dark hair he pushes back, a cropped salt-and-pepper beard, and an encyclopedic mind. "He can remember obscure details about all sorts of things," says an old school friend, Hector Proud, "like lines from *Blackadder* and Blaxploitation movies he watched twenty years ago. We call him the Jimternet."

Whyte holds an MBA and is a retail analyst. He is old enough, and successful enough, and earns more than enough to own plenty of things, but he is almost possession-less. All his worldly goods fit in the small, dingy room he rents in Earls Court, London. "I could fit all my stuff into four large suitcases," he will tell you, waving a hand at the things in his room. "Actually, probably three, as I'd throw things away while I was packing."

Whyte, you see, does not look for meaning in material possessions, or in what people tend to think of as the typical markers of success.

"If someone asks, 'How would you characterize the last forty years?' most people talk about family, friends, career, money. But for me, it's not like that. For me, it's the places I've visited, and the experiences I've had there.

"Like the elephant I came across in India in 1990, waddling down a side road. Or the angry crowd that gathered round me and the guy I was traveling with, Rob, in a square in Marrakech in 1991, just after the first Gulf War. Or the smell of Tahiti in 1999. I was sailing there from French Polynesia, and I'd been told you could smell Tahiti before you could see it—which sounded pretty implausible. But there I was, on watch, just before dawn, in the middle of the vast Pacific—and suddenly I could smell flowers. The island didn't emerge over the horizon for another couple of hours, by which time the air was almost Technicolor with perfume.

"These experiences are like markers for me. They're how I measure things. In twenty years' time, I'll only remember one thing about 2011, for instance. Everything else will have just faded away. For me, 2011 will always be the year I drove to Iran in a Citroën 2CV."

The trip was a fortieth birthday present to himself, and a reenactment, of sorts, of a rally from Paris to Persepolis, in Iran, that had begun two days before he was born, in 1971.

A few weeks into the trip, at the eastern end of Turkey's Black Sea coast, Whyte and his co-driver, a friend named Rupert, were motoring along the smooth modern road between the inky sea and the rain forest. As Whyte gazed out the window, he suddenly spotted a section of the old road, and a rare turn-off. "So I yelled at Rupert—above the noise of the engine—to take the turn-off," he recalls.

Rupert pushed the brakes, yanked the steering wheel. The car slowed, lurched, and the whine of engine over tarmac was replaced by a rougher sound, as the car bumpety-bumped along the forgotten side road.

"The original road!" Whyte says now. "It had been snaking alongside us for miles, heading out to headlands on its own. We had to have a look."

They drove for half a mile, to the farthest point, forty feet or so above the sea, and got out. Standing there, Whyte says, was one of the journey's highlights, more special even than seeing the ruins of Persepolis or meeting a mechanic who remembered the rally forty years before. "It was almost a spiritual experience," he says. "Seeing the old 1971 road like that . . . to think, those hippies had been here, forty years before. And now it was silent, overgrown with grass and creepers and vines. It was slowly turning back into rain forest."

Isn't it funny how, as many of us get older, we forget what truly makes us happy, and our spending shifts? We used to blow our money on extravagant adventures and memorable experiences, but we don't have the time or energy anymore. So instead, we reward ourselves for all that hard work by splurging on material consolations, on clothes, gadgets, and jewelry we don't need, have room to store, or time to wear. But, hey, we think, we've earned it so we might as well spend it.

Whyte doesn't. At the end of the week, he doesn't buy things to make up for the time he spent working. He can fit all his goods into three or four suitcases. Instead of buying things, Whyte spends his money on experiences. On the weekends, instead of shopping, he goes to the latest pop-up event or Secret Cinema screening. During his vacations, rather than taking a "fly-and-flop" trip, he does something eventful and meaningful.

Whyte shows that you don't have to give up your job and your home and your friends to live a life based on experientialist values. As such, he is a good representative of this growing tribe of people— the hippies with calculators—who are carrying on life as normal, still taking part in the current system, but whose values are shifting from materialism to experientialism.

THE RISE OF THE HIPPIES WITH CALCULATORS

In the past, people who rejected the mainstream system tended to downshift or drop out completely. Where else could they go? Today, in our connected world where the barriers to starting a business are lower than ever, people no longer need to make the black-or-white choice between staying on the treadmill or packing up for the commune. Now it is not so clear-cut. There are many more alternatives.

If you are fed up with your Monday to Friday, you can make a living as an eBay entrepreneur, using your bedroom as an office, and your garage as your storeroom—or even outsourcing the entire stock management system, as Tim Ferriss, the author of *The 4-Hour Workweek,* advises. Or you could swap your city-slicker suit for your pajamas—and trade the markets from your attic in Ireland, or your beach house in Mauritius. Or you could be an IT consultant from up a mountain, as Jeff Harris is. Or you could create a personal consultation business from wherever you find an Internet connection, like Marianne Cantwell does. Or you could run your restaurant remotely, as Bertrand Lenet does.

Today, there are many more experientialists, and aspiring experientialists, like Cantwell and the Lenets. There are, for instance, the 150,000-plus professionals who have joined a London- and New York–based organization called Escape the City since it launched in 2009. It works as a supportive social network and marketplace for people who are fed up with the sort of corporate life that Cantwell had had enough of, and would prefer to, say, develop a beach lodge in Ghana or work for a children's charity in Uganda.

Then there are all those in the social media scene in California's Silicon Valley. A researcher named Alice Marwick made a four-year study of their habits for her PhD. In her thesis, she noted that they eschew "typical status symbols like clothes and cars" and instead spend their money on "acceptable conspicuous consumption"— activities like rock climbing, cycling, and yoga, and going to conferences and festivals like TED, Sundance, Coachella, South by Southwest, and New York Internet Week.

In some circles it is now not only socially *acceptable* but also socially *expected* to prefer experiences over stuff. The ideas and values these hippies with calculators hold dear are already starting to spread from experientialist innovators like these people to the hundreds of millions in the mainstream, especially, I believe, because of one of the twenty-first century's most important innovations: Facebook.

10

Facebook Changed How We Keep Up with the Joneses

The last decades of the nineteenth century were a boom time in America. Trade and industrialization produced huge wealth for millionaire families like the Astors and the Vanderbilts. To advertise their standing in high society, these families held outlandish parties—a black-tie dinner eaten on horseback, for instance. And they decorated their mansions with the sort of details you would see in Italian *palazzi* and French *châteaux*—like the Louis XVI–style sports pavilion at the Astor country estate.

At the tail end of this era, which was named the Gilded Age, a sociologist by the name of Thorstein Veblen considered the society flourishing around him, and realized how similar, in some ways, it was to primitive societies. It did not matter, Veblen realized, if you were born in the caves of France in the Neolithic era, in a pole and thatched hut in the Middle Ages, or in an elaborate mansion in the nineteenth century, you would still spend a considerable amount of your energy displaying your fitness markers to other humans. And while barbarians did this through displays of physical strength, Veblen decided, the best way to do it in modern society was through wasteful displays of spending money. In his satirical 1899 book, *The Theory of the Leisure Class,* he gave this practice of buying things for social status, rather than practical value, a new name: "conspicuous consumption."

As wages rose and the cost of consumer goods like cars and radios fell in the twentieth century, conspicuous consumption became possible not only for rich families like the Astors, but for the masses as well. And just as Veblen had made fun of the leisure class, so another writer, a man named Arthur Ragland "Pop" Momand, mocked the working classes in a new comic strip in the *New York World* newspaper. The strip, which debuted in 1913 and ran for twenty-six years, was named *Keeping Up with the Joneses.*

Inspired by suburban life that Pop had seen in an outer borough of New York, *Keeping Up with the Joneses* starred Ma and Pa Mc-Ginnis. In one of the early stories, Ma is out shopping with Pa, whom she calls by his first name, Aloysius. We see Ma dressing him in ever more colorful clothes: pink socks, a red tie, yellow gloves, green spats, and, finally, a fuzzy hat.

"Ah!" she declares, happy at last. "Now my love we will show that Jones woman that her husband is not the only Adonis that can wear pink socks an' a fuzzy hat! Oh! You are so noble looking Aloysius!"

In the last scene, we see Aloysius, having escaped his wife, leaning on a bar. He holds his head in one hand, as he talks half to himself and half to the barman. "Curses on them Jones's an' th' pink socks!!!" he says. "Gimme another deep one Jerry!!"

Whether you join Aloysius and curse the Joneses and conspicuous consumption or not, there is no denying that it was a key element of the fuel that made materialistic culture take off. Moreover, it is really only our current culture's version of an essential animal and human trait. It is our way of shaking our manes, flashing our feathers, and howling like monkeys. If experientialism is to replace materialism as the dominant culture in the twenty-first century, it, too, will need a simple mechanism for people to display their fitness markers and their status. As it happens, there is already a way for people to do this.

THE EXPERIENTIALISTS WHO PRACTICE CONSPICUOUS CONSUMPTION

If you ask them, most experientialists would laugh at the idea that they try to keep up with the Joneses. Conspicuous consumption is something other people do, they would tell you. That is what materialistic people do when they want to show off that they have newer, shinier, or more stuff than their neighbors. Ask Sue and Bertrand Lenet, or Marianne Cantwell, or Jim Whyte, or Cliff Hodges, or any number of experientialists, and their responses would all be the same—that they do not do conspicuous consumption.

Talking to them, and hearing how little they value the traditional status markers of the twentieth century, like fancy watches, cars, and clothes, it is easy to understand why they would say that.

Yet one of the most counterintuitive things about experientialists in general is that, although they want nothing to do with keeping up with the Joneses in the traditional sense, many consume just as conspicuously as even the most status-conscious materialists. I blame Facebook.

Remember how friends used to tell you about their latest vacation? They would invite you over for dinner, and, as the after-dinner chocolates were passed around, pull out their photos and bore you for a bit. "There's Jean at the Acropolis, Jean in front of the Parthenon, Jean eating a souvlaki . . ." Then they would have other friends over and do the same. It was hard work telling everyone about their trip, but if they got the dates booked in before they went away, it was possible. They could usually do it within a couple of months.

It is not like that anymore. Now, with so many of us on social network sites—there are more than a billion on Facebook, more than a hundred million use Instagram each month—you do not have to wait till your vacation is over to get them back.

Now, using Facebook, Instagram, Twitter, and all the other social media sites, you can share every last detail of your trip in real time. You can let everyone know that, right now, you are watching the sunrise over Angkor Wat or the sunset from the rooftop of your riad in Marrakech, or that you are on a chairlift in the Alps, or that you have just finished packing and cannot wait to go. You need not, of course, broadcast your thoughts and updates only when you are on vacation. Why not share that you have just run a marathon, that you are at a Rolling Stones concert or a TEDx conference, or that you are thrilled because someone bought you flowers? Today, where you are, how you are feeling, what you are doing, and what you have done have suddenly become valuable social currency—just as they were before the twentieth century.

Then, most people lived in small communities. Everyone knew everybody else in the village. That meant everyone would just as likely know what you did with your time as how many possessions you owned, and how expensive and how good those possessions were. They would be as aware of the days you spent drinking in the local hostelry or chasing foxes on horseback as they would be of the horse-drawn carriage you owned. That meant, for signaling your status to others and establishing your place in the village's social hierarchy, what you did was as important as what you owned. To signal status, the conspicuous consumption of leisure—that is, experiences—was equal to the conspicuous consumption of goods.

It was the arrival of cities that changed all that. The mass migrations of the twentieth century, from small communities where everyone knew everyone else to large metropolises where you barely knew your neighbor, meant that what you did with your time became virtually useless as a way to signify status. In the relative anonymity of urban and, to a lesser extent, suburban life, your neighbors, friends, colleagues at work, and the people you passed on the street were much more likely to see what you owned than know what you did. They could admire the BMW you parked in your driveway. They might covet the Breitling watch on your wrist, the Prada handbag on your arm, or the Louis Vuitton wallet you used to pay. But how would they know what you did with your time? How would they be aware of the fact that, last weekend, you had been to the opera, the latest restaurant, or the coast?

There were exceptions to this rule, of course, like the suntan, the ideal way to turn an intangible and therefore, for status purposes, invisible purchase into a status symbol everyone could see. Consider the statement of the panda-eyes ski goggle tan. And why else would people waste so much of their vacation sweating under a burning sun, if not to show off that they had been away?

Generally, though, and suntans aside, a material possession could deliver far more status than an experiential purchase. And so, in the twentieth century, the conspicuous consumption of leisure was not nearly so effective as the conspicuous consumption of goods at telling others who you were.

Social media has turned this on its head. Now only a few people, relatively, might see your new sofa, or the car parked in your driveway. But with all your friends and followers on Twitter, Facebook, Pinterest, and Instagram, many more will now know you are partying in Ibiza, are in the front row of a Jay-Z concert, or that you have just completed a Tough Mudder assault course. And these people are more likely to be in your peer group, the people, in other words, whose opinion you are most interested in.

Social media also plays a vital role in making experiences appear more valuable, thanks to their pivotal role in the "rarity principle." According to this idea, the bigger the difference between the number of people who have access to something and the number of people who know about it, the rarer and more valuable the thing is. Anyone, after all, can buy most material goods, but not everyone can be at the event you are tweeting about or Instagramming a picture from. This explains the social status, for instance, of the principal TED conference. TED's videos have been watched more than a billion times, but there is still only one grandstand event, and only 1,500 can attend.

Of course, besides keeping your followers up to date with what you are doing, you could also post pictures of your new possession. But if you did that, you would soon lose followers. Remember the insight from the happiness researchers: we prefer to listen to people talk about things they've done—like their camping weekend—rather than their possessions—like their new sofa.

And you could argue that a limited-edition sneaker or handbag could be as effective at leveraging the rarity principle as a limited-capacity event, therefore offering a similar amount of social currency. But, once produced, even if the production run has finished, a material good is still out there somewhere and theoretically available. But experiences, because of the nature of time, have a built-in feature that makes them even more rare. If you were not there—in Berlin when the Wall came down, in Myanmar before the masses came, at Wimbledon when Murray won—you were not there.

Material goods, of course, still indicate status. But compared to the past, thanks to social media, more people now know about your experiences versus your stuff, and your experiences hold more social capital due to the rarity principle. As a result, experiences are now more visible, more tangible, and more valuable, and are more likely than material goods to contribute to status.

This matters, because, as we saw earlier, status doesn't only matter to big cats, exotic birds, and loud monkeys. It matters to humans. If you have high status, as the philosopher Alain de Botton observed in *Status Anxiety*, and a professor by the name of Ahmed Riahi-Belkaoui reported in *Social Status Matters*, you earn more, you live longer, you get invited out to more parties, people laugh at your jokes more, and you end up with a more attractive partner. In short, in the virtual game of Snakes and Ladders that is modern society, characterized by meritocracy and social mobility, status matters, and it matters more now than at any previous point in history.

In the old, materialistic consumerist system, where we played the game through the regular purchase and ritual display of our possessions, we tried to keep up with what the Joneses had, while they worried that they might not have as many and as nice possessions as we did. Now the rules of the game have been given a twenty-first-century, digital twist. Thanks to social media we want to keep up with what the Joneses are doing. Are we going to enough pop-ups, conferences, and concerts—like all our friends and acquaintances seem to be?

This concern has become so widespread that it has a new name: fear of missing out, better known by its acronym, FOMO. At the birth of the experiential era, four out of every ten people aged eighteen to thirty-four in the U.S. and U.K. say they sometimes worry that they are missing out. Facebook, you might say, is giving us a new way to keep up with the Joneses, and a new way to worry that we may not be keeping up.

DOES FOMO MEAN EXPERIENTIALISM IS A DOWNGRADE?

Fear of missing out is, at the least, problematic for experientialism. Because if this new way of living is just as likely to deliver anxiety and stress as materialism, how is it an improvement? Thought of in these terms, experientialism might even sound worse than materialism. That it is, in fact, a downgrade.

The old version of social Snakes and Ladders was not only different because it was based mostly on physical goods. It was also less stressful and easier to play. After all, most of the time you did not need to actively do anything. You would play by simply indicating your status, every now and then, by displaying your possessions. And you would get an update on other people's status each time you saw their Armani watch or Gucci handbag, or when you went to their house and saw what was on their sideboard—which is why having anyone over was such a big deal in those days.

But in today's hyper-connected, 24/7 world, the game has changed. Not only do we notice material status cues when we see people in the real world, we are also getting and giving status updates through Facebook, Twitter, and all the other social networks. And since we check these throughout the day—when we get up and when we go to bed, on the toilet, on the train, in the classroom, and in the office—that means that we are playing the game more regularly, and thinking about the game more too. As we do that, we are more likely to end up feeling anxious and stressed, and perhaps depressed, about status.

There is another change in the game that is having an even more damaging effect, I believe, on happiness. As we played the old version of social Snakes and Ladders, we would come across all sorts of status indicators. As we went about our everyday lives, we would not only see people with fancier cars and watches and clothes. We would also encounter people with cheaper, older, more threadbare, and less designer equivalents to the stuff we had. That mix would leave us feeling secure. It felt okay not being at the top of the social ladder, as long as you weren't at the bottom of the pile either.

Now, think about the last time you looked at a social network. Have you ever noticed how Facebook, and other social networks, sometimes brings to mind upscale magazines filled with the look-but-don't-touch lifestyles of the rich and lucky? It is like the people you know are living the airbrushed, stage-managed lives you see in luxury advertisements—which are deliberately designed to make you feel inferior.

Your friends' lives may well not be quite so perfect, of course. Life for most people, after all, is not a flawless timeline of weekends away and weddings in glamorous places. And if you stop to think about it, you know that. But it is hard to keep that in perspective and not be affected by all those sunsets, sunrises, and lunches on the veranda. And since we are all connected to so many people on Facebook, there is always someone jetting off to Miami, having lunch in Lima, lounging on a boat in the Mediterranean, or attending a wedding in the Caribbean.

So each time we check in, we cannot help but feel that our lives are so much smaller, hollower, and, frankly, more earthbound than those of our friends who are off doing glamorous things. This constant bombardment leaves us feeling that we are always at bottom of the pile looking up. And that, in a meritocratic system like ours, can leave us feeling anxious, stressed, and depressed.

So all of this puts Facebook and other social networks in the curious position of supporting the rise of experientialism, while also undermining its benefits. This suggests, ironically, that if you buy into experientialism, you could end up with just as much anxiety, stress, and depression as you would have had in gentler, more materialistic times.

If that was the last word on this, you might now be wondering if you should even bother trying experientialism. You might be questioning whether it could ever work for the mainstream, even if it has clearly worked for a few. (You might also be thinking about checking Facebook less often.)

But, and it is a very important but, even though keeping up with the Joneses through experiences has the potential to be anxiety-inducing, I still think experientialism is better than materialism, and that we should still think of it as an upgrade. Why?

WHY EXPERIENTIALISM IS STILL BETTER FOR YOU

To explain why experientialism is still better than materialism, despite the double-edged sword of social media, the best place to begin is by reminding ourselves of the five discoveries social scientists have made in recent years: that experiences are more likely to make us happy because we are less likely to get bored with them, more likely to see them with rose-tinted glasses, and more likely to think of them as part of who we are, and because they are more likely to bring us closer to other people and are harder to compare.

And even if experiences *can* be compared, the comparison is less clear-cut than it is with material goods, and that means you are less likely to think about the comparison, less likely to regret your choice afterward, and less likely to think about the status implications of what you do. So while competing through experiences could lead to some status anxiety, especially when the game is played out through social media sites like Facebook, it is likely to be a fuzzier, less acute version.

There are two further reasons why experiences are more likely to contribute to happiness, thanks to one simple fact: because you are *doing* something rather than *having* something, you are more likely to be in "flow" and your motivation is more likely to be "intrinsic."

Flow is a mental state, originally identified by a psychologist named Mihaly Csikszentmihalyi, that you get into when you are effortlessly engaged in whatever it is you are doing. This is what athletes mean when they talk about confronting a challenge and getting "in the zone." It is what spiritual gurus like Eckhart Tolle mean when they say you should be "in the present." It is what psychologists refer to when they say we are exercising competence. To see why experiences are better than material goods for achieving flow, and thus happiness, consider this comparison: would you find it easier to focus on a chair or a pair of shoes, or to concentrate when you are performing a task that challenges you, like playing tennis, singing in a choir, or reeling in a ten-foot shark?

Motivation matters because, as psychologists like Richard Ryan and Edward Deci have documented, it is one of the most important determinants of whether something will make you happy or not. They have identified two distinct motives. Either people do something because of intrinsic motivation, which means doing it for its own sake, because they personally find it interesting or enjoyable: eating an ice cream, say, or skimming a stone across water, or singing in the shower. Or people do something because of extrinsic motivation, which means doing it with some other aim in mind, like getting a reward or impressing people: eating kale, for instance, or filling in an expense sheet, or the ridiculous clothes you bought as a teenager so that people would think you looked cool. You are more likely to be happy, so studies have shown, if you do something for intrinsic reasons.

This is a useful insight, but a hard one to make use of, because it is difficult to look inside yourself and work out whether your motivation is intrinsic or extrinsic. Think about taking on a triathlon or buying a dress or a shirt, for instance. You might take on a triathlon for the challenge, to be physically fit, and because you enjoy thinking of yourself as a triathlete. But, truth be told, you also enjoy telling people you've conquered a triathlon. Now apply the same thinking to a dress or a shirt: you enjoy the feel of the material, and how it makes you feel when you wear it. But again, you are also aware of how it will affect the way others perceive you. So, in each case, are you really choosing it for yourself or to impress others? And which, if you are being totally honest, made you do it in the first place? Since it is hard to tell, it makes the insight that intrinsic motivation is better than extrinsic when it comes to happiness tricky to use—but not impossible.

Because, as psychologists have discovered, we are, on the whole, more likely to buy a material good for extrinsic reasons, and more likely to do something for intrinsic enjoyment. Therefore, if you want to be happier, save yourself the hard work of all that thinking, and just choose experiences instead.

This insight about motivation is also useful in light of Facebook's impact on experientialism. As you know from the pictures of your friends eating breakfast in Hollywood or drinking cocktails in Ibiza, it seems as if some people spend so much time posting updates that they are in it less for the enjoyment of the experience, and more so that everyone knows what they are up to. That sort of extrinsic motivation, in theory, should mean that those activities are less likely to lead to happiness.

But it doesn't even matter if your starting point is wanting to tell everyone about what you are doing, because every experience comes with a free virtuous circle of healthy, happy goodness. It will still bring you closer to other people. It is still more likely to lead you into a state of flow. Even if your starting point was to show off, you are still more likely to be happy if you choose experiences.

So, all these things considered, I don't think you should worry too much about the impact that social media can have on your status anxiety. If you care about your happiness, you should be an experientialist. Experientialism is better for you. Is it better for everyone else?

WHY EXPERIENTIALISM IS BETTER—FOR EVERYBODY

As well as all the evidence proving that doing will make you happier than having, if you also consider the problems causing Stuffocation, you will soon see why experientialism is better for everyone else as well. You can also see its appeal is likely to extend beyond a few pioneering hippies with calculators to the majority of those in the rich, currently materialistic world.

In a world underpinned by experientialism, where status and happiness and meaning are no longer based on material goods, we are likely to have far fewer environmental problems. Many experiences, of course, require material goods and create a footprint. Consider the carbon footprint of an experiential purchase like a vacation to Borneo, for instance. But since experiences are, by definition, less predicated on material possessions they are likely, overall, to create less environmental harm.

In an experientialist system we are less likely to accumulate possessions, which means less clutter and less of the stress that comes with all that stuff. Experientialism should be better able to cope with the growing population and the rise of the global middle class: since we are less interested in things, resource cost will be less problem-

atic. And experientialism, as an urban theorist named Richard Florida has noted, goes hand in hand with the trend for millions to
choose to live in cities rather than the countryside. Since accommo-
dations tend to be smaller and more expensive in cities, there is room
for less stuff, and experientialism makes far more sense there.

Experientialism could even restore some of the belief in the system that observers like the sociologist Ruth Milkman think has been
lost. In today's world, where success is measured in material terms, it
is clear who the winners and the losers are. That some have so many
more material goods than others aggravates a lot of people. But in a
world where our principal concern is not about material but experiential well-being, which is far harder to compare, fewer people will
be bothered that some have more, simply because who has more will
be a moot point.

If your reaction to that is that the experiences I have talked about
in this book have tended to be glamorous and expensive, that you
clearly need to be wealthy to be an experientialist, and that in an
experientialist culture there will still be a divide between the haves
and the have-nots—let me explain. Experiences like hauling your
family across a continent or flying around the world may only be
available to people with plenty of money. But I picked those examples simply because they illustrate the point. Experiences that cost
nothing—like walking in the park, chatting with a friend, going to
church, or dipping your toes in the sea—are all just as likely to lead
to happiness. The experiences of the average person are as valid as
the pop star's. The average person's life may not be as loud, or fre-
netic, or embellished with stadiums full of people, but from an experiential point of view, it counts just as much: after all, it is equally
likely to result in happiness, and it may well be more rewarding.

So it doesn't matter if you're rich or poor or anywhere in between. It makes no difference if you're being experientialist for the
planet, for yourself, for society, to post look-at-me pictures on Facebook, or to tweet something smart. I believe you should join the ex-

perientialist movement because it is better for you, for me, and for all of us.

BUT WILL EXPERIENTIALISM SOLVE STUFFOCATION?

In the early 1970s, engineers from the world's leading technology companies were busy inventing an incredible new system: a machine that, for the first time, would let people record programs on the television and watch them later at their own convenience. From our twenty-first-century viewpoint, in an era when we can pause live television and watch it not only whenever we want, but on whatever device we feel like, that does not sound so amazing. But at the time it was revolutionary, and it led to war.

The Japanese company Sony fired the first major salvo, launching its Betamax system in 1975. A rival, JVC, responded in 1976, with a format called VHS. To begin with, the battle went Sony's way. After grabbing 100 percent of the lucrative U.S. market in 1975, it remained in a market-leading position for some years. And so it should have, because Betamax was better. It offered higher-resolution images than VHS, a more stable image, and better sound quality. But as the home recorder war wound on, Betamax's dominance unraveled. By 1981, Betamax could only claim 25 percent of the U.S. market. By 1988, when the magazine *Rolling Stone* declared that "the battle is over," VHS owned 95 percent of the market.

Businesspeople have spent years analyzing why VHS beat Betamax. They have cited issues like cost, recording time, distribution, and marketing tactics. But whatever the ultimate reasons, what is most interesting to me is the point this story proves: that just because something is better, it does not mean that it will catch on and become dominant. In this case, it was a piece of technology, but the same can be said of many things, even ways of living. Social scientists like Tim Kasser have found that people who live simple lives are far more likely to be happier. And yet, as we saw earlier in the book, voluntary simplicity has not caught on. Could it be the same for experientialism? Could it be better, but not catch on?

The best way to answer this question is to ask the same questions we would ask of any trend. Has this sort of thing, a wholesale change in values and practices, happened before? We have already answered that: yes—for example, when our ancestors gave up their thrifty ways to become wasteful, materialistic consumers.

Next, we should return to the five key questions we should ask of any innovation to determine whether it will spread. We have already answered two of those questions. We have established that experientialism is better. We have also established that it is observable, since social media is making it much easier for other people to know what you are doing. If you consider how often people check their social media feeds and post status updates, you could say the practice of experientialism has become hyper-observable. After all, people spend more time on social media than any other activity online, and increasingly do that from the smartphones they carry with them.

How does experientialism hold up under interrogation by the three other key questions? The short answer is very well—because, to begin with, experientialism is simple to understand, and it is compatible with how we live now. After all, we already play sports and go to concerts and *do* things. To upgrade from materialism to experientialism does not require a sudden shift. It is not an all-or-nothing change. It is not like flicking a light switch on or off. All it requires is a shift of attention: less having, more doing. And experientialism is easy to try: you could try it this month, or even this weekend, simply by spending what you normally would, but with the goal of having nothing new at the end of the month or the weekend—except for the memories and stories from the things you did. (For a guide to how you can try out and practice experientialism, see the appendix, "The Way of the Experientialist.")

Experientialism, then, clearly has a lot going for it. It not only looks better than materialism, but also like the sort of innovation that is likely to spread. And I believe it will. But if I am to make that claim, and you are to believe me, there should already be signs that materialism is waning and experientialism is spreading. Is there any evidence that this is happening? There is, and lots of it, if you know where and how to look.

IN THE FOOTSTEPS OF THE EXPERIENTIALISTS

In a perfect world, spotting and forecasting trends would be simple. There would be clean, clear information about what everyone is thinking and doing—and I would not have a job. In the real world, though, trend analysts like me have to make do with noisy, imperfect information. Some trends, like color blocking or animal prints, are easy to spot, especially when they are seasonal and out in the open, in the mainstream press and everyone is wearing them. But if the trend you are tracking is a cultural change—a fundamental shift in the values that underpin the world we live in—and it is in its early stages, it will be far harder to detect. In these cases, we have to identify the trend through the shadows it casts and the footprints it makes. Fortunately, the movement away from materialism and toward experientialism has been casting plenty of shadows, and is making unmistakable footprints.

There is the suggestion, for a start, in the survey results I mentioned in the introduction. But as well as the finding that two out of every three people in general are in the habit of de-Stuffocating their lives by getting rid of things, the survey found that three out of every four of the innovators and early adopters said that they get rid of things. Since, as we know from the S curve, it is the innovators and early adopters who represent the future, we can infer that more will get rid of things in the future.

Then, there is the well-marked, forty-year-old trail that leads directly to these statistics, in the work of the political scientist I also mentioned in the introduction, Ron Inglehart. The research that he began in 1970, and that has been conducted ever since and is now called the World Values Survey, shows that we have been becoming less materialistic for more than four decades.

And think, for a moment, about the changing makeup of our economy. "If you look at items on those first national income accounts in 1934," the late economist Robert Fogel told me, "eighty percent of the things on it, like food, clothing, and shelter—you could touch them. They were material. Now, though, those things make up less than a third. We have a lot more money to spend on other things. Today, most of what is entered into the national income is immaterial [such as tourism, banking, health care, education, and entertainment]. You can't touch it." So there is a long-term shift in our economy away from material goods.

There is new evidence that not only is the relative importance of material goods in our national income accounts falling, but that the absolute level of material goods is falling too. We have reached, as the man who discovered this, an ex-McKinsey consultant and environmental analyst, Chris Goodall, says, "peak stuff." Goodall's detailed analysis shows that Britain has been consuming less water, concrete, and paper, and fewer cars and clothes, since 2003 at least. And he has also seen signs that other countries, including France, Sweden, and the United States, are consuming less as well. Remember that most of this reduction in material use happened during a time when our economies were rising. We were spending more, in other words, but not on goods that were material. Instead, we were spending more on things like communications, entertainment, and tourism—on things like mobile phone contracts, going out for dinner, and going away for the weekend.

We may have reached the apex of our (over)consumption on clothes as well. After decades of going up, perhaps we have reached "peak clothes." In 2007, the average American bought almost twice as many items of clothing as they had in 1991. But by 2012 the number had stopped rising, and even fallen slightly, from sixty-seven to sixty-four items.

I have found more evidence throughout our society and economy—in surveys I conducted in the U.K. and Ireland that show people prefer experiences to material goods, in the demise of the hardback and the rise of ebooks, in the plummeting sales of recorded music and the boom in live music and festivals, in the fact that people in their sixties spend more on vacations than any other age group, in the emergence of extreme sports, and in the expanding health care market. "In 1929, we spent three percent of GDP on health," Fogel told me. "Today we spend sixteen percent. Forecasts suggest that by 2040 we could be spending thirty percent."

There are also indications of the rise of experientialism in the luxury market. In 2011, luxury consumers—who, with their high economic status, tend to be ones who try things first and whom the rest of society emulates—spent more, for the first time, on experiential luxury goods, such as vacations, than any other sector, according to research from a company called the Boston Consulting Group. The trend for what the company calls "experiential luxury" has continued. "In an era of overconsumption, people are realizing that there is more than just buying products," said Jean-Marc Bellaiche, a senior partner at Boston Consulting, in 2013. "Buying experiences provides more pleasure and satisfaction." His comments were echoed by his colleague Antonella Mei-Pochtler a year later. "Luxury," she said, "is shifting rapidly from 'having' to 'being'—that is, consumers are moving from owning a luxury product to experiencing a luxury."

There are other signs of the shift in what the next generation of consumers, people in their twenties and thirties whom marketers call millennials, are doing, and in what they are not doing. They are no longer buying cars like their parents did, and they are choosing to live in small, city-center apartments—which, by nature of their size and location, offer less room for stuff and more possibilities for experience—since one thing cities do is offer a far greater variety of experiences than the countryside. Rather than owning a thing—whether that's an album, a movie, or a car—they prefer access, through services like Zipcar, Spotify, Rent the Runway, and Netflix.

Rather than showing off through physical goods, like previous generations used to, they are expressing their identities and getting status through experiences they can share through social media. And, as we've seen, they are not the only ones: there are 140 million people sharing their experiences on Twitter and more than a billion posting theirs on Facebook.

There are, as you can see, and even if they are unevenly distributed, a lot of signposts that suggest the practice and values of experientialism are spreading. Before we conclude, though, that experientialism will be the answer to Stuffocation, we should also bear in mind that the last time the underlying value system of our world changed, the ones who chose the path we would all follow were those who held power: the captains of consciousness in government and big business.

While there has been a shift, in terms of the structure of power, from the pyramid to the pancake, the government and big business are still exceptionally powerful. Before we can be sure which way the world will turn, we should also find out what they think about experientialism.

11

We Love to Count Too: The New Way to Measure Progress

After the terrorist attacks of 9/11, the leaders of the free world encouraged their citizens to keep calm and shop. "This great nation will never be intimidated," George W. Bush declared. "People are going about their daily lives, working and shopping and playing, worshipping at churches and synagogues and mosques, going to movies and to baseball games." And Tony Blair told the British people "they should go about their daily lives: to work, to live, to travel, and to shop."

There is a good reason why Bush and Blair did this. It is because the key way that governments and the countries they run are judged is by the size and growth of their economies, and by the key figure that represents economic health: gross domestic product, better known by its initials, GDP.

You can think of GDP as a little like the mark you see on your child's report card. But rather than reporting on your child's education, it reports on the country's financial situation. And just as you are keen to see how your child is doing at the end of the term, so politicians, economists, businesspeople, and the general public look out for the quarterly GDP statement—because the better the economy is doing the more money the country and the government have to maintain and improve standards of living. It works just like your own household budget. The bigger your budget, the more you have to spend on food, rent, evening classes, clothes, and holidays. And the higher GDP goes, the more people in general have to spend on those things, and the more the government has to spend on firefighters, teachers, roads, and the weapons and warriors who keep us safe from anyone who might threaten our way of life.

Governments first started measuring GDP around the beginning of what I think of as the materialistic age. The national income accounts, of which GDP is a key constituent, were first published in 1934, in the United States, in response to the Great Depression. Their aim was to enable the government, for the first time, to make reliable estimates of the size, and rise, or fall, of the economy and its constituent parts. The measures were not perfect: they were, as their creator, Simon Kuznets, wrote in the first report, an "amalgam of relatively accurate and only approximate estimates." But the accounts still gave the government a better indication about which sectors of the economy were working and which were not, and by how much. That meant that the government was in a better position to act like a clear-sighted general: one who could see where his army was strong, where it needed reinforcement, and how many troops to send. If demand was particularly low in one area, for instance, the government could send help to stimulate demand.

There were other consequences. For one, this new way of counting, as Robert Fogel observed, raised economics from a speculative and ideologically riven discipline into an empirically based social science.

For another, it promoted economics and economists to the heart of government. The income accounts that this new method produced proved indispensable throughout the 1930s, as the government sought to solve the problems of the Depression. And they were vital again in the 1940s, in the war effort. Through information gleaned from these income accounts, economists assessed the U.S.'s capacity to produce the military goods that were essential in arming the country and its allies. They also designed the financial instruments that paid for them, and they planned the air force's bomb strikes on Germany so as to cause the most damage to the Nazi war effort. Their input proved so valuable that the economist Paul Samuelson would later claim that the Second World War had been "the economists' war."

That may have been overstating the case, but by the time peace returned the discipline of economics and its practitioners had arrived. In 1946, Congress established the Council of Economic Advisers to the president, cementing the role of economics at the heart of government—and building on the good work that the captains of consciousness had begun a few decades before. As the council's chairman, Raymond J. Saulnier, said, when talking of the American economy in 1959, "its ultimate purpose is to produce more consumer goods."

By the late 1950s, with backing from the International Monetary Fund, the method of national income accounting that the United States used was adopted by all countries. Since then, national income accounting—which includes GDP in its reports—has become the principal method by which a country measures its economic performance. The logic for that is simple. But also in the years since the late 1950s, national income has become the de facto way that politicians measure a country's general progress. The logic for that is not nearly so simple.

WHAT HAVE THE ECONOMISTS EVER DONE FOR US?

It is Palestine, sometime in the early part of the first century A.D. The Roman Empire stretches from Hispania in the west to Judea in the east. Or rather, strictly speaking, it is Tunisia, 1978, and we are on the set of *Monty Python's Life of Brian*. We are in a dusty room with ragged curtains, as the Pythons film an iconic scene that will later be known by one question: "What have the Romans ever done for us?"

Dressed in black robes, sitting at a table, and addressing a handful of followers sitting cross-legged on the floor, are John Cleese, Michael Palin, and Eric Idle. They are, respectively, Reg, Francis, and Stan—though, to be strictly accurate, that should be Reg, Francis, and *Loretta* because, at the local colosseum a few scenes ago, Stan announced that he would like to be a woman, and be known from now on as Loretta. So, Reg, Francis, and Loretta are the leaders of an anti-Roman terrorist group called the People's Front of Judea, the PFJ—and not the Judean People's Front (JPF), or the Popular Front (PF), or the Judean Popular People's Front (JPPF). That lot, as they said at the colosseum, are all "wankers" and "splitters." No, Reg and Francis and Loretta are the People's Front of Judea, and they really, really hate the Romans.

"They've bled us white, the bastards," says Reg, trying to wind up the PFJ's followers. "They've taken everything we had, and not just from us, from our fathers, and from our fathers' fathers."

"And from our fathers' fathers' fathers," Loretta chimes in.

"Yeah," agrees Reg.

"And from our fathers' fathers' fathers' fathers," says Loretta, getting into this now.

"Yeah. All right, Stan. Don't labor the point," Reg answers. "And what have they ever given us in return?!"

"Sanitation?" one of the recruits pipes up.

"Roads?" says another.

"Irrigation."

"Medicine."

"Education."

"Wine."

"Public baths."

"Yeah. Yeah, that's something we'd really miss, Reg, if the Romans left," says the third PFJ leader, Francis.

"And it's safe to walk in the streets at night now, Reg," adds Loretta.

"Yeah, they certainly know how to keep order," says Francis. "Let's face it. They're the only ones who could in a place like this."

Reg grudgingly admits all these, and tries one final time.

"All right," he says, "but apart from the sanitation, the medicine, education, wine, public order, irrigation, roads, a fresh-water system, and public health, what have the Romans ever done for us?"

"Brought peace," one of the recruits says.

Reg, exasperated, gives up.

Given everything the captains of consciousness—the industrialists, economists, and politicians—have done for us, sometimes the people who complain about the system can seem a little like Reg, the leader of the Judean People's Front—sorry, People's Front of Judea. However, today, we not only worry less about wine, fresh water, and the other material basics of life. In this time of abundance, and so much stuff we are suffering from Stuffocation, many of us are losing patience with the captains of consciousness. In particular, we are getting fed up with the economists, and losing faith in the idea that economic success should be seen as a benchmark for the general progress of society.

ARE WE ALL DRUNKS LOOKING FOR OUR KEYS?

GDP was never supposed to comment on all aspects of society's progress. Yet, as we can now see, the unintended consequence of having a useful way to calculate economic progress is that, in the absence of any other agreed measure, it has become the definitive way to benchmark society's progress. Why?

The simple answer is that, to begin with at least, it did tell us how well our societies were doing. By focusing on GDP, the economists solved the huge, debilitating problems of scarcity that had plagued humans since people first settled down into complex societies. So in terms of solving the problem of scarcity—which also happens to be the stated goal of the discipline of economics—a rise in GDP, and especially GDP per capita, did mean progress.

Moreover, increases in GDP per capita do improve well-being, up to a certain level. So up to that point GDP per capita does measure progress, but after it—which research suggests is an annual salary of around $75,000 in today's money—the returns are vastly diminished. Many, like Richard Easterlin or Australia's foremost well-being champion, Bob Cummins, believe that level was reached years ago. "Mature markets," says Cummins, "arrived some decades ago at the point at which there was no further benefit in increasing material wealth, as far as the majority of citizens are concerned at any rate. Increasing wealth has done nothing to make people happier in America, Australia, and the U.K."

There are two other reasons why GDP has become the benchmark for progress. It is relatively easy to count and it is simple. To understand why these are so compelling, consider two insights from social science called the drunkard's search and substitution.

The drunkard's search, which some call the streetlight bias, was first described by the philosopher Abraham Kaplan. In his 1964 book, *The Conduct of Inquiry,* Kaplan told the tale of a drunkard searching under a street lamp for his keys, which he had dropped somewhere else. Asked why he was looking there and not where he had dropped them, he replied, "It's lighter here!" Is measuring GDP like the drunkard looking for his keys? Does it really measure what matters to us? Or are we just looking where it's lighter?

Substitution is the sort of mental shortcut that people use to avoid the time-consuming hard work of making complex decisions. Instead of answering a difficult question by the long, rational route, we look for a simpler version of the original question. Perhaps this is what we are doing at a societal level with GDP, swapping an easier question for a demanding one. Instead of answering a tricky question like "Are we making progress?," we prefer to answer a simpler substitute: "Is GDP going up?"

The simplicity of GDP makes it a very attractive measure for progress. It is, after all, only a number, one that tells us three essential facts about the economy. How big is it? Is it getting bigger or smaller? Is ours bigger than yours?

The simplicity of GDP is also its Achilles' heel, as a measure of general progress at any rate. It counts goods and income, but it has no opinion of them. It counts quantity of stuff, even when all that stuff does is pollute the air and blot the landscape, or helps us keep up with the Joneses but does nothing for our well-being. But GDP does not measure quality of life. It has nothing to say about better health, living longer, or sledding on a school day.

Remember those days when you'd wake up and the snow was so thick the roads were blocked, the trains would not run, and the weatherman said stay at home? You'd put on some warm clothes and get hold of a sled—ideally your gear would include ski gloves and one of those wooden sleds Austrians use, but you would have just as much fun wearing woolly gloves with yellow marigolds to keep your hands dry, and a sled made of red plastic. Then, wrapped up warm, you would go sledding for a stolen day of magic. The next day the paper would scream that the cost to the economy was billions. *The economy?* you'd think. *Who cares about the economy? We were sledding.*

When the problem we faced was scarcity, GDP made sense as a measure of progress. Today, though, expecting GDP to reflect the health and direction of society is like looking at your reflection in one of those wobbly fairground mirrors. In other words, GDP has a distorted view of progress. How could it not, when it counts business and busyness, but has nothing good to say about sledding?

Economists, ecologists, psychologists, and others have been trying to right the wrongs of GDP, and work out more appropriate measures of progress, since the 1960s. They have come up with many alternatives. There is the Environmental Sustainability Index (ESI), the Environmental Performance Index (EPI), and the Genuine Progress Indicator (GPI). There is the Index of Economic Well-being (IEW), the Measure of Economic Welfare (MEW), and the Sustainable Measure of Economic Welfare (SMEW). There is even an Index of Sustainable Economic Welfare (ISEW).

Each of these has its merits. Each has fueled the debate. But there is something about them that sounds, to me at least, a little like the People's Front of Judea (PFJ), the Popular Front (PF), the Judean People's Front (JPF), and the Judean Popular People's Front (JPPF).

Meanwhile GDP and the materialistic system it measures and promotes, like the Roman Empire, has marched on unchallenged—until now.

THE DANCE OF PROGRESS

It was a Frenchman with a lavish name, a contemporary of Voltaire's named Bernard Le Bovier de Fontenelle, who first pointed out one particularly important aspect of progress. Each age, Fontenelle observed, has the advantage of not having to rediscover things that have previously been discovered. So if you picture progress as a journey up a mountain, with some ideal of perfection at the peak, each generation does not have to start at the bottom, but from the level their ancestors reached.

From our vantage point, when cars, phones, and soap powders are new and improved with each passing generation, and when we have the sort of air-conditioning, air travel, and even airports that our ancestors could only dream of, this idea seems so obvious it's barely worth mentioning.

But I bring it up for two reasons. First, progress, the idea that things can and should and will get better, is one of our most deeply held beliefs. It gets us up in the morning. It fires us up at work and in our personal lives. It inspires us to make better products and better business models, to bake a better cake and cook a better pad thai, to be better at Pilates or *Grand Theft Auto,* and to create a better world for our children. If progress was a brand and someone gave it a slogan, it would go something like this: We believe in better. And if progress and better are so important us, we ought to be clear what better really means and the sort of progress we want.

The second reason I mention this well-worn view of progress is because if we blindly follow it, it could lead us astray. Based on the Latin words "go" and "forward," the concept of progress is an oversimplified model for how society changes—because change is not necessarily linear, and it is not always positive. Society is not always going steadily up the hill. Sometimes, instead, we get stuck and stay at the same level. At others, like in the game of Snakes and Ladders, we scramble up or slip back swiftly.

Consider, for example, the stop-start journey of the car. First, we took a great leap forward when the engine was created. We took another when mass production dropped the cost in the first years of the twentieth century, and opened the door for millions to own a car. From then till now, though, the car has been cruising. There have been incremental improvements—a few percent more efficient here, some new sensors there. But the fundamental shape has not changed much, nor have the basics of what is under the hood. That, in the long run, has caused the sort of problem you would have to call a step backward. Gas-guzzling cars used to sound throaty and powerful and good. Now they just sound like clunkers causing pollution and climate change. But the exciting news is that we may be about to leap forward again, as the very real possibility of a new era of post-gasoline engines and self-drive cars comes ever closer.

Mostly, though, progress is not just forward or back. Usually, it is more like a dance: like the schoolboy-at-a-disco side to side shuffle, perhaps, or maybe the sort of slow-quick-quick, left-and-right, to-and-fro steps a ballroom dancer makes. How else would you view, for example, the rise of social media? In some ways, it has brought us closer to more people. In others, we spread ourselves more thinly.

Or consider the instant access of the Internet. It is no doubt a boon for finding what we want when we want it, but it also raises questions: Are we drowning in too much information? Is it destroying our ability to concentrate?

If you consider society over the last hundred years, there is no doubt there have been vast changes. There have been incredible advances, in transportation, health care, and material comfort, for instance. And their progress has been expertly measured, in large part, by GDP. But what we really need now is a new measure that can reflect progress not just in economic terms, but in terms of every shimmy, step to the side, and leap forward our society takes. As well as measuring material standards of living, we should also count experiential quality of life. It was another Frenchman who began the movement toward this idea in the twenty-first century.

NICOLAS SARKOZY HAS A PROBLEM

Toward the end of 2007, less than a year into his presidency, Nicolas Sarkozy had a problem—the financial crash, which, as it ran into other headwinds, like overconsumption, stagnating wages, inequality, and rising resources costs, was fast becoming the Great Recession. The fall in GDP was hardly his fault. The whole world was feeling the effects of the meltdown. But that did not matter to the people who had put him in the Élysée Palace, the French voters who would also decide if he would remain there after the next election. And they were rapidly falling out of love with him. His popularity rating was nose-diving—from a high of 65 percent approval just after the election in July 2007 to only 41 percent in February 2008—and his party was floored in the countrywide municipal elections the following month.

This was the issue vexing him as he stalked the vast halls of the Élysée Palace: how could he regain his people's support? The problem was not only GDP, he decided. It was, as he would later write, that "our world, our society and our economy have changed, and the measures have not kept pace."

The French people, he thought, would not only judge him on GDP and standards of living, but on how good, happy, and satisfied they felt with life. They were not only bothered, in other words, about quantity of stuff, they were interested in quality of life.

So Sarkozy decided to construct a measure of progress that would do a better, more accurate job than GDP—and be acceptable to the wider community. He gathered a team of public intellectuals, like the behavioral psychologist Daniel Kahneman, and economists like Jean-Paul Fitoussi and Joseph Stiglitz. They produced a report and a book of their findings, *Mismeasuring Our Lives: Why GDP Doesn't Add Up*. And Sarkozy implemented the ideas almost immediately. In 2010, France became the first leading nation to measure not only the size and rise of its economy, but the well-being of its people. It became the first major country, if you like, to not only be concerned with the material well-being of its people, but to also ask what their experience of life was like.

The next year, 2011, the U.K. government started asking its citizens about their experience of life too. Other countries are now following suit: Germany, Australia, Canada, and the United States are now all working out better ways to measure well-being and track progress—and two states, Maryland and Vermont, have already adopted new ways of measuring progress.

Like the national income accounts when they were first introduced, the well-being measures are not perfect—nor are they universally accepted. Some question whether it is possible to measure happiness at all. Others say it is simple. "You just ask people," says Bob Cummins. He thinks you can determine someone's mood happiness with a handful of questions, by asking them, for instance, how satisfied they are with their standard of living, their health, whether they feel part of a community, and how safe they feel.

Some worry about substitution. So when the government asks, "How happy are you with your life nowadays?," most of us are likely to substitute that hard question with an easier question, some version of "What is my mood right now?" Others worry that there is a difference between the person who answers those questions, the "remembering self," and the person actually doing the living. (Does this explain why the Lenets treasure the memory of the forty-eight-hour bus trip across Bolivia even though it was deeply unpleasant at the time?)

How will we solve these disagreements to find a methodology for measuring well-being that is acceptable to everyone? And how will we agree on a system for measuring progress? Because at present there are as many methods as there are countries. The new, official system in Canada, the government's Indicators of Well-being in Canada (WIC), contains ten domains, like work and family life, and more than sixty indicators, like weekly earnings, marriage, divorce, and age of mother at childbirth. The citizen-backed Canadian Index of Wellbeing (CIW)—which is arguably better respected—is based on fewer domains—eight—including the quality of the communities people live in and what people do with their time, but a similar number of indicators. Australia's system, called Measures of Australia's Progress (MAP), contains even more indicators—eighty. Not to be outdone, the United States' federal government's new way to measure progress, the State of the USA, or SUSA for short, looks like it will contain as many as three hundred different indicators.

If these sound like another set of Judean terrorist groups, that is because at this point they are. They are all a bunch of splitters—because not only do they not agree with one another, they have all bypassed the other, internationally sanctioned challengers of GDP as measures of progress, like the Better Life Index used by the Organisation for Economic Co-operation and Development (OECD), based on eleven topics, the U.N.'s Human Development Index (HDI), featuring three dimensions and four indicators, and the granddaddy of all well-being measures: Bhutan's Gross National Happiness (GNH), which was created by Bhutan's Dragon King in 1972 and is based on four "pillars."

It is all, as you can see, a long way from the simplicity of GDP's headline figure, a simple number that tells us if things are good, bad, up, down, and better, or not, than our neighbors. And we are still a long way from finding a dominant method for measuring society's progress, as GDP does for economic progress.

It is easy to poke fun at the current state of the debate on measuring progress. But at least it is a step in the right direction. There is already broad agreement, for instance, about the essential elements of progress, like well-being, the environment, and quality-of-life factors such as how safe people feel.

More important, it is not only the captains of consciousness in the government who will debate and decide this time: the U.S. and Australian governments, for instance, are asking their citizens for input. "Till now, this has been the debate of the elite," says Chris Hoenig, who is CEO of SUSA. "But now, with our system, everyone can get involved and have their say."

Besides, it may be easy to laugh now, but this is how the economic measures began. As Hoenig says, "This is the beginning of the debate, not the end of it." It was not when Kuznets created national income accounting that there was a single method of measuring material progress. That did not happen until the late 1950s, a quarter century later, when it was accepted by all members of the International Monetary Fund.

Today, we are a long way from solving all the disagreements. And that is perfectly okay. You could argue that what economists and psychologists are doing today for the measurement of well-being and progress is very similar to what Kuznets did for economics in the 1930s—transforming them from speculative and ideologically riven disciplines into empirically based social sciences. Given this shift from material to experiential progress, psychologists are also likely, at some point in the near future, to become as important in government as economists are today: a psychologist named Barry Schwartz recently proposed a psychological parallel to 1946's Council of Economic Advisers called the "Council of Psychological Advisers."

Does all this mean that, just as Kuznets's paper in 1934 led to the acceptance of a global benchmark for material progress, we will have a new internationally agreed-upon standard for measuring well-being in the same time frame? That we will have one within the next quarter century, that is, by 2040? I believe we will.

This will be an important breakthrough, but even as things stand at present, even if there is not yet one agreed-upon system, and even though the methods are not perfect, governments can use the new measures today to improve the progress of society—just as Kuznets's national income accounts, despite the fact that they were only relatively accurate and approximate, raised the fog and helped governments work out where to apply their efforts. They can use happiness surveys, for instance, to raise the general level of well-being. Bob Cummins offers some useful examples. "When we do national surveys we can identify groups of people who have lower levels of mood happiness than they should have," he says. "They might lack important resources of some kind. Those could be financial, or they could be to do with the relationships they have. Or, it could be something about how safe they feel. Once we identify the group, we can do something to help. For example, there's an informal crisis of people looking after disabled family members. They have some of the lowest levels of mood happiness in Australia. But knowing this means we could provide them with more resources and get them functioning normally. Another example is middle-aged men living alone. They have perfectly adequate salaries but many of them are pretty bad at forming nonsexual supportive relationships."

This is why measures of well-being matter. Just as the introduction of the national income accounts enabled the government to do a better job of caring for its citizens in a time of scarcity, so these measures are helping today's governments do a better job of caring for their citizens in a time of abundance. Armed with information from the well-being surveys, governments can help their people avoid unhappiness, and increase the general level of well-being in society.

That, to me, and to a great many people today, sounds a lot closer to human progress than working to increase GDP.

So Sarkozy was right. People today, in rich, developed countries at least, are more interested in their quality of life than measuring the quantity of things they have.

Just as the creation of the national income accounts in 1934 re-flected, signaled, and encouraged the age of materialism, so these new well-being measures are doing the same for this new era of ex-perientialism. As we know from the law of unintended consequences, it does not matter whether the people in charge realize it or not: by measuring experiential progress they are not only reflecting the emergence of experientialism, they are encouraging it—because, as Joseph Stiglitz says, "what we measure affects what we do."

12

What About the Chinese?

How do you say "keeping up with the Joneses" in Mandarin or Cantonese? In Hindi, Urdu, or Brazilian Portuguese? In Tamil, Thai, or Bahasa Indonesia? Not so long ago, no one needed to know. Except for a tiny minority, conspicuous consumption was a Western phenomenon. Now, though, that is changing, and fast.

When twenty-something Liu Dandan and her husband, Zhou Zhou, wake each morning in their apartment in Beijing, they are surrounded by designers. Philippe Starck designed the gold AK-47 lamp on the table in their lounge. Paul Smith made Zhou Zhou's shoes. They have handbags, wallets, watches by Louis Vuitton, MCM, Cartier, Burberry, Fendi, Prada, Tod's, Hermès. They keep all the pristine boxes each item came in. They drive a Mercedes-Benz. They dress their baby in designer clothes. If material goods could talk—

and social scientists say they do—Liu and Zhou's possessions would scream conspicuous consumption.

So would the shoes that another Beijing resident, Richard Lu, has accumulated. His multicolored collection features around fifty pairs, by brands like Valentino, D&G, Prada, Tod's, and YSL. What pair will he wear today? The spring green suede ankle boots? The white bowling shoes with black laces? A pair of suede loafers perhaps, but which color to choose: red, burgundy, mustard, cornflower blue, French navy blue, imperial purple, deep purple, or ivy green?

Liu, Zhou, and Lu are influential. They are trendsetters, and not only because of Lu's shoes. Zhou works at the Chinese version of *Esquire* magazine. Lu runs a public relations agency. They represent the future of China, and the future of a vast swath of the rest of the world. Because their lifestyle, and the labels, logos, handbags, and shoes that come with it, is one many others now aspire to. It is also a lifestyle, or an approximation of it, that many millions will soon have. Because in the next few decades more than a billion people in countries like India, Indonesia, Vietnam, Nigeria, and Brazil will be joining them as middle-class, conspicuous consumers.

As that happens, those billion or so people will for the first time be able to afford to enjoy a lifestyle that you and I would recognize. As they make the march, from country to city, from hardscrabble poor to having disposable income to spend on life's little luxuries, these people will get their first chance to buy a television, a car, a mobile phone, a week's worth of shirts, and a washing machine to wash them in. In other words, there will be a lot of people getting their first taste of materialism. A few lucky million may even get the chance to buy the sort of shoes that would fit in Richard Lu's collection.

As the new middle classes enjoy the sweet side of materialism, they will also experience its sour twist. They will feel the status anxiety that comes with the Snakes and Ladders game of conspicuous consumption. From Lima to Lagos, Kolkata to Jakarta, Chongqing to Beijing, they will look across the corridor or fence or street. They will take note of what their neighbors have. They will want something a little newer, fancier, and better, and they will buy it sooner than they strictly need it. They will try to stay ahead of or, at least, keep up with the Silvas, the Kapoors, the Wangs, and the Lius—or whatever those pesky Joneses next door are called in their country.

IS STUFFOCATION MIDDLE-AGE ANGST?

As conspicuous consumption becomes the global norm, so we will witness a similar surge in standards of living in the developing world to that which came with the rise of consumerism in the West. At the same time, the rise of the global middle class over *there* will make the sense of Stuffocation we feel over *here* become even more pronounced, especially since two of the most pressing problems causing Stuffocation are resource scarcity and the environment. These are going to become much worse with a billion new people clamoring for their piece of the materialist pie on our finite planet.

This growing tribe of eager, first-time materialists is like the proverbial bull, elephant, and eight-hundred-pound gorilla in any meaningful discussion about Stuffocation. This billion-strong group gate-crashes its way in by calling into question whether we should even bother trying to solve problems like overconsumption and our impact on the environment. Because just as fast as we wealthy few try to curb our collective footprint and reduce our consumption, there will be a billion or so others queuing up to take our place and make their mark on the world by gobbling up its resources with their new cars, motorbikes, microwaves, washing machines, shirts, and blue suede shoes. Does that suggest, therefore, that Stuffocation is merely the middle-class, middle-age angst of a waning Western society worried about its place in the world—and that we may as well just get over it?

THE NEXT GREAT LEAP FORWARD

Stuffocation may well be the middle-age angst of a maturing society on the downturn today. But if we take into consideration what we have learned from the past and our knowledge of the present, we can make a realistic forecast about China and the other emerging nations. That forecast is this: that they will follow similar development curves to those we did in the West, only their curves will be steeper, and their revolutions will come quicker.

In the West, it took 150-odd years from the start of the Industrial Revolution to lead to overproduction. After that, it took just under eighty years or so in the West for the consumer revolution to lead to overconsumption and Stuffocation.

A similar journey—from industrial revolution to mass production and overproduction, from consumer revolution to mass consumption, overconsumption, and Stuffocation—is likely to happen in the emerging nations. But it is likely to happen far quicker.

Industrialization in the West happened in fits and starts and incremental steps, as new discoveries were made over decades, and those innovations took time to spread. The emerging economies have evolved from agricultural communities to industrial societies far more rapidly. They have benefited from all the dead ends, wrong turns, and blind alleys that the pioneers over here made—and have been able to avoid them. At the same time, they have been able to treat all the knowledge, inventions, and scientific advances like useful signposts that point them to the best way forward. Internationalization has also meant ready markets for all the goods their new factories can produce.

Despite these advantages, as China has rapidly industrialized and production has increased, the country has started to face problems that sound very similar to those the United States confronted in the 1920s and 1930s: the twin specters of overproduction and underconsumption. In 2012, for instance, there were overproduction problems in industries ranging from coal, cotton, and shipbuilding to clothing, solar cells, and construction.

And this problem, of overproduction, is compounded by the fact that people in China today share some strikingly similar traits with the people in America in the early twentieth century. Famine and austerity have taught generation upon generation of Chinese to be careful with their possessions and thrifty with their money. While our newspapers herald the arrival of the new Chinese consumer, and tell tales of relaxed visa requirements and Chinese tourists splurging on luxury goods, the great majority of Chinese are not—yet— consuming on the scale and in the manner that the country's new mass-producing system requires.

As in America almost a century ago, commentators have been weighing in with their worries, and a set of solutions that also sound very similar. Just as back then America's captains of consciousness worried, "Are the consumers consuming fast enough?," so a business journalist named Bill Saporito asked an almost identical question in a recent article in *Time* magazine, "A Great Leap Forward: Can China's Famously Thrifty Workers Become the World's Big Spenders?" Another business journalist, Dhara Ranasinghe, turned the question into a statement in a report for CNBC called "Chinese Consumers Are Still Not Spending Enough." Economists have similar concerns. For stability and growth—China's as well as the world's—the World Bank and the International Monetary Fund both want the Chinese masses to become, like the bees in Mandeville's fable and like their counterparts in the West, high-spending consumers.

Just as the government and business leaders in the U.S. solved overproduction by deliberately turning their country's once thrifty citizens into wasteful, conspicuous consumers, so China's captains of consciousness are doing the same. Advertising, the industry most likely to engineer consumers rather than products, is exploding. In 1976, there weren't even ten advertising agencies in the whole country. By 2001, there were 70,000. By 2010, 234,000. And by the end of 2012, that had shot up to 377,000.

The Chinese government is explicitly intent on creating consumers as well, and borrowing ideas from the American experiment of the twentieth century. The government plans to improve wages, so people spend more. It is making credit easier to come by, so people spend more. It is improving the welfare system, letting its people worry less about the future, so they save less and spend more. It is also improving the country's parcel delivery system, so people spend more on e-commerce. Are these policies working? Consider this: the value of e-commerce in China in 2012, from a standing start a few years before, was almost the same as the entire economy of the Republic of Ireland.

As those hundreds of millions of Chinese, and the new middle classes in India, Indonesia, and all the other emerging nations become better off, and buy more things in stores and online, all the factors that have caused Stuffocation over here—the safety net of affluence and a functioning welfare state, the move to cities, aging populations, environmental degradation, equality, and overconsumption—will concern them too. They will also suffer from Stuffocation.

The early signs, in fact, are already there. There are the frequent demonstrations and riots as people put their environment and quality of life before growth: some observers say that pollution is now the main cause of social unrest in China. There is the problem of stalling levels of happiness. Since 1990, the average Chinese person's material living standard has increased by four times. Yet over the same period happiness has not increased at all, according to a recent study by the man who discovered back in 1974 that having more didn't make us any happier, Richard Easterlin. Then there are the young, who are already evolving away from materialism. "China in general is in a grossly materialistic phase," Ron Inglehart told me. "But post-materialism is already beginning to emerge in a young, significant minority." And then there are the wealthy, who already have enough. They are even now beginning to prefer experiences over material goods. In China, the experiential luxury sector—which includes days out at spas, playing golf, and going on vacation—is growing around 25 percent faster than the personal luxury goods sector.

Once the Lius and Zhous and Lus have accumulated enough and gotten over the initial thrill of their LV wallets, Prada bags, and Paul Smith shoes, they, like the rest of us, will veer toward experiential, rather than material, goods. Once the hundreds of millions in China, and all the other emerging nations, not only satisfy but also sate their basic material needs, their preferences will also shift, I believe, from material to experiential goods.

Since the emerging economies are on steeper development curves, it is likely to happen soon—within the next few decades. It took China around a third of the time it took the West to go from the start of its industrialization to overproduction—around sixty years. If it continues to follow a similar, accelerated path, it will reach overconsumption by 2037.

As materialism builds up, as consuming turns to overconsumption, and as they run into all the other problems and opportunities that make up Stuffocation, today's new materialists will make the next Great Leap Forward, and become tomorrow's experientialists.

13

The Gypsy, the Wasp, and the Experience Economy

Not long ago, I found myself at the end of a long, dark corridor, in a warehouse somewhere in central London, like Alice when she first arrived in Wonderland, rubbing my eyes with surprise. I was in a square room, a bit smaller than a squash court, with wood-paneled walls. On each of the walls was a deep recess with the sort of collectibles you might see in the country home of a gentleman traveler: carved statues, tusks, the skulls of hunted animals. To my right was a floor-length, blood-red, gold-braided velvet curtain. In one recess, on the far side of the room, a small painted man was doing a slow-motion ballet dance or, perhaps, some version of Tai Chi.

As I stood watching him, I felt a hand on my arm, pulling me sideways out of the square room, behind the red curtain, and into a cubby hole that looked like a Gypsy trailer. Behind a writing desk covered in exotic knickknacks sat a woman in her early twenties, gazing up at me with plaintive, intense green eyes, a bandanna holding her dark hair back.

The wasp, she says, had a good life. It had been happy. It had traveled far. Oh, how she had loved that wasp! I frantically struggled to keep up with her story while trying to take it all in, but my head was spinning. It felt like I was listening to her from the bottom of the sea. As she went on, telling me more about this wasp she had loved—too much, I think she said—she stretched her bare arm out, freeing it from her shawls and silks, and in her hand was a small, mottled egg, or half of one anyway. It was cracked with a jagged edge. "Look!" she said. "Take it." Mesmerized, I took it. I held it. Inside, in some kind of frozen gel—like a mini-insect-equivalent of a Damien Hirst cow in formaldehyde—was a dead wasp.

When I turned back to look at her she had thrown open her shawls and wore nothing but a bra, but what I really remember, more than anything, was her big, swollen belly, and thinking, "Oh, she's pregnant." Then, I felt a hand on my arm again, and I was pulled out of the cubbyhole trailer, back into the other room. By the time I had blinked and turned to look, the curtain was already still.

THE PILOT AND THE PIG'S EAR

Not long after my encounter with the Gypsy, I found myself in another windowless room, this time with a floor of black and white marble squares. The ceiling was painted cyan, crisscrossed with gold stars, and dotted with hanging lamps that looked like the scales of justice. The walls were of white, cream, and pink marble, veined with gray, black, and red. Dark wooden benches lined two sides of the room. At one end was a throne. This, by the way, was not a movie set. It is an old Masonic temple, lost for decades, rediscovered a decade or so back.

I'm sitting in the center of this room, at a heavy, antique mahogany table. On my left is an actress with long, wavy hair like Jessica Rabbit's. On my right is a man with a pencil-thin 1940s Spitfire pilot mustache who introduces himself as Commander of Special Operations.

Dinner is served. The first course is pig's ear soup. I splash around in the bowl. Yes, there, and not quite swimming, is, as advertised, a pig's ear. I had been warned. As I had descended the steps on the way in, Sam Bompas, the impresario of this event, had held my arm and whispered, "Gird your loins. The first two courses are rather savage."

The menu continues to raise my hackles, along with those of the other diners. After the pig's ear soup, we have veal, snails, and blood marrow pudding, but, truth be told, our focus is not even on the food.

On a giant makeshift screen, opposite the throne, they are showing a surreal movie from 1973, called *The Holy Mountain*. The director took LSD to prepare for the filming, and had the actors take magic mushrooms for some scenes. A limbless dwarf and a gang of children attack a man who looks like Jesus. A woman says she makes mystical weapons for Buddhists, Jews, and Christians. A man who looks like an early 1970s cult leader—his long elder's hair and white robes are paired with a dark Freddie Mercury mustache and white platform boots—collects feces in a glass jar from the naked Jesus man. Then he cooks it as a white pelican struts about and a bare-skinned, tattooed woman plays the double bass. After the feces have boiled, steamed, and morphed into a pile of shiny, yellow metal, the cult leader announces: "You are excrement. You can change yourself into gold."

It was a little after that scene that the Commander of Special Operations leaned in to tell me something. "I have seen this movie many times," he says. "I like to make love as I watch it."

"EVERYONE IS AN AUTOBIOGRAPHER NOWADAYS"

Do these two tales sound like nightmares to you? The opening to surreal David Lynch movies, perhaps? They are, in fact, neither. They are real scenes from the make-believe world of the "experience economy." They are examples of "experiential marketing."

The first event, where I met the Gypsy with the wasp, was created for the luxury brand Louis Vuitton by a theater company called Punchdrunk. At a Punchdrunk play, instead of sitting down in seats and watching actors perform a play on stage, members of the audience wander corridors, go upstairs, downstairs, are pulled into random rooms, never quite sure what is happening or where they should be going. As they do, they come across what seem like impromptu, slightly surreal mini-plays. Actors whisper and shout, wander in and push through, argue and fight, tell stories and kiss and caress one another and even, sometimes, you. There is an overarching story, but it is less linear than a formal, regular play. Part of the magic of a Punchdrunk play is that every member of the audience goes to different places, sees different things, and has a different experience. Everyone has a different story to tell at the end of the night.

Since its first event in 2000, Punchdrunk has won awards and drawn praise on both sides of the Atlantic, for productions like *Faust, The Masque of the Red Death,* and *Sleep No More.* The company has also, now and then, created events for brands. It has launched a PlayStation game, a premium beer, and, as on the night I met the Gypsy, a new store. That night, Louis Vuitton was opening on London's New Bond Street. They staged this event for their biggest spenders, for A-listers like Jerry Hall and Gwyneth Paltrow, and for journalists like me. The question is: why? If Louis Vuitton wanted to let people know about its new shop, why not just have a launch party at the store, tell the press about it, and advertise in luxury magazines?

The second scene, with the pig's ear soup and the pilot, was a far simpler, smaller event. In many ways, it was just a regular night of drinks, dinner, and movie, even if it was more memorable than an ordinary evening's entertainment. It was an "experiential dinner," created by a company called Bompas & Parr, supported by the Andaz hotel chain and Hendrick's gin. The question, again, is: why? Why do these brands bother to stage an experiential event when they could simply advertise the way brands used to?

Perhaps Sam Bompas, the man who warned me about the savagery of the food on the way in, and his partner, Harry Parr, might have the answer. Visiting their London office is a little like going down a rabbit hole and arriving in a real-world Wonderland. You go down a narrow lane, turn right into a parking lot, and there, around the back, inside a boxy, unremarkable, two-story building, is their Bat Cave of half-baked ideas-in-progress.

In the main room, a colossal, green, friendly dinosaur's head pokes through one wall like a hunting trophy. Next to it a banner proclaims "the four horsemen of the oesophagus." On shelves nearby are the sort of plastic trophies you would win on a night of ten-pin bowling, and Jell-O molds in shapes you might recognize—the Reichstag, the Empire State Building, St. Paul's.

Bompas and Parr are both turning thirty. They are old friends from Eton. Parr, with salt-and-pepper hair and a wide grin, resembles a quieter and not-at-all-evil version of the Joker. You get the sense that behind his polite smile far more important work is being done, the sort of work that involves putting potions in vats and doing odd things with Victorian bicycle parts.

Bompas is the front man. The glint in his eye is the glint of a Barnum, or a Willy Wonka—the Gene Wilder version. When you see him, he might be wearing a military greatcoat, or a floor-length bear fur cape. He will most likely be sporting one of his forty bow ties, and a pair of bright blue, red, or yellow Turnbull & Asser socks.

Going to see Bompas and Parr, in other words, is quite an experience, especially when Bompas starts talking about their latest plans. He might tell you how they want to give people religious experiences at will, to make roses that flame and change color as you hand them to your date on Valentine's, and to create a way for people to not only talk to, but really communicate with, plants. These are not just hopes and dreams. Bompas knows how to whip up a bit of PR just as well as he knows how to make a twelve-course Victorian breakfast, but there is also substance behind the talk.

When I last saw them, Bompas and Parr had found a physicist who had a solution for those flaming roses. They had just commissioned an environmentalist and programmer to write an algorithm that would turn human words into the sort of piezoelectric signals that plants understand. They were going out that afternoon to meet a neuropsychologist at a haunted house, to find a way to induce religious experiences. They often turn their fantastical ideas, you see, into real events—more often than not paid for by a big brand.

Why? Why do brands—like Louis Vuitton, Andaz, and Hendrick's, among many others—commission these events rather than simply advertising as they did in the past?

It certainly is not only for fun. The people who control marketing budgets have to justify everything they do just as much as people did in the past. In today's digital era, when everything is more trackable, it is even more imperative. They still have to show they are getting a decent return for their investment. They are still trying to sell stuff.

The answer lies in Stuffocation. We live in a cluttered world of too much information and too much stuff. How can brands cut through the noise and stand out? With the same old marketing clichés—by shouting louder and saying it more often than their competitors, by offering more for less, free gift with purchase, two for one, buy one, get one free?

The problem with all these, to begin with, is that they have all been done. But more important, they no longer work as well today, especially with the more discerning, ahead-of-the-curve consumers that so many advertisers want to reach. These consumers are not only important—because they are influencers whose habits others follow—they are also most likely to be busy, and have more than enough material possessions already. The last thing they want, in other words, is more stuff clogging up their homes. But they still want status, and they increasingly know they are more likely to find it in the sort of experiences that enhance their sense of who they are, and give them a story to tell.

"Everyone is an autobiographer nowadays, it's like everyone is actively writing their own biography all the time," says Bompas. "So stories are becoming even more important. In the 1980s, people wanted a fast car. Now they want a good story to tell."

At present, of course, businesses are creating these experiences in order to get people to buy tangible things—like handbags, beer, and cars. But as we know from the law of unintended consequences, it does not really matter, strictly speaking, what they mean to do. Although they are using experiences to get people to buy physical products, what they are also doing is teaching people to value the experience more than the stuff the experience was designed to sell. As they evolve their positioning, marketing, and offer to stay ahead of the curve and appeal to the influencers, today's businesses, whether it is their intention or not, are encouraging the movement from the material to the experience economy. There could be a problem with that.

14

Can You Be an Experientialist and Still Love Stuff?

The modern economy is predicated on growth. We need growth for stability and prosperity. We need it like a boat needs water. Without growth, the system would run aground and keel over. Since the modern economy is, largely, the consumer economy—consumer spending makes up around 65 percent of the British and 70 percent or so of the U.S. economy, for instance—we really need people to keep spending.

But what would happen if tens of millions of people gave up their materialistic ways and bought a lot less stuff? What would happen if more businesses encouraged people to value experiences instead of material goods? What if millions followed the experientialist example set by Jim Whyte and his three suitcases, or the Lenet family, with their lives stuffed into backpacks? If millions followed them, there would be far less stuff needed. That could be devastating to many industries—like the shoe business, for instance. There would be less leather and rubber required, so fewer people needed to herd the cattle, tan the hides, tend the plantations, transport the raw materials to the factory, work in the factory, and make the packaging. We would not require so many people to import, distribute, market, make ads for, and sell the shoes. If millions of people gave up their materialistic ways, there would be far fewer jobs.

As Bernard Mandeville explored in *The Fable of the Bees,* and the architects of our system realized, those things we buy create a lot of work, wealth, and material well-being. As Christine Frederick pointed out in the "American paradox," we have more when we spend more. Seen this way, a few becoming experientialists and buying fewer goods is clearly okay. But if experientialism became the dominant value system it would be nothing short of a shipwreck.

Supporters of materialism—especially those grumpy old men at the helm of the current system who profit so handsomely from it—are quick to turn to this sort of argument to explain why materialism is better than any alternative. This is one reason why the captains of consciousness turned consuming into a patriotic act: most people today believe that buying stuff is in the same ballpark as singing the national anthem, flying the flag, and laughing in the face of anyone who might want to destroy our way of life. (Think about what Bush and Blair said after 9/11.)

So, given the collateral damage experientialism could do to the world we live in, is being an experientialist the lifestyle equivalent to sleeping with the enemy? Put like that, it would be hard to argue for experientialism. Who doesn't want to support the society we live in? Then again, thinking that there is only one way, and that this way is the one we already know, sounds suspiciously like a lack of imagination to me.

After all, arguing that the current system is best is how some people always react to any newfangled idea that threatens the world they know and, especially, their livelihood. This is exactly why English textile workers were protesting in the early nineteenth century, for example. They were so worried that less-skilled, low-wage machine operators would take their jobs that they smashed wool- and cotton-making machines, and burned down mills. They named themselves after a man who, in a pique of anti-machine rage, had smashed one to pieces. His name was Ned Ludd. They were the Luddites.

Where do you sit on all this: are you for or against trying a new way of being? By asking this I do not mean to imply that if you worry about the shift to a new system you are a Luddite. The stability of society, after all, is a good thing. Just because there is a new way of doing things does not mean it is better. And there is no point rocking the boat we have just for the sake of it.

But if the problems are coming in waves, and already threatening to overturn our system—as is happening in this time of Stuffocation—it seems like a good idea to at least consider an alternative that looks, in many ways, like it might be better. Instead of ignoring the issues, and blindly sticking with the current course, the questions we should be asking ourselves are: Is materialism the only value system that can give us stability and growth—or could experientialism provide that too? Can you be an experientialist and still contribute to the economy's growth?

And then, even if it turns out that you can be an experientialist and a patriot at the same time, you also have to ask the question of whether, in the final analysis, you would really, honestly, want to be an experientialist. Because, even if the basic idea appealed to you, wouldn't that mean you had to give up all the good stuff you've gotten used to? If you decided to be an experientialist, could you never again enjoy the smell of a leather handbag, the swish of a silk scarf, or the thrill of new clothes? Would you have to say goodbye to the righteous feeling of pushing the pedal to the metal in a car? Could you never again get excited about a new toy? Or can you be an experientialist and still enjoy all these things? Can you, even if it sounds counterintuitive, be an experientialist and still love stuff?

THE SECRET LOOT IN THE EXPERIENCE ECONOMY

My wife and I had our papers, as per the instructions in the email invite, so when we arrived at a former cinema called the Troxy in East London, we had no problems with the soldiers of Vichy France. They waved us through.

We wandered down a deserted corridor, past a row of potted palms, and entered a vast auditorium—"Rick's Café Américain," a blue electric sign said. Beneath the sign, a man played the piano. Everywhere, people were in trilbies and suits and vintage dresses.

A French policeman with a false mustache approaches our table and tells us not to cause any trouble, but if we come across any letters of transit we are to inform him. I tell him he is a Nazi stooge and that he should be ashamed of himself. A minute later, the policeman is back, this time accompanied by the Nazi Major Strasser—the chief baddy in *Casablanca*—and two henchmen in SS uniforms.

"Zis is ze man!" the French policeman says, pointing at me.

"Vot is the meaning of ze zings you said?" Strasser demands.

"You'll never win this war!" I say. (This is fun. I've always wanted to tell a Nazi that.)

"Take him," he says, and his two SS henchmen grab me by the shoulders, haul me off my seat, push me to my knees.

"Vot did you say?" one SS man demands.

"You'll. Never. Vin. This. Var," I say. It is all I can do not to laugh—yet at the same time, pushed to the floor, my knees on old carpet, two ruffians in uniform holding me by each shoulder, I'm kind of scared.

Strasser stares at me with hatred, his face turns puce.

"Bring him viz you," he stammers, turning on his black-booted heel and goose-stepping through the amazed crowd.

And the two men frog-march me after him, until we come to a small table. They roughhouse me into a big chair.

"Vill you," the major says menacingly, "svear allegiance to Heil Hitler?"

"Never," I vow.

"Zen you vill drink zis as your punishment," he declares, pouring a shot of Jack Daniel's into a glass.

I take it.

"Churchill!" I declare, and down the drink.

"Go," he says, dismissing me. And I wander off back to my seat and my wife.

By the time the movie starts, an hour or so later, more actors have appeared, playing out more scenes from *Casablanca* around the room. I have attended an impromptu rally where Victor Laszlo has stood on a chair, roused the crowd to pledge our allegiance to "free France!," and, with hand on heart and tears in his eyes, sung the "Marseillaise": "Aux armes, citoyens! Formez vos bataillons! Marchons, marchons!" Rick and Ilsa have talked by the piano. Sam has played "As Time Goes By." He has played it again. I have obtained letters of transit and passed them surreptitiously—keeping a keen eye out for that policeman and those Nazis—to Laszlo.

By the time the curtains open on the screen, the suspension of our disbelief is complete. We, like Laszlo and Ilsa and Rick, are sitting in Rick's Café in Casablanca in 1941. We hate the Nazis. We understand Ilsa's torment. We feel the nobility of Laszlo's struggle. We know how important those letters of transit are.

One Secret Cinema event, and you are hooked. If only every time you saw a movie it could be as immersive, memorable, and, quite frankly, amazing as this. It is not just seeing the movie, it is a complete experience. No wonder people treat a Secret Cinema production as if their favorite band has come to town. They cross the country to attend, they stay in hotels near the venue, they take the day off work the next day.

Like Punchdrunk and Bompas & Parr, Secret Cinema is a prime example of how the experience economy might work in the future, and how it is already working. This idea, of the experience economy, was popularized in the late 1990s by a pair of business consultants called Joe Pine and Jim Gilmore. In an article for the *Harvard Busi-*

ness Review and then a book, Pine and Gilmore set out a persuasive case that every business—including yours—should use experiences to sell more to more people. They also proposed that, after the agrarian, manufacturing, and service economies, the experience economy is the logical evolution of capitalism. By that, they meant that, just as the creation and delivery of food and drink were the hallmarks of the agrarian system, and the people who owned the means of production were the wealthiest—and just as the creation and delivery of material goods were the pillars of the manufacturing economy, and the people and businesses that owned the factories were the most successful, and so on for the service economy—so the creation and delivery of experiences will be the essential characteristics of the experience economy.

The difference between a service and an experience, to be clear, is that while both are intangible, that is, you cannot touch them, service is only that—whereas an experience is also designed to be memorable. It is something that engages you, as Pine and Gilmore wrote, "on an emotional, physical, intellectual, or even spiritual level." As with the other aspects of the economy, there is often some overlap, but with a little consideration you can see the difference. Food is a useful way to illustrate how each sector is distinct. When you shop for ingredients—like asparagus, potatoes, and steaks for dinner—this is part of the agrarian economy. When you buy prepared food, like a ready-made pizza, you are purchasing a manufactured good. When you buy dinner in a restaurant, you are supporting the service sector. And when you eat in a pop-up restaurant in a former Masonic temple, or have a picnic on a deserted beach where you have been dropped by speedboat, you are spending money in the experience sector.

It is worthwhile understanding this difference, because the experience economy—where businesses make the staging of memorable, engaging events their priority—is the sector growing fastest. In the past fifty years or so, it has grown, according to Pine and Gilmore's calculations, 38 percent faster than the manufacturing sector.

Secret Cinema is a stellar example of that growth. Besides *Casablanca,* the company has staged many other movies. At its performance of *The Shawshank Redemption,* the audience became convicts—they swapped their civvies for regulation uniforms, and prison guards shouted at them and locked them in cells. For *The Grand Budapest Hotel,* the audience, dressed in dapper suits, flapper hats, and furs, became guests of a kitsch 1930s Eastern European hotel, sipping vodka and Galliano cocktails as purple-suited bellboys handed out pastel-pink macaroon boxes.

The Secret Cinema formula—pick a movie, find a venue, and stage an experience based on that movie—is proving popular. When the company hired forty actors and forty crew to turn a London warehouse into a spaceship, and made 25,000 people over twenty-eight days become boiler-suited crew members of Ridley Scott's *Prometheus,* the company took in more money than London's IMAX theater. Secret Cinema, as its founder, Fabien Riggall, once boasted, is a good way to get people to pay £50 each to see a film.

Was someone at the back worrying whether there was money, and jobs, and growth, in the experience economy?

THE MILLIONAIRE MINIMALIST WHO LOVES STUFF

It was Olga who opened Graham Hill's eyes.

Now in her mid-thirties, and originally from Andorra, the pretty mountain principality between France and Spain, Olga Sasplugas has brown eyes, olive skin, and long legs. She is a ballet dancer and a dance therapist who teaches orphans. She was the first Andorran to be awarded a Fulbright Scholarship to study for a master's degree in the U.S. She took a course in performing arts in New York. It was there she met Hill.

After they had been dating for three months, Sasplugas's visa ran out and she had to leave the country. Hill did what any sensible man would have done. He followed her. First stop was Barcelona, and

Sasplugas's student apartment, a run-down place about a million miles from the loft Hill—a technology millionaire—had in Manhattan. The interior was just as ramshackle. Sasplugas had decorated it with things she had found on the street: people leave their unwanted furniture outside on Tuesdays in Barcelona. "The couch was a bed, the table was a wooden door—nothing went with nothing!" says Sasplugas. "And here was Graham coming from his fancy apartment in SoHo—I was absolutely scared!"

Hill did not mind though. They had a dream summer. They cycled to the beach. They ate *pimientos de Padrón*—spicy green peppers, deep-fried and served with salt. They had dinner parties on the roof. Sometimes, when it was cool, they would work up there too: to make the Wi-Fi reach, Hill strung a wire out of the window, up the side, and onto the top of the building.

Sasplugas was soon off again, to northern Cambodia, to teach dance therapy in an orphanage. The Internet connection was terrible, so Hill went as far as Bangkok. At least they could see each other on Sasplugas's few days off each month.

Then they went to Mysore, India, for Sasplugas to learn yoga. They rented an apartment in an old colonial house. It had three bedrooms, two bathrooms, a meditation room, a kitchen—but no hot water, no Internet, and not a single piece of furniture. They borrowed a mattress from their neighbors. Hill worked from the local Internet café. Next stop was Buenos Aires. Sasplugas learned tango. They stayed in a tiny top-floor apartment, far above the cobbled streets and jacaranda trees of a district called Palermo Viejo.

By the time they got back to New York, the last thing they wanted was the hassle of a designer loft. So they rented a three-hundred-square-foot sixth-floor walk-up. "The toilet was in the back, the shower was in the kitchen," Hill recalls. "At least it had a curtain around it though," says Sasplugas. "One of us could shower while the other cooked."

Then Hill ran into a problem, one that most people dream of. When he sold his business—an eco-site called TreeHugger.com he had set up from Sasplugas's place in Barcelona—he made the sort of money that would buy a loft in SoHo, fix it up, and fill it with brand-new stuff. Luckily though, he had faced this problem before. That time, he had bought a vast, 3,600-square-foot house and, because he was too busy working, hired a personal assistant to buy all the things it needed. At first, Hill had loved it. He had rented out rooms to friends, and hosted barbecues and parties. But he soon realized how much hassle a house was, and he had sold it. This time, he was older and wiser.

"When I'd been with Olga, I'd been working really hard, but always in a different place and always having cool new experiences," he recalls now. "And I guess I just realized—that was a really great way to live, and that I just didn't need that much stuff."

Hill did not want a big house this time, but he did want a place to call home. The obvious solution was a small apartment, like all those places he had shared with Sasplugas. But then, he had loved having people over for dinner and friends to stay at his old place. Could he, he wondered, have both—a really small place with almost no stuff and no hassle, but also somewhere he could have friends over?

To answer that question, Hill posted a challenge on a crowd-sourcing website called Jovoto: he wanted someone to create a design for a 420-square-foot apartment he had bought that would allow him to live and work there, host a sit-down dinner for twelve, and have a couple of friends to stay, while still giving them some privacy. To encourage people, he offered $70,000 in prizes. It worked. The Jovoto community responded with three hundred designs, seventy thousand people voted on their favorite, and Hill found a design he liked. He now lives there, in a place that has been called a "Swiss Army apartment" and a "Transformer home"—as every one of its 420 square feet shape-shifts and multitasks from morning to night. Everything seems to double up as something else, and hides away until it is needed. There is a pull-down bed, a pop-out desk, and, for when friends stay, a pull-out wall. There is an extendable table so ten—not twelve, but who's counting?—can have a sit-down meal.

Hill cannot bear having too much stuff. He calls himself a mini-malist. His brand of minimalism, as you can see, does not look any-thing like deprivation. And it does not come cheap. The push-out table that telescopes out to seat ten? $3,950. His pull-down queen-size bed? $15,000. The overall cost of creating his apartment—just for the renovation, not the cost of the real estate—$315,000.

Hill is not the only one practicing this type of minimalism. This is the minimalism favored by the social media set that Alice Marwick wrote about in her dissertation, and the one practiced by the wider tech community. Consider Colin Wright, for instance, an entrepre-neur from Los Angeles we met earlier who gave up a six-figure salary and thriving business to live with only 51 things. "If you're only going to have one of something, it should be your favorite of that thing—and that means upgrading to higher quality whenever you can," he says. "It's important to recalibrate and not to get stuck with one brand. At the moment, I have a Mac computer, an Android phone, and a Canon camera. But I won't always. I always try to make sure I have the best from each category for me, the thing that makes me happiest."

This point of view, the one that Hill and Wright advocate, is fas-cinating when you think about it. It is a perspective that manages to marry two ways of thinking that seem, at first glance, diametrically opposed. First, they are committed minimalists. They are not inter-ested in accumulating material possessions. Things, they believe, weigh them down. Things do not bring happiness. Stuff cannot con-fer status. But, at the same time, Hill and Wright are enthusiastic consumers. That makes them similar to the materialists of the last century. But the difference is that their way of consuming feels far more discerning and sophisticated. Instead of gathering more, they only want the best. While the materialists, you could say, are inter-ested, principally, in quantity, these "consumer minimalists" are in-terested in quality.

These people matter, because Silicon Valley matters. We live in a flatter world today, but there are people and places that stand out and wield far more influence. The bright ideas that originate in Silicon Valley, and in all the other Silicon Somethings around the world, in particular those that come from the consumer technology and social media scenes, influence what people all around the world think. If they are more interested in getting status by having fewer but better things—and conspicuously consuming experiences, as Alice Marwick showed—then more people will think and behave this way.

Besides this, the consumer minimalists are more proof that a value system other than materialism could still deliver stability and growth. As you can see, the consumer minimalists—who, like all minimalists, are ultimately interested in experiences rather than stuff—would deliver stability and growth by buying fewer goods, but ones that cost a whole lot more.

This, of course, is great news, for experientialism, for society, for us. But, while answering one question—can you be an experientialist and still love stuff?—it raises another. Because it's all well and good for a tech millionaire like Hill to live a pared-back life of far less but much better stuff, but what about the rest of us? What about those of us who don't have $4,000 to spend on a now-you-see-it-now-you-don't telescopic table? Can we be experientialists too?

"YOU CAN'T HAVE THE EXPERIENCES WITHOUT THE STUFF"

One bright, sunny Sunday morning some years back, Sarah Howell found herself at the edge of a cliff in the Morialta Falls area outside Adelaide, Australia, trembling like a gum tree leaf in the breeze. Admittedly, she was wearing a safety harness, and that was attached to a rope held by a man who knew what he was doing. So she was completely safe. But still, as she perched on that edge, about to rappel for the first time, she had to wonder—what the *bloody hell* was she doing here?

"I'm just not the sporty type," she says now. "I love food markets, finding new recipes, and testing out menus with chefs. And I'm used to feeling like I'm in charge! Standing at the top of a cliff, my feet shuffling backwards towards the edge, peering over that edge and looking down, I was petrified. Adrenaline was pumping through me. There was *no way*. I just did *not* want to walk down a cliff backwards!"

But at least this was different from the usual dates she went on. Most guys who were attracted to her pale skin, ruby red hair, and English-rose looks would take her for drinks and dinner. Since she was a restaurateur, that was a lot like going to work. When a cocky DJ named Ben had said he would pick her up Sunday morning, and that she should wear track shoes and gym clothes, she thought he might be different. She soon realized he was. He did not seem to care too much about clothes. He always wore the same khaki pants and some sort of pineapple print surf shirt. Also, he never tried to impress her with money. And instead of talking about *having* things, he would talk about *doing* things: skiing, kiteboarding, climbing—and taking her rappeling.

"Ben was great that day in Morialta Falls," she remembers. "He talked me through it, told me I'd be all right. I felt really vulnerable, but he knew what he was doing." Looking back, it is clear he did. He and Red—as he calls Sarah because of the color of her hair—got together, got married. They have a daughter, five-year-old Poppy. They haven't changed much since they met all those years ago. She is still a restaurateur. She runs a Spanish restaurant, an Italian osteria, and a pop-up place called Ruby Red Flamingo that opened in 2013. He still prefers doing to having. He owns as few possessions as he can get away with.

"Don't own a watch, never have," Ben Howell says. "I only have three pairs of shoes—a pair of leather work boots, a pair of sneakers for jogging, and a pair of dress shoes in case Red makes me dress up to go to an awards ceremony with her. Actually, I have four pairs, if you count my thongs."

(For the non-Australian reader: those thongs are not g-strings. Ben is not really that type. "Thong" is the Aussie term for flip-flops.)

The Howells are a typical twenty-first-century experientialist family. "We put experiences first," says Sarah. She fulfills her passion for food and hospitality at work and in her spare time. Whenever they pass a food market, they stop. Their overseas trips often include foodie elements, like visiting the fish markets in Tokyo, or finding great foie gras in Paris. Ben, meanwhile, spends his money and the spare time he gets away from his marketing job learning sports like surfing, kiteboarding, and, his latest hobby, dirt biking.

And here we have come across one of the counterintuitive aspects of experientialism. Because, while Ben prefers experiences to things, and is not someone you would ever call materialistic, he likes some things very much.

If you were to visit the Howells in Australia, and take a look around, you would soon see what I mean. You would notice, first of all, that they are not materialistic. Their home is nothing special. It is a regular, suburban house, in need of a bit of renovation, in the leafy foothills of Adelaide. Inside is a good-sized, open-plan living area. Though there are record turntables in one corner, and high-end stainless steel gadgets in the kitchen, it is, as Sarah points out, "definitely not cluttered" with material possessions.

But take a walk out back, yank up the creaky garage door, and you would realize there is a very different material story in there. It is bursting with stuff. There are surfboards and wet suits. There are windsurf boards, sails, booms, and masts. There are kiteboards, a power kite, a foil kite, a kite harness, and sets of flying lines. There is a rock-climbing harness. There is a dirt bike and a motorbike helmet. There are also lots of shoes. But these are not fashion items, which look good one season but you cannot wear the next. This is technical footwear, like motorbike boots, windsurf boots, and climbing shoes.

Though Ben cannot see the point in accumulating ordinary material possessions, he loves things that give him experiences—and he does not hesitate to spend on them. "I spent $12 on a pair of shoes the other week, and it really annoyed me—they should have cost

$10," he once told me. "But then I went out the next day and blew $1,700 on a great new kite."

And here, we have come across another typical aspect of the Howells, and most experientialists. They are not materialistic, but they have no problem with, and therefore pose little threat to, the overall system we live in. They fully intend to keep working and earning and spending. As Sarah says, "You can't have all the experiences Ben has without all the stuff, and the money to buy that stuff."

Given the chance, the Howells and most experientialists will continue to play their part in "have more by spending more" consumerism, and do their bit for growth. But they will increasingly do that by spending their money on experiences rather than objects. "Red and me, we still see ourselves as capitalists," Ben says. "A lot of things we do cost a fair bit of money. But rather than buy some pointless thing, like a fancy shirt or a black BMW, we invest our money in experiences—like jumping out of a plane or going skiing."

It's fair to say that not everyone has enough money to choose between a ski trip and a BMW, like the Howells—just as very few of us are rich enough to even think about spending $4,000 on a dining table. But we can all relate to choosing between an experience and a material good—yet another pair of shoes against a night out with friends, for instance. That's why the Howells prove that living an experientialist life is not only good for the economy and society as a whole, but that it is also possible for the rest of us.

To be an experientialist, whatever your level of income, all you need do is choose experiences over stuff whenever there is a choice. But as this story about the Howells shows, that doesn't mean you have to cut stuff out of your life completely. To be an experientialist there's no need to take a "vow of stuff-less-ness," or expel the very idea of things—the way a monk takes a vow of silence, or an emperor sends an enemy into exile. As an experientialist, you can still enjoy, and even love, stuff. How?

HOW TO BE AN EXPERIENTIALIST AND STILL LOVE STUFF

As these stories about Hill and the Howells make clear, the rise of experientialism does not mean the end of stuff. We will still buy, use, and use up products—for all the reasons we looked at earlier that prove stuff is good. As we respond to Stuffocation, though, our tastes will evolve, and the things we choose will change.

To begin with, we will increasingly buy "experiential products," those that, as the psychologist Ryan Howell has recently discovered, provide as much happiness as experiences—because we buy them not so much for the tangible, material object but for the experiences they provide. Think of musical instruments, computer games, tennis rackets, and books. If the government does ever decide that products should carry information labels to nudge us to buy the ones that are good for us and avoid the ones that are bad, these experiential products will no doubt be the products that get the thumbs-up and the green light. They are, if you like, the fruit and vegetables of the product world.

We will also prefer goods—products, services, and solutions—that are more experiential, less wasteful, and less harmful to the environment, and create less clutter. Where possible, they will occupy no physical space at all. Instead of owning physical objects, we will sign up to services that give us access to them. And we will gravitate, in particular, to those services that create conversation and community, and that contribute to a better, happier world.

Does this sound like an idealistic dream to you? It shouldn't. While projections of the future you have come across before may have felt like wishful thinking—involving an enlightened, post-paranoid race of people who have given up the status game of Snakes and Ladders—this forecast does not ignore our need to express status. Experientialism may well help solve the problems of Stuffocation, but it will not do so by hoping we forget all about signaling our position in the social pecking order. "People still want to keep up with the Joneses," says Jim Gilmore. "Before, they wanted goods that were shinier, faster, more powerful. And they still want to keep up in the experience economy. But now they want things that are different—more durable, say, or more egalitarian, or more participatory."

Moreover, the experience economy should not feel like hopeful idealism because, even though it is still unevenly distributed, there are many signs that it is already happening. Here are a few of my favorite examples.

The shoe company TOMS and sportswear brand Puma have each introduced novel ways to create less clutter for their customers. TOMS has done this by turning a classic twentieth-century, materialistic marketing idea—"buy one, get one free"—and giving it an experientialist twist. TOMS does, in fact, operate a "buy one, get one free" model. But they give that free pair to a child in need. So instead of getting your attention by giving you more clutter-causing stuff, TOMS incentivizes you to buy by giving you something invisible, intangible, and so much more valuable: the feel-good sense that you have helped someone out.

To really comprehend the magic of one of Puma's ideas, picture the typical scene in your home just after you have gotten back from shopping, when you find yourself surrounded by bags and packaging. To solve that problem, Puma created a bag that, rather than add to the clutter in your home when you stash it away, or the guilt you feel when you throw it out, simply disappeared. Put the Clever Little Shopper in hot water for three minutes and it harmlessly dissolves, so you can pour it safely down the drain.

There is more post-materialist magic in a recent campaign by the outdoor brand Patagonia. In its Common Threads Partnership with eBay, the company encourages its customers to repair, resell, or recycle its goods. For me, though, the highlight of the campaign was something the company's founder, Yvon Chouinard, said. He asked his company's customers "to not buy something if they don't need it." This is, if you think about it, a revolutionary statement. It is the antithesis of the "spend more to have more" idea that the captains of consciousness encouraged in the past. Imagine, for a moment, taking that idea to your boss: "Let's ask our customers to buy less from us." Yet it is the sort of statement that makes sense in a world suffering from Stuffocation. By genuinely caring about the environment, Patagonia is far more likely to connect with people concerned with the state of our planet and suffering from Stuffocation.

A company in the Netherlands named OAT that makes baby shoes has taken the idea of ecological impact a step further. Rather than reduce the impact it has on the planet, the company aims to increase its impact but make it positive rather than negative: each pair of its shoes is biodegradable and contains wildflower seeds. So when your child is finished with a pair, instead of adding to landfill, you can plant them, as if they were a pet that had passed on, in your garden. The shoes then decompose and, in their place, daisies, poppies, and snapdragons grow.

You may be surprised to hear that I think Apple is a good example of the shift from material to experiential. Of course, Apple turns out a lot of hardware. But Apple is on my list because of its ruthless focus on experience. Think, for a moment, how easy it is to operate an Apple device, and how slim the operating manual is. How different is that to the manual that came with, say, your VHS recorder in the 1980s? Do you remember how complicated it was to record a TV show back then? Jonathan Ive and his designers at Apple not only consider the experience of using their product though. They try to make everything pleasant, from the stores to the moment you open the box. "Not only do the guys at Apple make sure their products are products people love to use," says Joe Pine. "They even think about the packaging, about the 'box-opening experience,' so even that is unique and engaging."

Apple also makes a product that causes less clutter and lowers environmental impact. The company's iPad, like other e-reading devices, means fewer trees cut down, lower carbon footprint, and fewer magazines and books and newspapers cluttering up the house or your bag.

You might be wondering if, as people always seem to be upgrading to the next iPad, Kindle, Kobo, or Galaxy device, e-readers are actually adding to the problem of Stuffocation—both in terms of more e-waste damaging our general environment and of more clutter clogging up our homes. There is, regrettably, no simple answer to this. In theory, these devices should be ideal. A year's worth of newspapers uses 67 times more water and produces 140 more CO_2 emissions compared to their digital equivalent. It takes 78 times more water to produce a physical book than an ebook. But, of course, you have to weigh these impressive statistics against the footprint in the manufacture of the machine.

The best answer available at present is that today's gadgets *can* reduce clutter and environmental impact, and are more likely to in the future—thanks to a new mode of production called "remanufacturing." Around 50 percent of the material components in most of today's mobile phones could be reused, and device makers are investigating how they can make new phones by reusing these recycled components. In the long term, remanufacturing may well help e-reading fulfill its potential to reduce clutter and environmental impact. In the meantime, you can do your bit by loving the e-reader you have that bit longer—and, as with the Patagonia campaign, when you are done with it, reselling or recycling as best you can.

The last example in this list is one of the clearest signposts of the shift away from materialism and toward experientialism. It is known, from slightly different angles, as the "sharing economy," "collaborative consumption," "dis-ownership," and "the shift from ownership to access." Whatever you call it, the result is the same: thanks to new attitudes, behaviors, and technologies, you can now enjoy the experience of many of the things you love about modern life, without all the hassle that comes with physically owning them. By sharing, in other words, you can be an experientialist and still love stuff.

You can be an experientialist and still enjoy one of the most potent symbols of the materialistic era: the car. Thanks to car-sharing schemes, like Zipcar, DriveNow, and the Classic Car Club, you can still love and drive a VW, a BMW, and a Jaguar E-type, while avoiding all the regular costs and hassles of car ownership. Moreover, you feel good for playing your part in de-cluttering your city—research suggests every shared car takes up to thirteen others off the road.

By sharing, you can be an experientialist and still love lots of the other stuff that makes modern life fun. Love movies or music, but don't want all those DVDs and CDs taking over the room? Access them instead through Netflix, Hulu, Deezer, or Spotify. Love clothes but can't handle the wardrobe clutter? Rent the latest Diane von Furstenberg or Victoria Beckham design through Rent the Runway or Girl Meets Dress. Like DIY but don't have the room to store a ladder, a power tool, or a lawnmower? Borrow them through Neighbor-Goods or rent them through Zilok. And if you pine for a dog, but can't face the full-time hassle of owning one, now you can just take one for a walk through Borrow My Doggy. Something you love not on this list? Chances are it will be at some point in the future: as more people adopt these ways, the model is likely to spread to cover more categories.

The best of these sharing services are the ones that not only reduce clutter and costs but also generate conversation and create community. Take home- and ride-sharing services like Airbnb, Lyft, and BlaBlaCar. When you ride-share through Lyft, so a journalist named Drew Olanoff wrote, "You feel like you're in the car with a friend. . . . Whether it's bringing someone a sandwich for the ride or letting them choose the music in the car, Lyft drivers have their own budding community growing."

In this time of Stuffocation, what people want from the goods and services they buy is evolving. This will cause some industries and businesses, like ships in a storm, to sink. Others will be bailed out. The smartest captains of industry—who may be lazy, greedy, or frightened, and who are certainly looking for easier, more profitable, and safer ways of ensuring the success of their business—are reimagining their products, services, and business models to keep their companies afloat in a changing world. Take the German carmaker

BMW: the company is aiming for more than a million members, in Germany alone, for its DriveNow car share service by 2020.

Inspired by pioneers like Bompas & Parr, Secret Cinema, Patagonia, Airbnb, and Lyft, the smartest businesses are putting their material offer in the background, and making experience the star. As they do, they are not only passively reflecting this change in values, they are actively creating the shift from the material to the experience economy. They are showing that you can be an experientialist and still contribute to society—not by spending money on shiny, materialistic stuff, but by buying and sharing goods that have much less material and are far more experiential. And they are proving that it is perfectly possible to be an experientialist and still love stuff.

LIVING IN AN EXPERIENTIAL WORLD

When in 1984 Madonna appeared in a pink silk gown and long pink gloves on a lipstick red stage in the video for "Material Girl," she was paying homage to Marilyn Monroe's 1953 performance of "Diamonds Are a Girl's Best Friend." Just like Monroe, Madonna was dripping in diamonds. Her every step was followed by a troupe of handsome men. Her hair was in big, blond Marilyn curls. But Madonna was channeling far more than the 1950s idol. Through the look of the video and the lyrics of the song—"we are living in a material world, and I am a material girl"—she was also personifying the idea that defined the era: materialism.

Strictly speaking, Madonna was talking about money—especially when she sang that "the boy with the cold hard cash is always Mister Right." But she didn't mean "cold hard cash" for its own sake. It was about the conspicuous, materialistic, diamond-encrusted, and fur-filled life that money could provide. After all, the song's heroine was a material, not a financial, girl.

In this century we will be ever less impressed by the diamonds and furs that excited Monroe, Madonna, and millions of others in the age of materialism. It is not only our aspirations and possessions that will change, though. Alongside the experience economy, we will also see the rise of an experiential, as opposed to material, world. What will that look like? What will experientialism mean for other aspects of our lives? How will it change, for instance, how we work, rest, and play?

Work will change dramatically. Instead of viewing work as a way to gather cold hard cash to buy things we don't need to impress people we don't like, we will think of it more as a stage to express ourselves and realize our passions. A *Harvard Business Review* columnist, Tammy Erickson, summed this idea up in the phrase: "Meaning is the new money."

To reflect this shift, and attract the best talent, businesses will judge their success in more meaningful terms than just money. You can already see this happening in the rise of benefit corporations. First created in 2010 in Maryland, and better known as "B corporations," these companies are not concerned with maximizing shareholder value alone, as traditional companies are. Instead, they measure success not only by the profit they create, but also in terms of their impact on society and the environment. Following a similar ethos, the B Team was founded in 2012 by two business leaders, Sir Richard Branson and Jochen Zeitz, to encourage more businesses to put people and the planet on a similar level to their profits.

Offices will change, as we come to think of work, according to a workplace expert named Jeanne Meister, "as an 'experience' rather than merely a place to go to every day." There will be three new models for the new workplace.

I think of the first as the "Hotel California model": you can come into the office anytime you like, but the facilities and the time you have there will be so good, you can never really leave. The offices of the search company Google and the shoe retailer Zappos are great examples. At Google's campus in Mountain View, California, for instance, there are bikes, pool tables, gourmet coffee stations, smoothies, a lap pool, and volleyball courts—and all free to use. Zappos also has free facilities, like a nap room, for instance, but it is the company's radical culture that really turns the idea of work on its head. In the old world, work was that place you had to go in between spending time with friends and family. But in the Zappos version of the new world, work is where you go to see your friends and, as some employees genuinely call their coworkers, family.

I think of the second as the "Martini model," with reference to the 1980s commercial. The tag line was "anytime, anyplace, anywhere." The best ad featured a waiter in a white tuxedo in Cannes, taking drinks down to the beach and into the sea, to deliver them to glamorous people sitting, ankle-deep, at a table there. In this technology-enabled version of the future of work, you will work the Martini way—"anytime, anyplace, anywhere." This is the model Marianne Cantwell chose when she ditched her old life. It is the way Jeff Harris earns a living, working for a company in Texas from his home in New Mexico. It is the way many millions are now working, wherever and whenever they want.

There is a problem with this way of working, and it is giving rise to a third version of the future, which I think of as the "Third Place" work model. Although many people say they want the Martini model, in practice mobile workers often miss the social strokes that happen in a regular workplace: the friendships, for instance, and someone asking how your weekend was on a Monday morning. As a result, many are now taking their private working lives back into public places that offer Hotel California–like benefits. Consider Fueled Collective, for instance, an eighteen-thousand-square-foot coworking space in New York that, besides the desks, water, and Wi-Fi, also gives out free ice cream and has a whiskey room and Ping-Pong tables. There has been a significant trend for these Third Place coworking spaces in recent years. In the U.S., there were forty of them in 2008, three hundred in 2011, and eight hundred in 2013. Picture how those numbers would look on the sort of graph a cultural forecaster would use, and you can clearly see the beginnings of an S curve.

Besides why and where we work, how much we work will also change. As our focus shifts from quantity of stuff to quality of life, we will choose to spend less time at work, and more time at leisure. After all, when you have more than enough, and you know that every extra penny is going to deliver ever less happiness, why bother sweating for more when you could be enjoying what you've already got? That could translate into longer holidays, fewer working hours, and a radically shorter working week. If you earn enough in four days, or even three, why not make every weekend three or four days long? Or instead of taking an increase in pay, perhaps more of us will prefer to take regular sabbaticals instead.

As work changes, so our homes, holidays, and communities will change too. Our homes will, in general, be smaller. Not all of us will live in homes quite as tiny as Tammy Strobel's, but we will become less concerned with square footage, and more interested in our homes' ability to deliver experiences, whether that is through the technology and flexibility inside them, or their location—for instance, being near a park or the beach or great restaurants.

How we think about our homes will change too. As we become collaborative consumers, we will think of our homes as we would any other sharable good that can be managed and maximized. In order to appeal to the widest demographic—and yes, we will think about our home's target markets—we will design and decorate our homes differently. Flexibility will be key. We will want coffee tables that pop up for dining, walls that pull down for sleeping, and chairs that fold away—just as Graham Hill has in his apartment. As home sharing becomes even more common we may even begin to think more about the "shoot-ability" of our homes. We will not only tidy up every seven years when the real estate agent's photographer comes around, but every time we upload photos to a home sharing site, and each time someone rents the place.

What we do in our free time will change. We will prefer to do things that give us social and experiential currency to help us stand out in an experiential world. The signs have been with us for some time. Think of the rise of triathlons and extreme sports events like the Marathon des Sables and Tough Mudder. Or the growing popularity of festivals like South by Southwest, Benicàssim, and Coachella. Or the emergence of experiential theater and immersive games as seen in Punchdrunk's productions and New York's Escape the Room, where teams solve clues and complete challenges to get out in less than sixty minutes. Or the thriving experiential travel market, where you can sign up to go thrifting with a fashion designer in Barcelona, dine with a food blogger in Queens, paraglide into a hotel in Oman, or meet local tribespeople in Papua New Guinea.

The way our communities are organized, finally, will also change. Just as Lyft is bringing people together, so other shared services will encourage us to trust and like one another more. What shared services exactly? "I'd mention," says Neal Gorenflo, editor of a sharing economy publication named *Shareable*, "the surge in local, community-based sharing projects like tool libraries, repair cafes, coworking spaces, complementary currencies, food forests, cooperatives, community-supported agriculture farms, hacker spaces, fab labs, time banks, bike sharing, and more." All of these will create stronger, better communities. Think of the pro-social benefits of the tool libraries, for instance, community-oriented places where people lend their power tools and other DIY equipment to others. They are popping up all around the world, from Australia to Belgium and the United States. Or consider Seattle's community-run, seven-acre Beacon Food Forest, where every plant, from the blueberry and raspberry bushes to the plum and walnut trees, produces something edible.

As we move from the age of materialism to the new era of experientialism, then, much will change. We will have more fun, and spend less time, at work. We will live in smaller, more flexible, and better-designed homes. We will have better connections with more people, and create better communities. We will, in short, be happier, healthier people, leading more sustainable lives on a less damaged planet.

If this all sounds like some utopian vision that is too good to be true, think how today's world would have sounded to someone a few generations ago. Could your grandmother's mother have imagined a map that knows where you are and can tell you where to go next? Would she have believed that one of society's most pressing problems would be that there was so much food and affluence that it is making millions sick? If material advances like these were possible in the twentieth century, why are experiential breakthroughs not also probable in the twenty-first? The good news, of course, is that the signs are already here.

The road to experientialism will not be quite as simple as this brief description makes it sound. There will be unexpected bumps, twists, rain clouds, hail storms, and sunny spells along the way. There will be unintended consequences from the changes happening now. But in the ongoing dance of progress, we will, in general, be moving in a positive direction, taking steps up the hill to a better future.

In the beginning, it may only be possible for those of us in the wealthy West. But once the new materialists in the emerging economies get enough stuff and feel their own sense of Stuffocation, they will want to join us, and become experientialists too. And then everybody will be living not in a material but in an experiential world.

Conclusion

Why You Need Experience
More Than Ever

On January 27, 1940, it was a quiet night in London. The blackouts were in place. There was snow on the ground. In the north of the city, near where Tottenham Hotspur play soccer, a man in a suit and bow tie stepped out of a dance hall leading a woman by the hand. He leaned in and kissed his new bride, Pam.

"Come on," Jack said, squeezing her hand. "Let's go home."

With that, he led her to their first home, just two rooms on the ground floor of a tiny, two-story, Victorian-era terraced house that had an apple tree in the garden. They shared the kitchen and bathroom with the owner of the house, a spinster called Miss Burt, who lived upstairs.

A few years later, they had a son, Alan. When Alan was too big to share the bedroom with them, they gave it to him. Each night at bedtime, Jack and Pam would open out a camp bed and make it up for themselves in the living room. Every morning, before Alan left to deliver papers, he would wake to the smell of bacon, eggs, sausages, and fried bread. Jack cooked that for him every day, until he left for Liverpool University in 1962.

Alan was the first person in the family to reach higher education. (His Aunt Lulu had been offered a place at Oxford in the 1930s, but the family had been far too poor to send her.) He made the most of it. He played for the university football team. He saw the Beatles and the Rolling Stones before they were famous. He graduated with an engineering degree. Afterward, he joined IBM, got promoted, married, had kids.

Jack was my grandfather, Alan is my father. This is my backstory. Why am I telling you all this? Because Jack and Alan are typical. Just as the families in the CELF study are characteristic of the middle class today, and the case studies in this book exemplify others, so Alan and Jack are representative of their generations. And because the shift in circumstances from Jack to Alan to me reflects our society's journey from scarcity to abundance, and illustrates the effect that has had on our attitudes, values, and behaviors. In our ordinary family tale, in other words, you can trace the story of this book: the rise of materialism, its subsequent demise, and the emergence of experientialism.

As an archetypal baby boomer, my father, who people say looks a bit like Harrison Ford, measured success in material terms and looked for happiness in material things, like the house he lived in or the car he drove. I recall how happy he was—we all were—every time he got a new car. At the sound of an engine on the anointed day, we would all rush to the front room, my brother and I on tiptoes at the window, our mother following us, looking for the latest symbol of our dad's success. I remember them all: the boxy, blue Triumph Toledo and the curvy, caramel Mark I Cavalier in the 1970s, and in the 1980s, the sharp-angled silver Mark II Cavalier SR, the tanklike gold Opel Senator, the red Porsche 911, and the gold Porsche 944.

My father does not value only material things, of course. Over the years, he has spent a great deal of his money on experiences, like watching the Spurs and seeing the Stones. But he and the rest of the baby boomers were brought up believing in the materialistic consumerist system, as it offered the straightest route from the poverty they had been born into to the plenty they were helping to create.

Like millions of us who came after the boomers, I grew up believing in that system too. But then something happened. Or, rather, many things did. They all added up to this problem I call Stuffocation. And so I, like millions today, started questioning the benefits of materialism. You can see that in the work I have done. I have bounced between materialistic jobs—like aggressively selling advertising space from a boiler room like the one in the movies *Wall Street* and *Glengarry Glen Ross*—and experiential ones, like ski guiding and travel writing.

One Sunday in January 2002, my father brought Jack and Pam over for a pub lunch in South London. We talked about the past: the tangy taste of the apples from the tree in their garden, days out on London's red buses, the family trip when Jack got everyone lost in Lisbon. We talked about the future as well, in particular, my dreams for success in advertising, the career I was then pursuing. Just before they left, Jack handed me an envelope. Inside was a £5 note—enough for two pints of beer in those days—and a message on a scrap of paper.

"27-1-2002," it read. "This date in 1940 Nanna & I tramped through snow to our first home. Memories live longer than dreams. Treat yourself to a nice momento [sic]. Good Luck."

Ten minutes later, as they were about to drive across the River Thames, Jack gasped, like he was choking, my father told me later, and slumped in his seat. His aorta had burst. My father did what he could. He roared through traffic, jumped the lights, got pulled over, and was then escorted by the police and their flashing blue lights in a race to get my grandfather to the hospital. They tried their best, but Jack died that day.

I have thought a lot about that note since then, especially since I started thinking about and researching the ideas in this book. Did my grandfather somehow know he was going to die that day? And what did he mean by "memories live longer than dreams": did he mean that the past is more important than the future? Or was he saying, as I have come to believe, that *material* dreams have their place, but that life is made up of memories, which come from *experiences*?

He might, but then he might not have. Perhaps this is just a reading that suits me. At the least, it was quite a parting shot. In that note he addressed, and gave advice on, one of the most important questions a person can ask, the question that is at the heart of this book: how should we live in order to be happy?

THOU SHALL COVET THY NEIGHBOR'S DONKEY

For most of the past two millennia the answer to that question was defined by circumstance, and, in the West at least, controlled by the Church. Circumstance remained fairly constant. Life, for most people, for most of those years, was a matter of scraping by, not much above the subsistence level.

The Church's message did not waver much either. Happiness, it said, would come in the next life, in heaven. To get there you had to live a good life of moderation, thriftiness, and poverty—after all, it was easier for a camel to pass through the eye of a needle than for a rich man to get into heaven. And you had to follow a set of rules. One of those was explicitly antimaterialistic: thou shalt not covet thy neighbor's house, wife, manservant, maidservant, ox, donkey, or, basically, any of his material possessions.

The Church's—and therefore society's—version of the good life remained the same for most of the next two thousand years. That ideal made a lot of sense when society was static, when, if you were born poor, as most people were, you would stay poor. What was the point, after all, of wishing for something you would never have?

But, as circumstances changed, especially from the sixteenth century onward, that version of the good life and happiness did not make nearly so much sense. Thanks to mining, banking, and trade, at first, and, later, the machines of the Industrial Revolution, Western society became increasingly prosperous.

That created a new problem. For the first time, for large numbers of people, there was tension between Church and circumstance, between the version of the good life they heard being preached from the pulpit each Sunday and the life they were living the other days of the week. Did material success in the here and now really mean they were not living a good life, and that they would not, ultimately, be happy? The Church's teaching on this was clear though, and its version of the good life remained the dominant one—until the early twentieth century.

Then the shift in circumstances began to happen more rapidly, especially in the United States, putting this set of teachings even further out of step with day-to-day reality. Worse, this advice, that people should be thrifty, moderate, and not materialistic, was not delivering the levels of mass consumption needed to keep up with mass production.

Fortunately, around this time, there was a new network, a direct competitor to the Church's pulpits, if you like: the mass media of magazines, newspapers, movies, and radio. The leaders of the secular world—the captains of consciousness—used that network to solve the problem of overproduction, and take advantage of the possibilities of mass production, by preaching a good life that was defined in material, consumer terms, like cars, toasters, radios, and dishwashers.

Happiness, according to this new gospel of consumption, could come in this life. To get it, you had to live a good life of profligate, conspicuous consumption—after all, the more you spent, the more work you would create for other people, and the more wealth you would create. To have more you had to spend more, you had to be materialistic: to covet the things thy neighbors, the Joneses, had—if not their oxen and their donkeys, certainly their cars.

This innovative idea was not only counterintuitive, because it flipped the old truth on its head. It was also revolutionary: it sparked the consumer revolution. More important, it worked. It took us on an exciting journey to unprecedented material progress. It has also, unintentionally, led us into the perfect storm of Stuffocation today. Which means it is time, once again, to open our minds to another innovative, revolutionary idea.

MANIFESTO: WHY WE NEED EXPERIENCE MORE THAN EVER

If our culture is to evolve and find the answer to Stuffocation, we will need to build a new value system. This new system will have to cast light on all the dark sides that came with materialism—like overconsumption, pollution, anxiety, and stress. It should also take advantage of all the opportunities available today—like the technologies that give us the benefits of access without the downsides of physical ownership.

The path we choose will have to appeal to everyone you would call a captain of consciousness in the twenty-first century—businesses and governments, you and me. Its starting point should be the realization that happiness is more likely to come from the enjoyment of experiences than from the accumulation of stuff. It should provide stability and prosperity: jobs for people, profit for businesses, and both taxable income and a useful benchmark for governments. It should also satisfy our innate desires for happiness, identity, and meaning, and, yes, a way for every one of us to shake our tail feathers.

Rather than defeatist and dull, it should be aspirational, inspiring, and fun. Instead of implying that we have reached the highest point of human evolution, and that from here on in we should just plateau, it should empower us to believe in a better future.

The way ahead, out of the storm of Stuffocation, is not minimalism, simple living, or the medium chill. Each of these has pointed us in the right direction. But minimalism is too negative, too reductive. Simple living is too regressive. The medium chill lacks aspiration. The new value system that will solve Stuffocation, I think, is experientialism.

Experientialism will work for all of us. By having less and doing more, we will be happier, healthier, richer, in every sense: less clutter, less regret, less anxiety, more meaning, more flow, more intrinsic enjoyment, better conversations, more connections, a healthier take on status, and a stronger sense of belonging.

To succeed in this new world, businesses, rather than trying to flog newly positioned but actually the same old stuff, will have to create genuinely new products, services, and adventures that streamline our lives and give us more social and experiential currency—that is, a story to tell and an experience worth remembering. And governments, instead of being fixated on GDP and material gains, should shift their focus to improving well-being and experiential progress.

A good start would be to raise psychologists to the same level of economists. We also need, alongside the new measures of society's well-being and progress, a new way to count personal progress that is as informative and simple as the figure that tells you your salary, but expresses your success in experiential rather than material terms.

If we all—you, me, businesses, and governments—dare to "believe in better," and embrace experientialism, we can achieve in this century what our ancestors did in the last. Just as materialism hauled billions out of poverty and delivered standards of living for the masses that would have sounded ludicrous in the first decades of the twentieth century, so experientialism, I believe, will do something similar this century. It will generate advances in well-being and quality of life that might sound, today at least, like they are the wishful thinking of an idealistic mind: less stress, less work, more enjoyable work, more time with family and friends, and more time doing things that really matter to us.

FORECAST: THE RISE OF EXPERIENTIALISM

For all these reasons, then, it is now time for a cultural revolution. We need to discard our materialist values and replace them with experientialist ones. And the good news is that there are already signs that the revolution is under way.

There is the political scientist Ron Inglehart's research, for instance, which shows that there is a long-term shift in our attitudes away from materialism. There is Chris Goodall's analysis, which demonstrates that our behavior is changing and we are now consuming less water, paper, and concrete, and fewer cars. There is the rising experience economy. There are the pioneer governments, measuring well-being and creating new benchmarks of progress. And there are all the signposts to experientialism in how people are spending their time and money: younger people living in smaller apartments in cities and not buying cars, older people spending more on vacations and health care, luxury consumers spending more on experiences, collaborative consumers renting rather than buying, millions reading ebooks instead of physical books, and billions sharing their experiences every day on Facebook, Instagram, and Twitter.

We are still at the start. As we travel further down this path, the dawn of experientialism will become easier for all to see. There will be more people opting to work less and play more, and more companies producing experiences instead of clutter. As the years pass, the signs of experientialism will become more evenly distributed, just as the hallmarks of materialism—like luxury label goods, oversized watches, and two-car garages—became more obvious as the twentieth century progressed.

The last time Western society came to a crossroads like this, we solved the headache of overproduction, and the age-old issue of scarcity, by becoming materialistic. Then, as materialists, we became part of the problem of Stuffocation.

Now, as we arrive at our crossroads, we are becoming part of the solution. As we become experientialists, we are using a new equation for happiness. We are lessening our ecological footprint, clearing out the clutter, reducing our reliance on stuff. We are displaying our fitness markers through experiences rather than objects. And we are starting to think of progress in experiential rather than material terms.

We have got enough, and we have had enough of stuff. We are realizing that, to live a life that is meaningful, to shake our tail feathers, and to be happy in the twenty-first century—you, me, and society in general—we all need experience more than ever.

Acknowledgments

"No author is an island," the poet John Donne almost wrote. That is especially true of nonfiction authors. A work of nonfiction may have only one name on the cover, but in truth it is likely to be the work of many people.

There are a huge number of people without whom the book you are holding in your hands would not exist. More than a hundred people gave up their time to discuss the idea with me over tea, coffee, lunch, dinner, beer, wine, telephone, video call, and email. There are the people, especially on America's West Coast and in Australia, who got up early or stayed up late so that the timing worked for them and me. There are the people whose work I have drawn on, both directly and indirectly. (I have tried to credit all those in the Notes. If any are missing, please let me know, and I will rectify the situation.)

So it may be my name on the front, but in many ways, *Stuffoca-*

tion stands on the hard work, good nature, and, yes, shoulders of many others. Given the fact that I wanted a clean cover, though, there was no way we'd have gotten all those names on the front.

I'm going to start by thanking my case studies, the people who shared the most, because they shared not only their ideas, but their lives. So, thank you: Ryan Nicodemus, Joshua Fields Millburn, Tammy Strobel, Graham Hill, Olga Sasplugas, Courtney Carver, Ben Howell, Sarah Howell, Marianne Cantwell, Jim Whyte, Sue Lenet, Bertrand Lenet, Dave Roberts, Jen Roberts, and Cliff Hodges.

And then there are my case studies' friends and families, who helped bring their wives', husbands', daughters', sons', mothers', fathers', and friends' stories to life by adding the sorts of details the case studies had forgotten, didn't think were appropriate, or, let's be honest here, hoped weren't mentioned. So, thank you: Logan Smith, Tina Smith, Derek Hill, Hannah Wray, Mark Tuttle, Ren LeVally, Jenn Oslawski, Katherine Tickle, Dan Bosscher, Don Hodges, Hilda Hodges, Kai McDonald, Kathy Hettick, Hector Proud, Sarah Whyte, Emma Hutchinson, Andrew Bird, Andi Norris, and Coni Battle.

Then there are all the people who gave up so much of their time but whose stories ended up on the cutting-room floor. Editing is a nasty process that takes no prisoners. They don't say "kill your darlings" for nothing. Please know that your stories did help me find the way forward, but there simply wasn't room to keep all of them in— even those stories that include the sort of breakups, breakdowns, breakthroughs, and gold bullion that make great reading. So, thank you: Rachel Jonat, Chris Wray, Colin Wright, Joshua Becker, Simon Smith, Jeff Dobbs, Chris Concannon, Neal Gorenflo, Nina Yau, Teresa Carey, Valeska von Mühldorfer, Ethan Segal, Fredrik Lofgren, Rakesh Banburi, Mike Benson, Deborah Richmond, and Roberto Gonzalez.

Then, there are all the experts, who have spent, in many cases, decades in their field. Your dedication to discovery, and to challenging the status quo and the conventional wisdom, is exactly the sort of thing that raises the fog a bit more, so that people like me can have a better view of the direction the world is turning. Thank you for that, and also, among other things: for your suggestions of more avenues to explore, for challenging and inspiring me over lunch and email and phone and Skype, for responding to far more fact-checking emails than strictly necessary, for patiently explaining how you do what you do, and for pushing me to reexamine whether I believed in what I believe—and whether I really was reading the data right.

So, thank you: Richard Thaler, Oliver James, Barry Schwartz, Stuart Ewen, Robert Fogel, Chris Goodall, Michael Schrage, Ron Inglehart, Ryan Howell, Jeanne Arnold, Darby Saxbe, Travis Carter, Leaf van Boven, Tom Gilovich, Brian Wansink, Geoffrey Miller, Danny Miller, Rupert Pennant-Rea, Garson O'Toole, Daniel Franklin, John Andrews, Rob Hyndman, Corinne Shefner-Rogers, Jim Dearing, Juliet Schor, Anna Coote, Benjamin Kline Hunnicutt, Pippa Norris, Trudi Toyne, Felipe Fernández-Armesto, Avner Offer, Peter Stearns, Joe Pine, Jim Gilmore, Grant McCracken, Blake Mycoskie, Rob Symington, Alice Marwick, Harry Parr, Sam Bompas, Jules Evans, Bob Cummins, Bernice Steinhardt, Chris Hoenig, Mark Tungate, Ann Mack, Albert Cañigueral, Anna-Maren Ashford, James O'Shaughnessy, Joe Goodman, Alastair Humphreys, Richard Layard, Tim Kasser, Vicki Robin, Gabriel Rossman, Janice Rutherford, Eve Fisher, Kelly Ransdell, Irving Kirsch, Michael Bonsall, Jean Twenge, Tam Fry, Jessica Vaughn, Kate Black, Paula Zuccotti, Stephanie Schorow, Richard Cope, and Gail Steketee.

Thank you to all the great people who put up with me being the worst of customers—stay for ages, spend very little—at the Hampshire Hog, the Thatched House, Brackenburys Delicatessen, Artisan, Street Eats, Carluccio's in Kensington, and La Caffetteria.

Also thank you to the various libraries that have housed and helped: the LSE Library, the Imperial War Museum, the British Library, Kensington Central Library, Shepherds Bush Library, the Schlesinger Library at Radcliffe (especially Ellen Shea), and the Herbert Hoover Presidential Library (in particular Spencer Howard).

Thank you to everyone who has believed in *Stuffocation* and helped make the first edition happen, in particular: Victoria Grand, Sean Daily, Marcus and Sarah Oliver, Pam Roderick, Johan de Kleer, Nora Boettcher, John White, Mitch Baranowski, Andy Gibson, Lucie Greene, Vashti Hallissey, Ian Carrington, Charlie Viney, Chris Lascelles, Sue Browning, Janice Rayment, Ruby Epsilon, and Patrick Mcaleenan.

Then there are all my friends, both old and new, who have inspired me, and who have helped with contacts, ideas, suggestions, data, Paleolithic, psychological, and economic knowledge, and the use of a Nespresso machine and a home to write in: Thiru and Raj Raj-manickam, Ewen Brown, Hugh Brown, Adrian Sandiford, Catherine Mayer, Dan and Jacqueline Bosscher, Marilyn Wallman, Julian Ellerby, James Kennedy, Daniel and Flip Antoine, Susan Herbert, Peter Markham, Gary Horne, Sophy Roberts, Nick Redman, Sean Thomas, Steve Tooze, Philipp Schwalber, George Collings, and, of course, Edwin Blanchard. The biggest thanks here are to Wendy Mandy, for helping me believe I had it in me, and Caroline van den Brul, for exceptionally insightful comments on an early draft.

A huge thank-you to the two people who took the book, shook the book, and showed me the way to make it so much better: Joel Rickett at Penguin in the U.K. and Jessica Sindler at Spiegel & Grau in the U.S. And thank you to the people who led me to them: Richard Lennon, Toby Jones, and Gavin Dawson.

Another huge thank-you to Jenny and Alan and Rob—for your love, my education, a love of stories, and myriad experiences.

A planet-size thank-you to my wife, for agreeing that we could bet the proverbial farm on the book and the movement I believe so strongly in, and also, as important, for your wise, head-spinning, thought-provoking, idea-challenging creative input. Without you, this book would not be.

Finally, thank *you* for reading my book. I think the ideas it contains are going to change the world. I hope that you agree, and that you have already started to see the signs of experientialism rising, both in your own life and in the lives of those around you.

Appendix

The Way of the Experientialist

Having reached this point in the book, you may well have decided that you want to join the experientialist movement, and that you are ready for all the benefits that come with experientialism. But you may be wondering about the practical next steps: How do I try out experientialism to see if it works for me? How can I be a successful experientialist in the long run? What, in other words, are the habits of highly effective experientialists?

The answers to those questions are simple: there are three steps, and there are seven habits. They are in the pages that follow.

THE 3 STEPS TO EXPERIENTIALISM

Step 1: De-Stuffocate

Get rid of the stuff in your cabinets and closets that you don't use: the shoes you don't wear, the clothes you've never worn, the chargers for all those gadgets you no longer use. There are many ways you can do this. Here are my favorite five:

I. The Bag-and-Box Method   Put everything you own in bags and boxes, as Ryan Nicodemus did. You are allowed to take anything out you like, whenever you need it. By the end of a month, you will know what you use, and what you don't. Dedicated players will get rid of everything that remains bagged and boxed up. Some may prefer to give a few things another month before committing. Note that you can play the extreme way where everything in your home that can be moved goes in a bag or a box, as Nicodemus did, or you can choose a room or a closet at a time. It is best to play this game with friends.

II. The "Did You Miss It?" Game   Best played by two people who get along well, like Courtney Carver and her husband, Mark Tuttle. It's a simple game: you hide something, and if the other person does not notice it missing after a set time period—a week, say, or a month—he or she clearly did not need it, so you can get rid of it.

III. The Reverse-Hanger Method   Works for de-Stuffocating wardrobes. Put all your hangers facing the same direction, and if you wear something, put it back on a hanger facing the other way. At the end of a month, you'll know how much of your wardrobe you use.

IV. The Month of Minimalism Game   Get rid of as many things as the corresponding number on the calendar. So you get rid of one thing on the 1st, two things on the 2nd until you get rid of 28, 30, or 31 things on the final day. Best if played with a friend, to see who can make it till the end of the month. (This idea comes from Ryan Nico-demus and Joshua Fields Millburn, and their blog, TheMinimalists .com.)

V. The Pick-a-Number Challenge Take on Dave Bruno's 100 Thing Challenge, and live with 100 items. Try the way Courtney Carver experimented with minimalism, by reducing the number of things in your wardrobe to 33. Or choose any room or cupboard in your house, pick a number, and see if you can get the amount of stuff you have down to that number. As before, best played with your partner or a friend.

Step 2: Don't Re-Stuffocate

It is easy, after getting rid of lots of things, to want to reward your-self by buying something. After all, you have just been "good" and have created empty space in your wardrobe or on your shelves. It is also very easy to see that space and wonder, "What am I going to put in there?," and then to go out and buy more stuff. That would be the most natural reaction in the world, since we have been raised as con-sumers to think and behave that way. Resist the temptation—even if there is a deal you feel like you can't pass up and the sale sign says, "Everything must go—80 percent off." Otherwise you'll end up back where you started.

As with most of the ways of tackling step one, it is best to take step two with a friend. The support will be helpful: phoning a friend could save you from buying another T-shirt, or pair of shoes, or throw pillow you really do not need.

These first two steps are important. But they will only really get you to the starting line. The real reason you need to let go of all that stuff is to give yourself enough energy, time, and money to stay the course and make the more fundamental changes required to take on Stuffo-cation. This next step is the best bit. It makes step one worthwhile, and it makes step two so much easier. This is the step that will change your life.

Step 3: Play the *Brewster's Millions* Game

This game is based on the 1902 novel and the 1985 movie *Brewster's Millions*. In the 1902 story, in order to win a fortune left in a will by an eccentric relative, Montgomery Brewster is challenged to spend one million dollars in a year and have nothing physical to show for it at the end. In the inflation-adjusted movie version of 1985, Brewster, played by Richard Pryor, has to spend thirty million dollars in a month and have nothing tangible to show for it. Brewster's challenge, if you think about it, was to be the ultimate experientialist— for a year in the book, and a month in the movie.

To play the version of the game I'm proposing, you should play, at first, for a month. You do not have to spend one million or even thirty million dollars in that month, but you do have to spend the *same amount* you would normally spend, and still have nothing physical to show for it at the end.

If you can't commit for a whole month, play for a weekend, or just play the next time you go to spend money on stuff you really don't need. Then, instead of buying it, remember the *Brewster's Millions* game and spend the money on doing something instead. Next, tell your friends what you've done, and make a note to yourself about how doing something makes you feel.

That is all you have to do to join the experientialists. If you play the *Brewster's Millions* game this month or next weekend or the next time you spend money, you'll have more stories, more status, and a greater sense of who you are. You'll have more fun when you shake your tail feathers, people will be more likely to talk with you and listen to you, and you will be happier.

Play the *Brewster's Millions* game and you will have taken your first steps away from materialism and the storm of Stuffocation. You will be more likely to see what my grandfather meant in that note he gave me: that memories live longer than things. And you'll be well on your way to adopting the 7 Habits of Highly Effective Experientialists.

See how others are playing the *Brewster's Millions* game, and share your journey to experientialism, at Stuffocation.org—and on Facebook, Twitter, Google+, and whatever social network you use. Where you can, add tags to your posts and photos like #experientialism, #brewstersmillions, and #stuffocation.

THE 7 HABITS OF HIGHLY EFFECTIVE EXPERIENTIALISTS

When I give talks about experientialism, people often come up to me afterward and ask: "Are you an experientialist?," "So, what do experientialists do exactly?," and "How can I be an experientialist?"

This section is for those people, and for everyone who is inspired not only to try experientialism for a weekend or a month, but to redesign their life and make experientialism the manifesto they live by.

As I have replied to these questions, I have gradually become aware that my answers contain a number of core ideas, and that those ideas are based on what I have learned from social science, and on the habits the experientialists live by. I have also realized that anyone can get the benefits of experientialism if they practice these habits. There are seven of them, and they fall into three categories.

The first two habits are tools for analyzing your life and figuring out if the path you are on is the right one. The next two are guiding principles, mental check-ins, if you like, to live by. The final three are decision-making shortcuts to help you spend your energy, time, and money better in any situation.

Adopt all seven habits and you will be happier and healthier today, tomorrow, and in the long run. You will have richer connections to your friends and your family, and a stronger sense of belonging to the community you live in. Your life will feel like it has more meaning. You will feel that you are working to live, rather than living to work. You will have more stories, and they will give you better conversations, more status, and a clearer sense of your own identity.

Commit to making these seven habits your habits, and you will be blazing a trail for the rest of society, leading everyone else—even your pesky neighbors the Joneses—along the most direct, aspirational, and fun road out of the storm of Stuffocation. Choose the way of the experientialist, and you will be part of the movement that is speeding the world from the weather-beaten old age of materialism toward the bright new era of experientialism.

THE 7 HABITS OF HIGHLY EFFECTIVE EXPERIENTIALISTS

Tools to analyze your life:
1. Know Your Stuff
2. Find Your Ladder

Principles to live by:
3. Be Here Now
4. Be Your Own Audience

Shortcuts to smarter spending:
5. Put People First
6. Spend Well and Feel Good
7. Choose Life, Choose Experience

Tools to Analyze Your Life

Habit 1. Know Your Stuff　Chiseled in stone, in the entrance of the temple to Apollo at Delphi, were the ancient Greek words for "know yourself." Philosophers, poets, and writers have given this maxim various meanings through the ages. The two that have stood the test of time are: one, that you should take time to find out who you really are, and, two, that you should know your place in society, and not seek to rise above your station. Experientialists live by an updated version of this maxim. Think of any of the case studies in the book, and you will see that they seek to know their possessions—how many they have, how much they use them, whether they really need them—and that they have hauled physical goods down from the pedestal that materialists had elevated them to, and put them back in their place.

Some experientialists do this after a road-to-Damascus-like revelation. Remember Ryan Nicodemus and Joshua Fields Millburn, and how they came across the idea that less, not more, would lead to happiness. Or Cliff Hodges, as he talked with his father in the hospital. Or Marianne Cantwell, that day on the tube.

For other experientialists, this is just something they have always done. Their possessions tend to be what psychologists now call "experiential products." Picture Ben Howell's garage of sports gear, for instance.

Experientialists, to be clear, are not anticapitalist or anticonsumerist. They are not even against stuff, but they are against having too much of the wrong kind of stuff. To make sure your possessions play a healthy role in your life, and that you *know your stuff*, ask yourself these questions:

    i. How often do I use my possessions?
    ii. How much stuff do I really need?
    iii. Do my things give me experiences that make me happy—or
        are they bringing hassle, debt, stress, and depression?

Habit 2. Find Your Ladder   This habit stems from the age-old cliché about how it is better to be anywhere on a ladder you want to climb than at the top of a ladder you don't. This is one of the experientialists' key beliefs. Think of Cliff Hodges, for instance, who realized that he felt dead inside in his dreary job of endless meetings and late night conference calls. But just because experientialists want to turn off the mainstream materialistic path, that does not mean they want to drop out of society altogether. These hippies with calculators, after all, still want to be good at what they do and make money. Hodges would like to buy his own piece of land in California, and Sarah Howell enjoys her job running restaurants and opening new ones.

The difference between materialistic people and experientialists is a matter of definition and emphasis. Experientialists are still motivated by success, but they define success differently. Their version of success places less emphasis on the goal, the destination, and the material, and more on the process, the journey, and the experience. So while a materialist might accept painful, uninteresting, or unpleasant work as the sacrifice for success, the experientialist would not.

When people discover experientialism, some change jobs—like Marianne Cantwell and Cliff Hodges. And others do not. Bertrand Lenet did not close or sell his restaurant. He mostly now manages it remotely, and sometimes comes back to make sure everything is running as he would like it. Jeff Harris has found work he enjoys that he can do remotely, from his cabin on a mountain in New Mexico. And Graham Hill did not give up being an entrepreneur after he shed his stuff. He started TreeHugger, after all, from Olga's flat in Barcelona. And he has recently started another business, called LifeEdited, that promotes the sort of multifunctional, ecologically aware apartment he lives in.

To be an experientialist, you do not have to change your world and give up your job—but you should do something you love. To *find your ladder*, or check that you are on yours, ask yourself these questions:

i. Do I love the ladder I'm on, that is, the work I do?

ii. When I'm with friends, do I talk about work as a passion, or do I talk about everything but the ladder I spend most of my time on?

iii. Do I aspire to be like my boss, or those above me in the company? Would I like to have their lives?

Principles to Live By

Habit 3. Be Here Now   Choosing experiences over material goods is, from a certain point of view, really only dipping your toe in the water of experientialism—because you can choose experiences instead of material goods and still be miserable. It's possible, you see, to treat experiences the same way materialists treat material goods: as items to check off or add to a list, and then wheel out at a later point to impress people. Think of country counters, for instance, those annoying people who visit a country less out of curiosity and more so they can put a check mark on their bucket list.

To get the most out of experientialism, especially the increased happiness it can bring, it is important not only to choose experiences but also to dive into them in the right way. The best way to do that is by being, as sports players say, "in the zone" or, as psychologists say, in "flow."—when you are so focused you forget the future, the past, your everyday concerns, and any lingering sense of self-consciousness. You are likely to be in flow when you: sing your heart out in the shower, ski, drive down a country road with the roof down, slurp down an oyster, climb a rock wall, see a great movie, ride on the neck of an elephant, cycle down a hill with your feet off the pedals, and when you swim, underwater, in a warm, clear, aquamarine sea.

Being in flow, if you think about it, is how the case studies in this book live. They not only choose experiences, they also throw themselves into those experiences. Consider Jim Whyte and his cross-country trip to Iran. Or the Lenets and the time it all went wrong in Peru. Or Aimée LeVally: fibromyalgia was disastrous for her physical health, but it lit a fire in her mind, giving her the determination to take it on, to take her family out of the system she thought was toxic, and to live a life that, as she says, is more intense, rewarding, and fulfilling.

You are more likely to notice flow after the fact than at the time. Ideally, you will be so absorbed in any activity that you won't need reminding. But in case your mind wanders, these questions should help you *be here now*:

i. Would I rather be doing something different from what I am doing now?
ii. Am I thinking about yesterday or tomorrow, or am I utterly absorbed, in the moment, and in the zone?
iii. Am I doing this for fun and the enjoyment of the experience, or for some future reward?

Habit 4. Be Your Own Audience   If you are watching the sunrise on the beach in Koh Pha Ngan or the sunset from the deck of a sailboat in Zanzibar, if you are landing in New York, or lunching with an A-lister in Hollywood—congratulations, because you are, without doubt, having one of the more exciting experiences life has to offer.

But watch out—if you spend too much time telling the world what you are doing, you will lose many of the upsides of experientialism, especially, again, the increased happiness it offers. Why?

The answer, so social scientists have discovered, and as described in Chapter 10 above, lies in the motivation behind your choices. There are two types of motivation. There is intrinsic, when you do something for yourself and for the enjoyment of the experience. There is extrinsic, when you do something to impress others or for some reward at the end. Motivation matters when it comes to happiness. Because if your motivation for doing something is intrinsic, it is more likely to make you happy.

Many of the experientialists in this book have goals and share their experiences with others. But these are not their primary motivations. Dave Roberts has written about what motivates him, but he and his wife, Jen, are clearly motivated not by what others think, but by what matters to them. And the Lenets have a blog to keep friends and family up to date with where they are. But they are not doing what they are doing to tell others about it. They make their decisions based on what is best for the family. Cliff Hodges's long-term ambition may be to buy some land to run his outdoor adventures on—but that isn't what drives him. And he will happily tell you about the time he almost got stamped into the ground by two bugling, rutting elks in Montana—but he didn't go out that day, and he doesn't go out any day, so that he can tell others about it. In fact, he doesn't even take photos. "I hate taking pictures," he says. "I feel that if you pick up a camera you take yourself out of the moment. You're no longer there, living it purely for the experience. You're trying to record it for someone else."

I am not saying that you should give up posting updates and taking photos. But they should, at the least, be your secondary consideration. With anything you do, it is vital that you do it, first of all, for yourself, and for the pure enjoyment of the experience itself. So like the most effective experientialists, put your camera phone down and do whatever it is you are doing as if no one else is watching. Use these questions to remind yourself to *be your own audience:*

    i. Am I doing this for myself?

    ii. Am I doing this to impress others?

       (Note: as per the discussion in Chapter 10, how hard it is to know the true answers to questions (i) and (ii)—and why this makes Habit 7 so important.)

    iii. If no one knew I was doing this, would I do it anyway?

Shortcuts to Smarter Spending

Habit 5. Put People First   Solitary confinement is one of the harshest punishments given to prisoners. There is a simple reason for this: as humans, we're social animals. We like social contact of all stripes. We like hugs. We like to be listened to. We like to think people understand us. We like to know people care. And we like to feel as if we belong. We are, you could say, people people.

The most effective experientialists, either consciously or subconsciously, recognize this. Through their life choices, they prioritize the relationships they have with their partners, friends, children, family, and the community in general. They put people first.

Think of Cliff Hodges again, and his reaction to his father's stroke: he stayed with his father for weeks until he recovered. Or Tammy Strobel, whose better choices vastly improved the relationship with her husband. And her smarter choices meant that when her dad died, she could spend quality time supporting her mother. And consider Bertrand and Sue Lenet. When they looked at their life and asked, "What is the point of it all?," they realized that, despite all the good things their hard work had brought them, they wanted to spend more time together. As Bertrand once told me: "Life is about spending time with the family. That is what matters: our family having experiences all together."

At the crossroads of any decision, these questions should help you *put people first*:

    i. Will I do this with others?
    ii. How might I do this with others?
    iii. Will spending this money, time, and energy keep me apart from, or bring me closer to, other people?

Habit 6. Spend Well and Feel Good   One of the most disappointing legacies of materialism is that it has made a monster out of the idea of spending well. In a time of scarcity, which was basically any time before the twentieth century, spending well meant using your resources carefully, frugally, and sustainably. But then, to feed the system that would turn scarcity into abundance, for many people spending well came to mean being showy, conspicuous, and wasteful.

This reckless way of spending was not confined to money. People wasted their energy worrying about whether their stuff was as good as the stuff their neighbors had. They spent their time carelessly and conspicuously: they lived to work, rather than worked to live, and they told anyone who would listen how hard they were working. The result, as we now know, is throwaway culture, the overconsumption causing Stuffocation, and a twisted definition of spending well that, rather than making people feel good, is weighing them down with regret, anxiety, and guilt.

Today's experientialists are redefining the idea of spending well. To them, it means using their resources carefully, consciously, and sustainably. It means being, in a word, smart.

By carefully, I mean that experientialists are mindful of their energy, time, and money. They do not, for instance, engage in retail therapy. Think about how Tammy Strobel weaned herself off her lunchtime shopping trips, and then found a more meaningful life. And if they do buy physical products, they make sure they are "experiential products"—the sort of products that you buy in order to do something, like a bicycle, or a guitar, or a video game.

When I say consciously rather than conspicuously, I mean that experientialists do not squander their time and money trying to buy their way up the social ladder through material goods. Remember Ben Howell's attitude toward one of the most conspicuous items a man can buy today, a watch. He has never had one. Or consider Jim Whyte's relationship with his computer. Rather than owning a top of-the-line laptop that will firmly place him in the social hierarchy, he is just happy to have one that works. Or think about Marianne Cantwell's take on clothes: she enjoys them, and she certainly does not avoid having nice things, but she does not obsess over them.

By sustainably, I mean experientialists spend with respect for the future—their own future, the future of society, and the future of the planet. Graham Hill, for instance, has used the millions he made from the environmental website TreeHugger to pioneer a way of living that has smaller footprints in all sorts of ways. And Cliff Hodges has channeled his love for nature into an ambition to buy a piece of land, so that he can look after it and run courses there.

A final point of clarity here: the aim of spending well is not to be, or appear to be, a good person. It is to *feel* good. Experientialists know they are making the right choices when those decisions do not make them feel regretful, anxious, or guilty. As an experientialist, you will know you have made the right decision because it will make you feel good.

These questions should help you *spend well and feel good*:

i. Will this purchase make me feel good, or will it lead to guilt, anxiety, or regret?
ii. Am I buying this for later, or for show, or to really *use now*?
iii. Am I spending my energy and time on what matters to me?

Habit 7. Choose Life, Choose Experience   Life is a series of events that you experience, one after another, like a daisy chain of moments.

Right now, you are experiencing reading this book. Earlier, you had the experience of waking, yawning, stretching. You tasted toothpaste, smelled coffee, and felt the floor beneath your feet as you padded down the hall. You have had, in other words, many experiences already today. Later, you will no doubt have a myriad more. So to say *choose life, choose experience* may sound silly at first, because you have no choice but to have experiences.

But the reason *choose life, choose experience* is the seventh, and most important, habit is that, for a long time, life and experience got pushed to one side. As a result of the industrial and consumer revolutions, people were redefined as dissatisfied, high-spending, hardworking cogs in the machine of materialism. They were like mechanical rabbits, mesmerized by the headlights of a million consumer goods and the promise of ever higher standards of living. They forgot what mattered.

Experientialists are remembering what matters. They are rejecting the goal-oriented, other-focused, material-minded rush and hurry of materialism. They are rediscovering the meaning of life and the value of experience.

As they do, the till now quiet revolution of experientialism is taking a stand, and finding a voice. Ask any experientialist, and she or he will respond with a defiant "No!" to the idea that we should look for status, identity, meaning, and, above all, happiness externally, in material objects. Instead you will hear a resounding "Yes!" to the idea that the best way to find status, identity, meaning, and happiness is internally, through the adventures and activities we experience. When you make that "Yes!" a habit, you are doing what highly effective experientialists do. You are choosing life and choosing experience.

Use these questions to make sure you *choose life, choose experience* with every spending decision you make today:

    i. Am I just buying this item for external status or validation, or am I investing in an experience?

ii. If I were playing the *Brewster's Millions* game with a friend, would this purchase count?

iii. Now think about my grandfather's note: "Memories live longer than dreams." If something about this experience goes wrong, will it have been worth it anyway? Could it at least create a memory?

Notes

Introduction. We've Had Enough of Stuff

ix **Ryan Nicodemus and Joshua Fields Millburn**
The best way to find out about Ryan Nicodemus and Joshua Fields Mill-burn, their books, their book tour (coming to your city soon), and how they help people get rid of what doesn't matter, is by visiting their fan-tastic website, www.theminimalists.com.

xv *The Story of Stuff*
Watch *The Story of Stuff* and read *The Story of Stuff, Referenced and Annotated Script,* which contains evidence for the video's statements, at www.storyofstuff.org.

xv **four out of five held materialistic values in 1970**
Ronald Inglehart, "The Silent Revolution in Europe: Intergenerational Change in Post-Industrial Societies," *American Political Science Review* 65, no. 4 (December 1971). For updates since then: see Ronald Inglehart, "Changing Values Among Western Publics from 1970 to 2006," *West European Politics* 31, nos. 1–2 (January–March 2008); also, the World Values Survey, www.worldvaluessurvey.org. Many make sense of the shift to

less materialistic values by referring to Abraham Maslow, "A Theory of Human Motivation," *Psychological Review* 50, no. 4 (1943). Also, read about a generational shift to post-materialism in David Brooks, "The Experience Economy," *New York Times,* February 14, 2011.

xv **advertising agency research**

The first set of research was conducted by an advertising agency called Euro RSCG Worldwide, which, in the time it's taken me to write the book and for the publisher to publish it, has become Havas Worldwide. The research paper is called *The New Consumer,* www.thenewconsumer .com. The second set of research was conducted by Havas Worldwide (so the same company, but with a new name): Havas Worldwide Prosumer Report, *The New Consumer and the Sharing Economy,* 2014.

I calculated the number of people who have had enough of stuff based on *The New Consumer* statistics that 67 percent believe most of us would be better off if we lived more simply, and that there are 63.23 million people in the U.K., and 313.9 million in the U.S. Sources for those figures: World Bank and U.S. Census Bureau.

xviii **Sherlock Holmes and the Mystery of the Krispy Kremes**

This account draws on direct correspondence with Tam Fry and a number of reports, including: Peter Laing, "Cops Tackle Krispy Kreme Traffic Chaos—and Pick up a Box of Doughnuts," *Deadline News,* February 15, 2013; Shiv Malik, "Krispy Kremes Cause Chaos in Edinburgh Streets," *The Guardian,* February 15. 2013; and Harriet Arkell, "Jam Doughnuts: Hundreds of Motorists Bring Traffic Chaos to M8 as They Queue for Opening of New Krispy Kreme," *Mail Online,* February 15, 2013.

Note that the Krispy Kreme store was also offering a year's supply of doughnuts. This incentive makes it clearer why people would queue to begin with, and it reinforces the main point of this section: why queue for a year's worth of something you know is not good for you?

To make sense of evolutionary psychology and how it relates to consumerism, read the funny and engaging Geoffrey Miller, *Spent: Sex, Evolution and the Secrets of Consumerism* (New York: William Heinemann, 2009). In the U.K., the paperback is Geoffrey Miller, *Must-Have: The Hidden Instincts Behind Everything We Buy* (London: Vintage, 2010). Not as funny, but as inspiring, and brilliant at helping us understand why we make (often bad) decisions on food, is Brian Wansink, *Mindless Eating: Why We Eat More Than We Think* (London: Bantam, 2006; reprint, 2010).

xviii **Krispy Kreme's Original Glazed nutritional information**

Krispy Kreme website, www.krispykreme.co.uk/wp-content/themes/thesis/docs/nutritional_info.pdf.

xx **We are now living in an age of material abundance**

For more, read Avner Offer, *The Challenge of Affluence* (Oxford: Oxford University Press, 2006); and John Kenneth Galbraith, *The Affluent Society* (New York: Houghton Mifflin Harcourt, 1958).

xx **A shirt, before the Industrial Revolution, would have been worth around $3,500 in today's money**

I asked Eve Fisher to explain. Here's the reply she emailed me: "Take a standard medieval man's shirt, à la Breughel's *Peasant Wedding*, etc., long sleeves, yoke, some smocking, band collar, hemmed, wrists, etc. Estimate it takes 7 hours to sew a shirt like that by hand—cutting the fabric, sewing, finishing inside and out, etc. Now, you have to have the cloth to sew. This would have been relatively fine, dense cloth. An historical reconstruction site (*National Geographic*) figured a good weaver could produce 2 inches an hour. It would have taken at least 4 yards of fabric, but you can't just have the 4 yards on a loom. It takes at least 1–2 feet at each end for a warp, and so $4 \times 3 = 12$ feet plus 3 feet at the end = 15 feet, $15 \times 12 = 180$ inches, divide by 2 = 90 hours. And you have to produce the thread/yarn to weave with. There would have been 15–20 threads per inch, we'll say he's poor and only gets coarse cloth, 15 threads. The fabric would have been a yard wide, so that would be $15 \times 36 = 540$ threads, each 15 feet long, just for the warp, a little less for the weft, but we'll just double it, so $1,080 \times 5$ yards = 5,400 yards of thread. This would have taken about 400 hours to weave. (This is also the reason why women were defined by spinning—'spinsters'—to make all that thread, fabric, etc., took a TREMENDOUS amount of time and energy.) So $7 + 90 + 400 = 497$, or round to 500 hours of hand labor to make one shirt. Multiply by minimum wage of $7.00 = $3,500.00 for a shirt. No wonder fabric was never, ever thrown out, but worn to pieces, and then cut down for the kids, and then turned into diapers, rags, etc. Also why peasants had one set of work clothes, and a set of 'best' clothes (Sundays, holidays, etc.). Because that of course is just the shirt—you'd still need breeches/stockings, vest and jerkin for a man; skirt, bodice for a woman. And a cloak would be nice."

xx **Stuffocation Is a Health Hazard**

This section is informed by various sources, including: Nanci Hellmich, "Obesity Can Trim 10 Years Off Life," *USA Today*, March 17, 2009; "Moderate Obesity Takes Years Off Life Expectancy," Oxford University press release, March 18, 2009; "Effects of Obesity and Smoking on U.S. Life Expectancy," *New England Journal of Medicine* 362 (March 4, 2010): 855–57; Pam Belluck, "Children's Life Expectancy Being Cut Short by Obesity," *New York Times*, March 17, 2005; Marc Ambinder, "Beating Obesity," *The Atlantic*, April 13, 2010; and "Stress Kills—Don't Take It Lightly," Heart MD Institute, www.heartmdinstitute.com, December 30, 2013.

xxii **"Cigarette smoking may be hazardous to your health"**

In the U.S., the Surgeon General's report was in 1964, and the first cigarette warnings appeared in 1966. The first warnings appeared in the U.K. in 1971.

xxiii **we have become less concerned about basic material needs like food and shelter**

For more, read Abraham Maslow, "A Theory of Human Motivation," *Psychological Review* 50 (1943): 370–96. But beware of referring too closely to the hierarchy of needs: today's psychologists only refer to the basic, physiological level as meaningful and useful.

xxiii **affluenza, "status anxiety," the "clutter crisis"**

For the best introduction on how mass consumption is leading to mass depression, read Oliver James, *Affluenza* (London: Vermilion, 2007). For the primer on the concept of status anxiety, read Alain de Botton, *Status Anxiety* (London: Hamish Hamilton, 2004). They are quite different in style. James's is chatty, like having a conversation with an intelligent friend. De Botton's is written like a philosophical conversation starter. Each is well worth reading. For more on the clutter crisis, read Chapter 1.

xxiii **An environmentalist will tell you**

For the environmentalists' view, read Greenpeace reports, most sensible newspapers, and the U.N.-commissioned Intergovernmental Panel on Climate Change report. For an alternative and fascinating view, read Peter H. Diamandis and Steven Kottler's *Abundance: The Future Is Better Than You Think* (New York: Free Press, 2011).

xxiii **aging population**

On the aging population's heightened interest in experiences rather than material goods, consider twentieth-century business success Malcolm

Forbes, whose maxim was "he who dies with the most toys wins." When, as the owner of a lot of very big, expensive toys, like a 151-foot yacht with a helicopter pad, he died in 1990, not long after a $2 million seventieth birthday party in Morocco, it didn't seem excessively unreasonable. It does now.

As people get older their priorities shift "from material things to ethereal things. Boomers are more interested in acquiring more experiences over more 'stuff'"—according to Matt Thornhill, an expert on older consumers who is coauthor of *Boomer Consumer* (Carlsbad, CA: Linx Corp., 2007) and founder of a consulting company targeting the elderly called Boomer Project. Source of this quote: Paul Hyman, "Baby Boomers: Every Silver Lining Has a Touch of Grey," *CRM Magazine,* February 2012.

People's consumption peaks around the age of fifty, according to the way Kenneth Gronbach, author of *The Age Curve: How to Profit from the Coming Demographic Storm,* reads U.S. Bureau of Labor statistics. That is the time, he says, when people's earnings and consumption are at their highest and when they own their biggest homes. Source: Hyman, "Baby Boomers."

xxiv **psychologists like Tim Kasser, Tom Gilovich, Elizabeth Dunn, and Ryan Howell**
The seminal paper here is Tom Gilovich and Leaf Van Boven, "To Do or to Have? That Is the Question," *Journal of Personality and Social Psychology* 85, no. 6 (2003). There are more references to the others' research about experiences not making us happier than material goods in the notes for Chapter 8.

xxiv **growing population**
There will be around nine billion by 2050, according to John Andrews and Daniel Franklin, eds., *Megachange: The World in 2050* (London: Economist, 2011). See also the French Institute of Demographic Studies (Ined)'s forecast that there will be 9.7 billion by 2050, up from just over seven billion today.

xxiv **the rise of the global middle class**
Consider, for example, the opening statement in Dominic Wilson, Alex L. Kelston, and Swarnali Ahmed, "Is This the BRICs [Brazil, Russia, India, China] Decade?," *Goldman Sachs' BRICs Monthly Issue,* 10/03, May 2010: "The last decade saw the BRICs make their mark on the global economic landscape. Over the past 10 years they have contributed over a third of world GDP growth and grown from one-sixth of the world economy to

almost a quarter (in PPP terms). Looking forward to the coming decade, we expect this trend to continue and become even more pronounced."

Or consider the final sentence in Catherine Wolfram, "Rising Middle Class Fuels Global Energy Surge," Bloomberg.com, January 17, 2012: "There is no doubt that the rise of the global middle class is a positive development. Yet, if we don't forecast and plan accordingly, it could lead to dire unexpected environmental consequences and cause dramatic increases in energy prices that ultimately diminish the very livelihoods we are trying to improve."

xxiv **the move to cities and fewer cars**

For more on the move to cities, consider the fact that humans officially became an urban species in 2007: since then, more than 50 percent of us have lived in cities. Source: Ricky Burdett and Deyan Sudjic, *The Endless City: The Urban Age Project* (London: Phaidon, 2007). Also: "One hundred years ago, 2 out of every 10 people lived in an urban area. By 1990, less than 40% of the global population lived in a city, but as of 2010, more than half of all people live in an urban area. By 2030, 6 out of every 10 people will live in a city, and by 2050, this proportion will increase to 7 out of 10 people." Source: World Health Organization.

Also, Ariel Schwartz, "We Are Approaching Peak Car Use," *Fast Company*, July 5, 2011; and Richard Florida, *The Great Reset: How the Post-Crash Economy Will Change the Way We Live and Work* (New York: Harper Business, 2011). For a quick introduction, read Richard Florida, "The Fading Differentiation Between City and Suburb," *Urban Land Magazine,* urbanland.uli.org, January 2013.

xxiv **a lack of belief in the system**

See Ruth Milkman, Stephanie Luce, and Penny Lewis, *Changing the Subject: A Bottom-Up Account of Occupy Wall Street in New York City* (New York: CUNY School of Professional Studies, 2013).

xxiv **rising costs, stagnating incomes**

See Richard Dobbs et al., *Resource Revolution: Meeting the World's Energy, Materials, Food, and Water Needs,* a report from McKinsey & Company (November 2011). Also, "Hitting Our Limits?," *The Economist,* October 14, 2011.

xxiv **A technologist might agree**

For examples of technology facilitating the shift from owning material things to experience, consider the success of Spotify, Zipcar, and the Kindle. Various sources, including: "All Eyes on the Sharing Economy," *The Economist,* March 9, 2013.

xxvii **status, identity, meaning, and happiness**

There are many things people want. I chose to stick with these four because I think they are a simple way to cover most of the basic human desires. For more, read Alain de Botton, *Status Anxiety* (London: Penguin, 2005); Roman Krznaric, *How to Find Fulfilling Work* (London: Macmillan, 2012); Tim Kasser, *Values and Human Wellbeing*, a commissioned research paper for the Bellagio Initiative (November 2011); Geoffrey Miller, *Spent: Sex, Evolution and the Secrets of Consumerism* (New York: William Heinemann, 2009); S. H. Schwartz, "Universals in the Content and Structure of Values: Theory and Empirical Tests in 20 Countries," in M. Zanna. ed., *Advances in Experimental Social Psychology*, vol. 25 (New York: Academic Press, 1992); and Steven Reiss, *Who Am I?* (New York: Berkley, 2000).

PART ONE. THE PROBLEM: STUFFOCATION

Chapter 1. The Anthropologist and the Clutter Crisis

Much of this chapter is drawn from the excellent, frightening, and very readable Jeanne E. Arnold, Anthony P. Graesch, Enzo Ragazzini, and Elinor Ochs, *Life at Home in the Twenty-first Century* (Los Angeles: Cotsen Institute of Archaeology Press, 2012).

4 **native tribe called the Chumash**

For more on the Chumash, read Jeanne E. Arnold, *Foundations of Chumash Complexity* (Los Angeles: Cotsen Institute of Archaeology Press, 2004).

5 **complex societies**

For more on complex societies—especially the discovery that a complex society could emerge from something other than an agricultural community—see Michael Moseley, *Pre-Agricultural Coastal Civilizations in Peru* (Burlington, NC: Carolina Biological Supply Company, 1977).

10 **Clutter Kills**

The information in this section is based on Darby Saxbe and Rena Repetti, "No Place Like Home: Home Tours Correlate with Daily Patterns of Mood and Cortisol," *Personality and Social Psychology Bulletin* 36, no. 1 (2010).

Why hasn't something so important had more coverage before? I have some theories: Does it not suit the media agenda, as Rachel Carson's discoveries did not in the 1960s? Or has it simply been overlooked? I don't know the answer.

13 **why the difference between men and women?**

See, for instance, Amy Tennery, "More Women Are in the Workforce—So Why Are They Still Doing So Many Chores?," *Time*, June 28, 2012; and Richard Chang, "Moms Feel Overwhelmed by Responsibilities: Poll," Reuters, June 15, 2011.

14 **Canada's Katrina**

This account was informed by various sources, including: William Stewart, "Highrise Horror," *Firefighting in Canada* 54, no. 8 (December 2010); Kate Allen, Kristin Rushowy, and Jayme Poisson, "Highrise Blaze Strands 1,200 People," *The Star,* September 25, 2010; and Stephanie Schorow, "The Dangers of Too Much Stuff," *National Fire Protection Association Journal,* January/February 2012. With particular thanks to Stephanie Schorow for all her assistance in terms of contacts and fact-checking (though any errors remain mine).

17 **The Secret Hoarder in You**

This section was inspired and informed by Randy Frost and Gail Steketee, *Stuff: Compulsive Hoarding and the Meaning of Things* (New York: Houghton Mifflin, 2010). With particular thanks to Gail Steketee for her assistance in terms of fact-checking (though any errors remain mine).

It was also informed by Jack Samuels, Joseph Bienvenu, et al., "Prevalence and Correlates of Hoarding Behavior in a Community-Based Sample," *Behaviour Research and Therapy* 46, no. 7 (July 2008): 836–44; Randy Frost, "Inheriting the Hoard: Greg's Story," *International OCD Foundation,* 2010; and Vicky Waltz and Devin Hahn, "When Stuff Takes Over—Gail Steketee on Hoarding Compulsion," *BU Today,* April 30, 2010.

To gauge how cluttered your home is with the help of some scientific images, take a look at Randy Frost's Clutter Image Rating at www .science.smith.edu/departments/PSYCH/rfrost/Hoarding_Images.htm.

18 **Langley and Homer Collyer**

The Collyer story was informed by various sources, including: Wikipedia; Andy Newman, "'Collyers' Mansion' Is Code for Firefighters' Nightmare," *New York Times,* July 5, 2006; Christopher Gray, "Streetscapes/128th St. and Fifth Ave., Former Site of the Harlem House Where the Collyer Brothers Kept All That Stuff; Wondering Whether a Park Should

Keep Its Name," *New York Times,* June 23, 2002; and "Langley Collyer Dead for Weeks; Police Find Body in Homer's Room," *Montreal Gazette,* April 9, 1947.

20 flashover

For more on flashover, read Christopher Flatley, "Flashover and Backdraft: A Primer," *Fire Engineering*, March 1, 2005; Jason Poremba, "Flashover: Time to Get Out," *FireRescue1.com*, June 10, 2009; and "Fire Test Video Shows That Hoarders at Greater Risk of Fire Death Brigade Warns," London Fire Brigade website, May 15, 2014.

21 hoarding fires

Watch a hoarding home go up in flames in this video by the London Fire Brigade: www.youtube.com/watch?v=pPWI24uvs4E. The scientific study on hoarding fires is Gregory Lucini, Ian Monk, and Christopher Szlatenyi, "An Analysis of Fire Incidents Involving Hoarding Households," Worcester Polytechnic Institute, May 22, 2009, http://web.cs.wpi .edu/~rek/Projects/MFB_D09.pdf.

Chapter 2. The Dark Side of Materialism

22 infamous scene

This scene is in "The Gold Violin," *Mad Men*, AMC, 2008.

23 The movement began

Rachel Carson, *Silent Spring* (New York: Houghton Mifflin, 1962), is quite a read.

24 environmental damage has only gotten worse through the years

U.N.-commissioned Intergovernmental Panel on Climate Change report.

24 the greatest extinction of plant and animal species since the dinosaurs died out

The Center for Biological Diversity, www.biologicaldiversity.org.

24 materialism is making millions of us feel joyless, anxious, and, even worse, depressed

Read these three works, by a philosopher, a psychologist, and an economist: Alain de Botton, *Status Anxiety* (London: Penguin, 2005); Oliver James, *Affluenza* (London: Vermilion, 2007); and Tibor Scitovsky, *The Joyless Economy: An Inquiry into Human Satisfaction and Consumer Dissatisfaction* (Oxford: Oxford University Press, 1976).

24 Richard Easterlin's research

Richard Easterlin, "Does Economic Growth Improve the Human Lot?

Some Empirical Evidence," in Paul A. David and Melvin W. Reder, eds., *Nations and Households in Economic Growth: Essays in Honor of Moses Abramovitz* (New York: Academic Press, 1974).

Easterlin, to be clear, was asking about economic growth rather than only material goods. But since the economy was driven by consumerism, and consumerism is largely driven by materialism, I think it is an acceptable proxy in this case.

Down the years, other scholars have challenged Easterlin's findings. For example, Betsey Stevenson and Justin Wolfers, "Economic Growth and Subjective Well-Being: Reassessing the Easterlin Paradox," *Brookings Papers on Economic Activity*, Economic Studies Program, the Brookings Institution 39, no. 1 (Spring 2008). The subject is now much debated. Who to believe and agree with? My current view is that the objective data can be given the subjective spin that suits your beliefs. If you consider other research, for example, Oliver James's *Affluenza*, it is clear which is correct.

25 **Jeremy Bentham**

Tibor Scitovsky, *The Joyless Economy: An Inquiry into Human Satisfaction and Consumer Dissatisfaction* (Oxford: Oxford University Press, 1976).

25 **Material goods . . . can be useful for self-expression**

For a very readable text on why material goods matter for self-expression and signifying status, read Daniel Miller, *Comfort of Things* (London: Polity, 2008). It is painstakingly researched, and brilliantly written.

26 **mental illness in children and adults in developed countries doubled**

Oliver James, *Affluenza* (London: Vermilion, 2007); Jean M. Twenge, Katharine Lacefield, Brittany Gentile, David R. Schurtz, and C. Nathan DeWall, "Birth Cohort Increases in Psychopathology Among Young Americans, 1938–2007: A Cross-Temporal Meta-Analysis of the MMPI," *Clinical Psychology Review* 30 (2010): 145–54. Also consider, Bruce Levine, "How Our Society Breeds Anxiety, Depression and Dysfunction," *Alternet/Salon*, August 26, 2013.

With thanks to Irving Kirsch, Oliver James, and Jean Twenge— author of *Generation Me* (New York: Atria, 2007)—for bearing with me while I double-checked the facts.

29 **Drawing a Road Map to the Future**

This section is inspired and informed by Peter N. Stearns, "Why Study History?," American Historical Association, 1998; Nate Silver, *The Sig-*

nal and the Noise (New York: Penguin Press, 2012); Rob Hyndman, "Why Are Some Things Easier to Forecast than Others?," September 18, 2012, on his blog, Hyndsight, www.robjhyndman.com/hyndsight; Martin Raymond, *The Trend Forecaster's Handbook* (London: Lawrence King, 2010); Alvin Toffler, *Future Shock* (New York: Random House, 1970); and Daniel Bell, *The Coming of Post-Industrial Society* (New York: Basic Books, 1973).

If you're not ready to read Nate Silver's *The Signal and the Noise* yet, read Nate Silver, "The Weatherman Is Not a Moron," *New York Times,* September 7, 2012.

29 **"The future is already here"**
Interview with William Gibson, "The Science in Science Fiction," *Talk of the Nation,* November 30, 1999, National Public Radio (quotation is around 11:50). With thanks to Garson O'Toole, aka the Quote Investigator (www.quoteinvestigator.com).

29 **a way of reading cultural change**
Everett M. Rogers, *Diffusion of Innovations* (New York: Free Press, 1962; 5th ed., 2003).

31 **How to Find the Future in the Present**
For more on Everett Rogers and his contribution to the field of diffusion analysis, read Everett M. Rogers, *The Fourteenth Paw* (Singapore: Asian Media Information and Communication Centre, 2008); Everett M. Rogers, *Diffusion of Innovations* (New York: Free Press, 1962; 5th ed., 2003); Thomas E. Backer, James Dearing, Arvind Singhal, and Thomas Valente, "Writing with Ev—Words to Transform Science into Action," *Journal of Health Communication* 10 (2005); Arvind Singhal, "Everett M. Rogers, an Intercultural Life: From Iowa Farm Boy to Global Intellectual," *International Journal of Intercultural Relations* 36, no. 6 (2012); and Arvind Singhal and James Dearing, *Communication of Innovations: A Journey with Ev Rogers* (Thousand Oaks, CA: Sage, 2006).

I have Corinne Shefner-Rogers to thank for many useful conversations, and for sending me Bruce Ryan and Neal Gross's original paper: "The Diffusion of Hybrid Seed Corn in Two Iowa Communities," *Rural Sociology* 8, no. 1 (1943).

There is an excellent analysis of the paper in Malcolm Gladwell, *The Tipping Point* (New York: Little, Brown, 2000). (But why did Gladwell never mention Everett Rogers, who had made sense of it all? I'm going to ask him one day.)

PART TWO. HOW WE GOT HERE:
THE ORIGINS OF THROWAWAY CULTURE

Chapter 3. The Original Mad Men and the Job of Creating Desire

37 **the original Mad Men**

To understand where the ideas came from that influenced the original Mad Men—people like Earnest Elmo Calkins and Christine Frederick—read Wilfred Trotter, *Instincts of the Herd in Peace and War* (London: Macmillan, 1916); Gustave Le Bon, *The Crowd: A Study of the Popular Mind* (London: Unwin, 1903); Edward Bernays, *Propaganda* (New York: Liveright, 1928; IG Publishing, 2005 ed.); Edward Bernays, *Crystallizing Public Opinion* (New York: Liveright, 1923); Stuart Ewen, *Captains of Consciousness* (New York: McGraw-Hill, 1976); Stuart Ewen, *PR! A Social History of Spin* (New York: Basic Books, 1996); and Matthew Hilton, *Consumerism in 20th-Century Britain* (Cambridge: Cambridge University Press, 2003).

To understand the birth of consumerism, read Mark Tungate, *Adland: A Global History of Advertising* (London: Kogan Page, 2007; 2nd ed., 2013); Frank Trentmann, ed., *The Oxford Handbook of the History of Consumption* (Oxford: Oxford University Press, 2012); Grant McCracken, *Culture and Consumption* (Bloomington: Indiana University Press, 1988); and Jan de Vries, *The Industrious Revolution* (Cambridge: Cambridge University Press, 2008).

The scene with Herbert Hoover was inspired by "Happiness Machines" and "The Engineering of Consent," *A Century of the Self,* Adam Curtis, BBC television, 2002. It was informed by "Hoover Sees Prosperous Era," *Houston Post Dispatch,* May 11, 1925; and "Advertising Is a Vital Force, Says Hoover," *Boston Daily Globe,* May 11, 1925.

Thank you to the Quote Investigator, Garson O'Toole, and to Spencer Howard, archives technician at the Hoover Presidential Library, for making sure the quotes in *Stuffocation* are correct.

38 **In the sixty years since the Civil War's end**

This, and much of this section, is sourced from a number of compelling accounts of this time: Jeffrey Kaplan, "The Gospel of Consumption," *Orion Magazine,* May/June 2008; Giles Slade, *Made to Break* (Cambridge: Harvard University Press, 2006); Vance Packard, *The Hidden Persuaders* (New York: Pelican, 1957), and Vance Packard, *The Waste Makers* (New York: Pelican, 1960). Simon N. Patten, *The New Basis of Civilization* (New York: Macmillan, 1907); and Victor Lebow, "Price

Competition in 1955," *Journal of Retailing,* Spring 1955, were also useful.

38 "need saturation"
Jeffrey Kaplan, "The Gospel of Consumption," *Orion Magazine,* May/June 2008.

38 By 1927, the country's textile mills
Ibid.

39 Bernard Mandeville
Read Bernard Mandeville, *The Fable of the Bees: or, Private Vices, Public Benefits* (1714) online.

40 "captains of consciousness"
The best place to find out about the role of the "captains of consciousness" in creating the "consumptionism" that has become the hallmark of twentieth-century society is Stuart Ewen, *Captains of Consciousness* (New York: McGraw-Hill, 1976).

40 Earnest Elmo Calkins
For a man who made a living writing simple copy that really spoke to people, Earnest Elmo Calkins's autobiography is very hard to read. Still, if you want to find out more about him, it's the thing to read: Earnest Elmo Calkins, *Louder Please! The Diary of a Deaf Man* (New York: Scribners, 1937). On Calkins's tilt toward obsolescence, read Earnest Elmo Calkins, "Beauty the New Business Tool," *The Atlantic,* August 1927; also, Roy Sheldon and Egmont Arens, *Consumer Engineering: A New Technique for Prosperity* (New York: Harper Brothers, 1932).

41 The question of how to stimulate consumption
Giles Slade, *Made to Break* (Cambridge: Harvard University Press, 2006); and Janice Rutherford, *Selling Mrs. Consumer: Christine Frederick and the Rise of Household Efficiency* (Athens: University of Georgia Press, 2003).

43 American men bought 70 million razor blades in 1915
"Safe. Cheap. Convenient," *Cutting Tool Engineering,* October 2003.

43 [American men] used and discarded 150 million throwaway collars and cuffs in 1872
Giles Slade, *Made to Break* (Cambridge: Harvard University Press, 2006).

44 "We want the man who buys one of our cars never to have to buy another"
The Henry Ford, www.thehenryford.org. Note that Ford did not go down the road that some other industries had: to make products with deliberately shorter lifespans, as, for instance, lightbulb manufacturers were doing.

44 **Christine Frederick**

For more on Christine Frederick, read Christine McGaffey Frederick, *Selling Mrs. Consumer* (New York: Business Borse, 1929); also Janice Rutherford, *Selling Mrs. Consumer: Christine Frederick and the Rise of Household Efficiency* (Athens: University of Georgia Press, 2003).

45 **The Kitchen Debate**

Sources for the account of Nixon, Khrushchev, and the kitchen include William Safire, "The Cold War's Hot Kitchen," *New York Times,* July 23, 2009; also, various articles at BBC.co.uk, in the *New York Times* archives, at History.com, and in old newscasts on YouTube.

Read the transcript—to which I've made minor alterations for the sake of grammar and ease of reading—at the Freedom of Information Act Reading Room, www.foia.cia.gov.

47 **in caveman terms, the slowest runners would not only miss out on lunch, they might become lunch**

I've borrowed this phrase from financial psychologist Brad Klontz. "[Keeping up with the Joneses] makes no rational sense but the animal brain tells us to think in terms of survival and it's a terrible idea to be left behind. The slowest runner misses out on lunch or becomes lunch," Klontz once said. "People think they need these things." Source: Craig Guillot, "The Psychology Behind Keeping Up with the Joneses," *Mint Life,* www.mint.com, January 23, 2013.

48 **Many, including the World Bank's president, Jim Yong Kim, even believe that we may have virtually wiped out poverty by 2030**

Read more about ending poverty in "Poverty: Not Always with Us," *The Economist,* June 1, 2013; and Mark Tran, "New UN Goals Call for End to Extreme Poverty by 2030," *The Guardian,* May 30, 2013.

48 **the best idea of the twentieth century**

For an excellent reading of the benefits of capitalism, read Michael Schuman, "How to Save Capitalism," *Time,* January 30, 2012; Martin Wolf, "Is the Age of Unlimited Growth Over?," *Financial Times,* October 3, 2012; and Stephen Moore and Julian L. Simon, "The Greatest Century That Ever Was: 25 Miraculous Trends of the Past 100 Years," *Policy Analysis,* No. 364, December 15, 1999.

Chapter 4. Barbra Streisand and the Law of Unintended Consequences

50 **Ken Adelman and Barbra Streisand**

The best place to read about the account of Ken Adelman and Barbra

Streisand is on Adelman's website, www.adelman.com. If you do, it's worth looking up some of the things Streisand's supporters said about Adelman.

51 **rabbits in Australia**

For a full version of the account of how rabbits came to Australia, read Mark Kellet, "Rabbits in Australia," *Australian Heritage,* Autumn 2006. The story of Thomas Austin was greatly helped by reading British History Online, www.british-history.ac.uk; also, "The Acclimatisation Society," *The Melbourne Argus,* April 21, 1864; and "The Late Mr. Thomas Austin," *The Melbourne Argus,* December 18, 1871.

52 **The Law of Unintended Consequences**

For more on Robert Merton's law of unintended consequences, read Robert K. Merton, "The Unanticipated Consequences of Purposive Social Action," *American Sociological Review* 1, no. 6 (December 1936).

53 **"Change is caused by lazy, greedy, frightened people"**

This is the "Morris theorem," from Ian Morris, *Why the West Rules—For Now: The Patterns of History and What They Reveal About the Future* (New York: Farrar, Straus & Giroux, 2010).

53 **From the Pyramid to the Pancake**

The idea of the pyramid to the pancake comes to me from two sources. The first was a lecture given by the political theorist Joseph Nye at the House of Commons. The second was something Dr. James Bellini said to me back in 2009. I thank both of them.

54 ***Fifty Shades of Grey* was rejected by professional agents**

Various sources, including: Ronald H. Balson, "Bestseller Success Stories That Started Out as Self-Published Books," *Huffington Post,* October 8, 2013.

54 **Jenna Marbles**

Watch the amazing Jenna Mourey get ready to go to work as a dancer in her "How to Trick People into Thinking You're Good Looking" video on YouTube.

54 **Tavi Gevinson**

Read about the time the twelve-year-old blogger sat front row in "Tavi Gevinson: 13-Year-Old Fashion Blogger Skips School, Attends Fashion Week," *Huffington Post,* November 17, 2009.

55 **the Internet has revolutionized politics**

For the impact of Facebook and Twitter on Egypt, Iran, and the Occupy Movement, consider Jose Antonio Vargas, "Spring Awakening: How an Egyptian Revolution Began on Facebook," *New York Times,* February

17, 2012; and Jared Keller, "Evaluating Iran's Twitter Revolution," *The Atlantic*, June 18, 2010.

PART THREE. THE CROSSROADS: SIGNPOSTS TO A BETTER FUTURE

Chapter 5. I Love to Count: The 33, 47, 69, and 100 Things of Minimalism

58 Tammy Strobel

Read more about Tammy Strobel at www.rowdykittens.com.

63 The 39 Socks

All the minimalists mentioned here have blogs. Some also write books about minimalism. Many also run courses to help people downsize their stuff and get more out of life.

Courtney Carver: www.bemorewithless.com

Ryan Nicodemus and Joshua Fields Millburn: www.theminimalists.com

Nina Yau: www.castlesintheair.com

Colin Wright: www.exilelifestyle.com

Chris Wray: www.twolessthings.com

Rachel Jonat: www.theminimalistmom.com

Leo Babauta: www.zenhabits.com

68 But minimalism is also achievable for families

Rachel Jonat: www.theminimalistmom.com

Leo Babauta: www.zenhabits.com

Chris Wray: www.twolessthings.com

Joshua Becker: www.becomingminimalist.com

69 de-cluttering is a good idea

For a smart, scholarly take on how many things we have—including toasters, towels, and clothes—and how we can change from a perspective of lack to one of plenty—read Juliet Schor, *Plenitude: The New Economics of True Wealth* (New York: Penguin, 2010). For a primer on the subject, and some useful statistics (e.g., about the towels and the toasters), read Stacy Mitchell, "Is Your Stuff Falling Apart? Thank Walmart," Grist.org, November 9, 2011. For the fashion angle, read Elizabeth L. Cline, *Overdressed: The Shockingly High Cost of Cheap Fashion* (New York: Penguin Portfolio, 2012). For more, especially statistics, read Julian M. Allwood et al., "Well Dressed? The Present and Future Sustainability of Clothing and Textiles in the United Kingdom," University of Cambridge Institute for Manufacturing, 2006; Sean Poulter, "In Every Woman's Closet, 22 Items She Never Wears—and the Guilty Complex That Stops Them Clearing Wardrobes Out," *Daily Mail,* January 26, 2011.

72 Stuff is good

Much of this section is inspired and informed by Danny Miller, *The Comfort of Things* (London: Polity, 2009). I should mention that Miller disagrees with some of the assertions I make in *Stuffocation,* because possessions, in some way, alleviate the general sadness that seems to be part of the human condition. This was one of the conclusions Miller came to after observing the people on one street in South London for seventeen months in the study that informed *The Comfort of Things.* "Above all, I sort of expected," he wrote, "but couldn't fully imagine, the sadness of lives and the comfort of things."

Miller believes, in fact, that possessions are an almost essential part of human relationships. As he also wrote in his introduction: "the closer our relationships are with objects, the closer our relationships are with people."

His studies support the importance of objects in our lives generally. Consider two case studies in *The Comfort of Things,* named only as George, and Mr. and Mrs. Clarke.

"George's flat was disorienting not because of anything that was in it but precisely because it contained nothing at all, beyond the most basic carpet and furniture." There is, Miller suggested, a "violence to such emptiness."

Contrast George with Mr. and Mrs. Clarke. Their house was the opposite of George's. Their Christmas tree, for instance, was adorned with eight hundred ornaments—fairies, sea horses, glass angels, and wooden nativity scenes from the Philippines. They were close, perhaps even devoted, to all five of their children, all ten of their grandchildren, and all of their many friends and neighbors. On Mr. Clarke, who collected stamps, Meccano sets, old cars, and people, Miller wrote: "The connection between the way he cares for stamps or Christmas ornaments and the way he has cared for people throughout his life is not just one of analogy."

72 Stuff is good, because it helps us express our identities and beliefs

Thanks to Oxford University's Michael Bonsall for help confirming this statement about animal fitness indicators. For how this concept manifests in human culture, read Geoffrey Miller, *Spent: Sex, Evolution and the Secrets of Consumerism* (New York: William Heinemann, 2009).

Chapter 6. The Simple Life and the Cage-Free Family

77 **chicken stock**

Kaayla Daniel, "Why Broth Is Beautiful: Essential Roles for Proline, Glycine and Gelatin," Weston A. Price Foundation for Wise Traditions in Food, Farming, and the Healing Arts, www.westonaprice.org/health-topics/why-broth-is-beautiful-essential-roles-for-proline-glycine-and-gelatin.

80 **Diogenes**

Read more about Diogenes of Sinope in Diogenes Laërtius, *Lives and Opinions of Eminent Philosophers*. Now out of copyright, it is available online and in various editions.

80 **Thoreau**

For a complete, and poetic, account of Thoreau's time in the woods, read Henry David Thoreau, *Walden; or, Life in the Woods* (Boston: Ticknor & Fields, 1854).

80 **Duane Elgin**

For more on Duane Elgin's discovery of, and research on, the voluntary simplicity movement, read Duane Elgin, *Voluntary Simplicity: Toward a Way of Life That Is Outwardly Simple, Inwardly Rich* (New York: William Morrow, 2nd ed., 1993). Another book I found useful was Vicki Robin and Joe Dominguez, *Your Money or Your Life* (New York: Penguin, 1992, 2008).

82 **Taos weather**

Taos Ski Valley Chamber of Commerce.

85 **people do not necessarily behave in a rational, logical way**

To understand this, read Daniel Kahneman, *Thinking, Fast and Slow* (New York: Penguin, 2011); Dan Ariely, *Predictably Irrational* (New York: HarperCollins, 2008); and Richard Thaler and Cass Sunstein, *Nudge* (New York: Penguin, 2008). For the best visualization of how the two parts of the brain work together, read about the elephant and its rider in Jonathan Haidt, *The Happiness Hypothesis: Putting Ancient Wisdom to the Test of Modern Science* (London: Arrow, 2007).

85 **3D televisions**

Okay, so maybe people aren't buying 3D TVs, but the concept of upgrading is valid. The current vogue thinking is that the technology after HD is 4K, which is also being called Ultra HD.

86 **LeVally and Harris did not give up**

To read a more complete account of how LeVally and Harris came down

from the mountain, and struggled with that decision, read www.cage
freefamily.com.

Chapter 7. The Medium Chill

88 the medium chill

Read about the medium chill from the man who created it in his two
seminal posts: David Roberts, "The Medium Chill," Grist.org, June 28,
2011; David Roberts, "The Medium Chill, Revisited," Grist.org, May 1,
2013.

For more on the working week, read Benjamin Kline Hunnicutt, *Work
Without End and Free Time: The Forgotten American Dream* (Philadel-
phia: Temple University Press, 2013); Benjamin Kline Hunnicutt, *Kel-
logg's Six-Hour Day* (Philadelphia: Temple University Press, 1996); and
Benjamin Kline Hunnicutt, *Work Without End: Abandoning Shorter
Hours for the Right to Work* (Philadelphia: Temple University Press,
1988). Also see Anna Coote, Andrew Simms, and Jane Franklin, *21
Hours* (London: New Economics Foundation, 2010); John Quiggin,
"The Golden Age," *Aeon Magazine,* September 2012; and Sharon Beder,
Selling the Work Ethic: From Puritan Pulpit to Corporate PR (Mel-
bourne: Scribe, 2000).

94 Paleolithic woman

The account of the average Paleolithic woman comes from Geoffrey
Miller, *Spent: Sex, Evolution and the Secrets of Consumerism* (New
York: William Heinemann, 2009).

95 clock-time

For the rise of "clock-time" and what the Industrial Revolution did to
our working week, read Benjamin Kline Hunnicutt's works mentioned
above: Benjamin Kline Hunnicutt, *Work Without End and Free Time:
The Forgotten American Dream* (Philadelphia: Temple University Press,
2013); Benjamin Kline Hunnicutt, *Kellogg's Six-Hour Day* (Philadelphia:
Temple University Press, 1996); and Benjamin Kline Hunnicutt, *Work
Without End: Abandoning Shorter Hours for the Right to Work* (Philadelphia: Temple University Press, 1988).

96 "threshold earners"

For more on threshold earners, see Tyler Cowen, "The Inequality That
Matters," *The American Interest,* January/February 2011. For an excellent deconstruction of that article, read political columnist Reihan

Salam, "Threshold Earners and Gentleman Hackers," *National Review,* December 28, 2010.

96 **There is no sign of the tipping point that would suggest that the medium chill is set to make the leap along the adoption curve**

I spent a lot of time thinking about this. I know a number of people who deliberately do not seek to maximize income, and prefer time and life instead. Then there are the numbers of part-time workers rising dramatically in recent years. But I think much of that has been forced on people. So although I think we will see a rise in people choosing the medium chill, and it could become much more important as a value system and lifestyle choice, I do not think the evidence is convincing enough yet to make me try to convince you. As it stands, the medium chill is a subset of this wider idea of experientialism.

PART FOUR. THE ROAD AHEAD: THE RISE OF THE EXPERIENTIALISTS

Chapter 8. To Do or to Have? That Is No Longer a Question

The most important paper for this chapter is Tom Gilovich and Leaf Van Boven, "To Do or to Have? That Is the Question," *Journal of Personality and Social Psychology* 85, no. 6 (2003).

This chapter is also informed by interviews with psychologists, including Tom Gilovich, Ryan Howell, Leaf Van Boven, Joseph Goodman, Tim Kasser, and Travis Carter, and a number of academic papers, including:

Leonardo Nicolao, Julie R. Irwin, and Joseph K. Goodman, "Happiness for Sale: Do Experiential Purchases Make Consumers Happier than Material Purchases?," *Journal of Consumer Research* 36, no. 2 (2009).

Elizabeth W. Dunn, Daniel T. Gilbert, and Timothy D. Wilson, "If Money Doesn't Make You Happy, Then You Probably Aren't Spending It Right," *Journal of Consumer Psychology* 21, no. 2 (April 2011).

Tim Kasser, *The High Price of Materialism* (Cambridge: MIT Press, 2002).

Tim Kasser et al., "Materialistic Values: Their Causes and Consequences," in *Psychology and Consumer Culture: The Struggle for a Good Life in a Materialistic World,* eds. Tim Kasser and Allen D. Kramer (Washington, DC: American Psychological Association, 2004).

Leaf Van Boven, "Experientialism, Materialism, and the Pursuit of Happiness," *Review of General Psychology* 9, no. 2 (June 2005).

Elizabeth Dunn and Michael Norton, "Don't Indulge. Be Happy," *New York Times,* July 7, 2012.

Elizabeth Dunn and Michael Norton, *Happy Money: The Science of Spending* (New York: Simon & Schuster, 2013).

Travis Carter and Thomas Gilovich, "I Am What I Do, Not What I Have: The Centrality of Experiential Purchases to the Self-Concept," *Journal of Personality and Social Psychology* 102, no. 6 (2012).

Travis Carter and Thomas Gilovich, "The Relative Relativity of Material and Experiential Purchases," *Journal of Personality and Social Psychology* 98, no. 1 (2010).

Ryan T. Howell, Paulina Pchelin, and Ravi Iyer, "The Preference for Experiences over Possessions: Measurement and Construct Validation of the Experiential Buying Tendency Scale," *The Journal of Positive Psychology* 7, no. 1 (January 2012).

Emily Rosenzweig and Thomas Gilovich, "Buyer's Remorse or Missed Opportunity? Differential Regrets for Material and Experiential Purchases," *Journal of Personality and Social Psychology* 102, no. 2 (2012).

Tori DeAngelis, "Consumerism and Its Discontents," *American Psychological Association* 35, no. 6 (June 2004).

Tim Kasser and Allen D. Kanner, eds., *Psychology and Consumer Culture: The Struggle for a Good Life in a Materialistic World* (Washington, DC: American Psychological Association, 2003).

Peter A. Caprariello and Harry T. Reis, "To Do with Others or to Have (or to Do Alone?): The Value of Experiences over Material Possessions Depends on the Involvement of Others," *Advances in Consumer Research* 37 (2010).

Chapter 9. The Experientialists

109 **By the 1950s, when you could see the Jet Age and the Space Race**

For example, the 1955 Chrysler 300F, the 1957 Chevrolet Bel Air Convertible, and the 1958 Aston Martin DB4.

109 **Dirk Jan De Pree**

For an introduction to the story of Dirk Jan De Pree and the cubicles, read Julie Schlosser, "Cubicles: The Great Mistake," *Fortune,* March 22,

2006; and Marc Kristal, "An Idea Whose Time Has Come," *Metropolis Magazine,* June 2013.

113 **Marianne Cantwell and the free-range lifestyle**

For more on the free-range movement, see www.free-range-humans .com, and Marianne Cantwell, *Be a Free Range Human* (London: Kogan Page, 2013).

116 **Bertrand Lenet**

When you are in London, visit Bertrand Lenet's restaurant. It may be a cliché to say it, but it is like a little bit of France in London. It scored 4.1 out of five stars on Google when I last looked. (I recommend the steak frites.) Gastro, 67 Venn St., London SW4 0BD. Telephone: +44 (0) 20 7627 0222.

123 **Rally from Paris to Persepolis**

If you want to drive from London to Ulan Bator, you can do it with the Mongol Rally.

125 **Escape the City**

Join Escape the City today at www.escapethecity.com.

125 **Alice Marwick**

Alice Marwick has now turned her PhD dissertation into a book: Alice Marwick, *Status Update: Celebrity, Publicity, and Branding in the Social Media Age* (New Haven: Yale University Press, 2013).

Chapter 10. Facebook Changed How We Keep Up with the Joneses

For the seminal work on consumption and status, read Thorstein Veblen, *Theory of the Leisure Class* (New York: Macmillan, 1899).

126 **black-tie dinner eaten on horseback**

This was held by millionaire C. K. G. Billings on March 28, 1903, for thirty-six of his closest male friends in Sherry's restaurant in New York.

126 **Louis XVI–style sports pavilion at the Astor country estate**

Visit the Vanderbilt Mansion National Historic Site in Hyde Park, New York, www.nps.gov.

127 *Keeping Up with the Joneses*

To read one of the very first *Keeping Up with the Joneses,* see Alex Jay, " 'Pop' Momand Profiled by Alex Jay," *Stripper's Guide,* http://strippers guide.blogspot.co.uk/2011/02/pop-momand-profiled-by-alex-jay.html.

131 **TED conference**

If you haven't already, watch a TED lecture at www.ted.com.

131 **If you have high status**

It surprises me how people bristle at the mention of status. Yet it is incredibly important to us. Consider this from a report called "Reaching for a Healthier Life—Facts on Socioeconomic Status and Health in the U.S." by researchers at the MacArthur Research Network on Socioeconomic Status and Health: "Your position on the ladder predicts how long you live and how healthy you are during your lifetime. . . . The risk of dying before the age of 65 is more than three times greater for those at the bottom than for those at the top. . . . The power of social status to impact the most precious resource we have—life itself—is enormous and pervasive."

For more, also read Alain de Botton, *Status Anxiety* (London: Hamish Hamilton, 2004); Ahmed Riahi-Belkaoui, *Social Status Matters* (Charleston: BookSurge, 2009); Meg McCabe, "Respect Brings More Happiness than Money Does, Study Shows," *Daily Californian,* July 3, 2012; and Alice Park, "Study: Money Isn't Everything—But Status Is!," *Time,* March 23, 2010.

132 **FOMO**

See the FOMO reports by advertising agency JWT: *Fear of Missing Out,* May 2011, and *Fear of Missing Out (FOMO),* March 2012 update. Take particular note of figures 2F and 2G in the Appendix of the March 2012 update. If you compare them you can see how social media is speeding the shift from materialism to experientialism—as people are more able than ever to get status from experiential rather than material goods. My reading, of course, is that conspicuous living is replacing conspicuous consumption in its importance for our status and our lives.

133 **we are more likely to end up feeling anxious and stressed**

For more on social media making people anxious, read Nicola Kemp, "Why Social Media Is Constructing a Reality Unworthy of Your Anxiety," *Media Week,* July 29, 2014; and Marissa Maldonado, "The Anxiety of Facebook," *Psych Central,* May 12, 2014.

135 **"flow"**

For the best text on flow, read Mihaly Csikszentmihalyi, *Flow: The Psychology of Optimal Experience* (New York: Harper Perennial Modern Classics, 2008).

135 **Motivation matters**

Read more about the importance of intrinsic motivation in Edward L. Deci and Richard M. Ryan, *Intrinsic Motivation and Self-Determination in Human Behavior* (New York: Springer Science & Business Media, 1985). Also see www.selfdeterminationtheory.org.

136 **This is a useful insight**

Interview with psychologist Leaf Van Boven.

138 **Experientialism could even restore**

For Ruth Milkman's view on why people are disillusioned with capitalism, see Ruth Milkman, Stephanie Luce, and Penny Lewis, *Changing the Subject: A Bottom-Up Account of Occupy Wall Street in New York City* (New York: CUNY School of Professional Studies, 2013).

139 **Betamax v. VHS**

For more on the Sony/Betamax versus JVC/VHS format war, read Brad Williams, "VHS Versus Betamax: The Great Format War of Our Time," LikeTotally80s.com, September 24, 2012; Stanley M. Besen and Joseph Farrell, "Choosing How to Compete: Strategies and Tactics in Standardization," *Journal of Economic Perspectives* 8, no. 2 (1994): 117–31; and James Megis, "Beta Is Out but Format Battle Rages," *Rolling Stone*, February 13, 1987.

141 **survey results: de-Stuffocating**

Havas Worldwide Prosumer Report, *The New Consumer and the Sharing Economy,* 2014.

141 **Ron Inglehart**

Again, Ron Inglehart, "The Silent Revolution in Europe: Intergenerational Change in Post-Industrial Societies," *American Political Science Review* 65, no. 4 (December 1971). To see the shift away from materialistic values, refer to the World Values Survey, www.worldvaluessurvey.org.

142 **the changing makeup of our economy**

Compare the type of items in Simon Kuznets, *National Income, 1929–32* (Cambridge: National Bureau of Economic Research, June 1934) with those in today's economies. Consider also Francisco J. Buera and Joseph P. Kaboski, "The Rise of the Service Economy," *American Economic Review* 102, no. 6 (2012). For an easy introduction, see the video infographic "The iPhone Economy" at www.nytimes.com.

For the definitive text on consuming fewer materials, read Chris Goodall, "Peak Stuff," *Carbon Commentary,* 2011. And read Chris Goodall, *Sustainability* (London: Hodder & Stoughton, 2012). Keep up with the latest news via Goodall's excellent blog, www.carboncommentary.com.

This chapter was also informed by Tyler Cowen, *The Great Stagnation* (New York: Dutton, 2011); and Robert J. Gordon, "Is US Economic Growth Over? Faltering Innovation Confronts the Six Headwinds" (Centre for Economic Policy Research, September 2012).

142 **In 2007, the average American bought almost twice as many items of clothing as they had in 1991. But by 2012 the number had stopped rising, and even fallen slightly, from sixty-seven to sixty-four items.**
Sources: Juliet Schor, *Plenitude: The New Economics of True Wealth* (New York: Penguin, 2010); Elizabeth L. Cline, *Overdressed: The Shockingly High Cost of Cheap Fashion* (New York: Penguin Portfolio, 2012).

143 **People in the U.K. and Ireland prefer experiences to material goods**
This statement is based on survey data from nationally representative surveys conducted in December 2012 (with thanks to James Kennedy). We asked: "Please think of the last time you spent money on something that made you really happy. Was this an 'object' or an 'experience'?"

In the U.K., 30 percent said object, 12 percent said they could not remember making a purchase that made them happy, 7 percent said not sure, and 51 percent said experience.

In the Republic of Ireland, 40 percent said object, 5 percent said they could not remember making a purchase that made them happy, 4 percent said not sure, and 51 percent said experience.

143 **the demise of the hardback and the rise of ebooks**
For example, Alison Flood, "Hardback Sales Plummeting in Age of the Ebook," TheGuardian.co.uk, August 12, 2011.

143 **plummeting sales of recorded music and the boom in live music and festivals**
Thomas K. Grose, "Live, at a Field Near You," *Time*, November 14, 2011.

143 **people in their sixties spend more on vacations than any other age group**
A report published January 2013 from a website called TravelSupermarket questioned five thousand vacationers. The report found that the over-sixties are most likely to spend the most money on vacations, and that they spend an average of £794 (about $1,300) on travel and accommodation each year. See "The Silver Pound: Holidaymakers in Their Sixties Spend More than Other Age Groups," *Daily Mail*, January 28, 2013. Also, research from the International Council of Shopping Centers, a trade body, reports that over-fifty-fives spend more than 50 percent of the money spent on vacations in the U.S.

143 **the emergence of extreme sports**
See, for instance, Geoffrey Miller, *Spent: Sex, Evolution and the Secrets of Consumerism* (New York: William Heinemann, 2009); and Richard Askwith, "Tough Mudder: The Obstacle Courses for Adults That Are Now Worth $250m," *The Independent*, May 3, 2013.

143 **expanding health care market**

Consider predictions from two of the world's leading consultancies. PWC predicts, in a report called "Pharma 2020," that by 2020 the pharmaceutical market will more than double in value to $1.3 trillion. Another consultancy, Bain, states in its "Healthcare 2020" report that "the total profit pool [for the health care sector] will grow at a compound adjusted growth rate (CAGR) of 4%—from $520 billion in 2010 to $740 billion in 2020."

143 **Jean-Marc Bellaiche: "In an era of over-consumption"**

Andrew Roberts, "Building Luxury Brand Loyalty via Exclusive Experiences," *Bloomberg Businessweek*, January 31, 2013.

143 **Boston Consulting Group**

For more on the Boston Consulting Group's luxury reports, visit www.bcg.com.

143 **Antonella Mei-Pochtler: "Luxury is shifting rapidly from 'having' to 'being'"**

Zoe Wood, "Super Rich Shift Their Thrills from Luxury Goods to Costly Experiences," *The Guardian*, January 30, 2014.

143 **millennials not buying cars**

Consider Robert Wright, "Transport: Freed from the Wheel," *Financial Times*, October 6, 2013: "Young city dwellers are driving less, forcing the motor industry to rethink the role of the car." Also, read Jordan Weissman, "Why Don't Young Americans Buy Cars?," *The Atlantic*, March 25, 2012; and John Arlidge, "Baby, You Can Share My Car," *Sunday Times*, March 10, 2013, which reports that in 2008, only 30 percent of sixteen-year-old Americans held driver's licenses, down from 50 percent a generation ago, that 80 percent of under-twenty-fives in Tokyo do not have a car, and that in Germany the share of young households without cars rose from 20 percent to 28 percent from 1998 to 2008.

143 **millennials choosing to live in small, city-center apartments**

See Richard Florida, *The Great Reset: How the Post-Crash Economy Will Change the Way We Live and Work* (New York: Harper Business, 2011). For a rigorous analysis of the millennials' housing aspirations, read Nathan Morris, "Why Generation Y Is Causing the Great Migration of the 21st Century," on the website of a design firm called Placemakers, www.placemakers.com, April 9, 2012.

143 **Rather than owning a thing . . . they prefer access**

Various sources, including Tammy Erickson, "Meaning Is the New Money," HBR Blog Network, March 23, 2011; and David Brooks, "The Experience Economy," *New York Times*, February 14, 2011.

143 **services like Zipcar, Spotify, Rent the Runway, and Netflix**

For excellent introductions to how these companies operate, read Rachel Botsman and Roo Rogers, "Beyond Zipcar: Collaborative Consumption," *Harvard Business Review,* October 2010; and, for the rise of these services, read "All Eyes on the Sharing Economy," *The Economist,* March 9, 2013.

Chapter 11. We Love to Count Too: The New Way to Measure Progress

This chapter is informed by many sources, including Roger Cohen, "The Happynomics of Life," *New York Times,* March 12, 2011; and Richard Layard, *Happiness: Lessons from a New Science* (London: Penguin, 2011).

145 **George W. Bush, Tony Blair**

Note that the view that Tony Blair and George Bush simply encouraged their people to shop after the attacks of 9/11 has been challenged—for example, by political consultant Karl Rove—but I believe the point holds good: that politicians, and many of us too, had come to largely measure our progress, and certainly our national status, in terms of GDP.

146 **"amalgam of relatively accurate and only approximate estimates"**

Read the first national income accounts: Simon Kuznets et al., *National Income, 1929–32* (National Bureau of Economic Research, June 1934).

146 **raised economics from a speculative and ideologically riven discipline into an empirically based social science**

Read more about the rise of economics and the life of Simon Kuznets in Robert Fogel, *Simon S. Kuznets, April 30, 1901–July 9, 1985* (Cambridge, MA: National Bureau of Economic Research, 2000).

147 **As the council's chairman, Raymond J. Saulnier, said, when talking of the American economy in 1959, "its ultimate purpose is to produce more consumer goods"**

This quote is popularly misattributed to another economist, Arthur F. Burns. I have the Quote Investigator, Garson O'Toole, to thank (again!) for ensuring that my quote is correct. As the chairman of the Council of Economic Advisers, Saulnier said in a response to a question from a senator: "Let me interpolate by saying that, as I understand an economy, its ultimate purpose is to produce more consumer goods. This is the goal. This is the object of everything that we are working at: to produce things for consumers."

147 **the method of national income accounting that the United States used was adopted by all countries**

By "all countries," I am referring here to the major Western countries. Simon Kuznets's work was supplemented by many other economists, including, for example, Richard Stone and Alexander Eckstein. With thanks to three economists at the London School of Economics for their assistance with this: Olivier Accominotti, Steve Broadberry, and Tamas Vonyo.

148 **"What have the Romans ever done for us?"**

Monty Python's Life of Brian, with kind permission. For the sake of brevity, it has been edited slightly. With thanks to Jill Foster and Holly Gilliam for their assistance.

150 **increases in GDP per capita do improve well-being**

Daniel Kahneman and Angus Deaton, "High Income Improves Evaluation of Life but Not Emotional Well-Being," *Proceedings of the National Academy of Sciences* 107, no. 38 (September 7, 2010).

150 **the drunkard's search**

Abraham Kaplan, *The Conduct of Inquiry: Methodology for Behavioral Science* (San Francisco: Chandler, 1964).

150 **substitution**

Daniel Kahneman, *Thinking, Fast and Slow* (New York: Penguin, 2011).

151 **But GDP does not measure quality of life**

For a moving version of what GDP does not measure, look up Robert Kennedy's 1969 speech set to (almost) stirring music on YouTube.

151 **alternatives to GDP**

Tim Jackson, *Prosperity Without Growth* (London: Earthscan, 2009); and Joseph E. Stiglitz, Amartya Sen, and Jean-Paul Fitoussi, *Mismeasuring Our Lives* (New York: New Press, 2010). Also, Jules Evans, "Beyond GDP: Towards a Better Measurement of National Wellbeing in France and the UK," Franco-British Council report, February 2, 2011; and Jon Gertner, "The Rise and Fall of the GDP," *New York Times,* May 13, 2010.

152 **Bernard Le Bovier de Fontenelle**

Bernard Le Bovier de Fontenelle, "Digression on the Ancients and the Moderns," first printed in his *Poésies pastorales de M.D.F.* (Paris, 1688), 224–82, and reprinted in Robert Shackleton, ed., *Entretiens sur la pluralité des mondes et Digression sur les anciens et les modernes* (Oxford, 1955), 161–76.

154 **Sarkozy's popularity rating nosediving**

Crispian Balmer, "French Fall Out of Love with Smitten Sarkozy," Reuters, February 4, 2008.

154 **he stalked the vast halls of the Élysée Palace**

Cécile Alduy, "Life as Sarkozy's Secret Speechwriter," *The Atlantic,* March 26, 2013. Sarkozy's thoughts here are taken from his foreword in Joseph E. Stiglitz, Amartya Sen, and Jean-Paul Fitoussi, *Mismeasuring Our Lives* (New York: New Press, 2010).

155 **substitution**

Daniel Kahneman, *Thinking, Fast and Slow* (New York: Penguin, 2011).

The Wikiprogress.org pages on Subjective Well-being have been invaluable here, as has Bernice Steinhardt et al., "Key Indicator Systems: Experiences of Other National and Subnational Systems Offer Insights for the United States," United States Government Accountability Office, Report to Congressional Addressees, 2011. Useful websites for progressive measures of social progress include: www4.hrsdc.gc.ca for Canada's Indicators of Well-being in Canada (WIC); uwaterloo.ca/canadian -index-wellbeing for the Canadian Index of Wellbeing (CIW); Australian Bureau of Statistics's www.abs.gov.au for Measures of Australia's Progress (MAP); www.oecdbetterlifeindex.org for the Organisation for Economic Co-operation and Development (OECD)'s Better Life Index; hdr .undp.org for the U.N.'s Human Development Index (HDI); www.gross nationalhappiness.com for Bhutan's Gross National Happiness (GNH); and www.stateoftheusa.org for the State of the USA (SUSA).

157 **Barry Schwartz recently proposed a psychological parallel**

Barry Schwartz, "Move Over Economists: We Need a Council of Psychological Advisers," *The Atlantic,* November 12, 2012. Also consider Richard Thaler, "Watching Behavior Before Writing the Rules," *New York Times,* July 7, 2012; and Cass R. Sunstein, "The Council of Psychological Advisors" (published online September 15, 2014, and forthcoming in *Annual Review of Psychology.* It is available at http://ssrn.com/abstract=2496438).

159 **"what we measure affects what we do"**

Joseph Stiglitz, "The Great GDP Swindle," *The Guardian*, September 13, 2009.

Chapter 12. What About the Chinese?

The description of Liu Dandan, Zhou Zhou, and Richard Lu is taken from the photo shoot for Bill Saporito, "A Great Leap Forward: Can China's Famously Thrifty Workers Become the World's Big Spenders?," *Time,* October 31, 2011. Thanks here to Bill Saporito, Zohair Abdoolcarim, Adrian Sandiford, Austin Ramzy, and Chen Jiaojiao for their help looking for Liu Dandan, Zhou Zhou, and Richard Lu.

161 **more than a billion people in countries like India, Indonesia, Vietnam, Nigeria, and Brazil**

Various sources, including: Linda Yueh, "The Rise of the Global Middle Class," BBC.co.uk, June 19, 2013.

163 **In the West, it took 150 odd years**

I'm taking the start of the Industrial Revolution as around 1780, and the moment of overproduction as 1929, and pegging Stuffocation to 2013. Cultural sweeps are rarely neat, so these are slightly arbitrary estimates.

163 **In 2012, for instance, there were overproduction problems**

Various sources, including Colyapi, "The Danger of Chinese Overproduction," *China Daily Mail,* January 8, 2013; Walden Bello, "China and the Crisis of Overproduction," GlobalPolitician.com; and Dexter Roberts, "To Fix Overproduction, China Wants to Supersize Industries," *Bloomberg Businessweek,* January 25, 2013.

164 **As in America almost a century ago, commentators have been weighing in with their worries**

Read Bill Saporito, "A Great Leap Forward," *Time,* October 31, 2011; Dhara Ranasinghe, "Chinese Consumers Are Still Not Spending Enough," CNBC.com, May 29, 2013.

164 **For stability and growth**

Louis Kuijs, "How to Further Boost Consumption?," World Bank, 2012, http://go.worldbank.org/OGWG0M41K0; and IMF Press Release No. 13/260, July 17, 2013, in which the IMF's directors "underscored the importance of [China] transitioning to a new growth path that is more consumption-based."

164 **Advertising, the industry most likely to engineer consumers rather than products, is exploding**

Kong Liang and Laurence Jacobs, "China's Advertising Agencies: Problems and Relations," *International Journal of Advertising,* June 22, 1994; Ying Fan, "Advertising and Public Relations in China," in Sarah Oliver, ed., published as part of "Communicating with 1.3 Billion People in China," *Handbook of Corporate Communication and Public Relations* (London: Routledge, 2004); "China's Advertising and Marketing Industry Research Report," My Decker Capital, January 2012; and

"China's Ad Industry Rises to World's Second: SAIC," *China Daily,* April 27, 2013, which cites Zhang Mao, the head of China's State Administration for Industry and Commerce (SAIC).

165 **The Chinese government is explicitly intent on creating consumers as well**
Louis Kuijs, "How to Further Boost Consumption?," World Bank, 2012, http://go.worldbank.org/OGWG0M41K0.

165 **the value of e-commerce in China in 2012 . . . was almost the same as the entire economy of the Republic of Ireland**
This comparison is based on the value of e-commerce in China in 2012 at $210 billion, and the Republic of Ireland economy for that year, $220 billion. Sources: Eurostat; and Kenneth Rapooza, "China E-Commerce Rises 64.7% in 2012," *Forbes,* March 29, 2013.

165 **frequent demonstrations and riots as people put their environment and quality of life before growth**
Various sources, including: "Chinese Anger over Pollution Becomes Main Cause of Social Unrest," Bloomberg.com, March 6, 2013; J. T. Quigley, "Chinese Government Will Spend $277 Billion to Combat Air Pollution," *The Diplomat,* July 27, 2013; and Sui-Lee Wee, "China Offers Rewards to Six Regions to Fight Air Pollution," Reuters, October 14, 2013, which notes that "Protests over pollution in China are becoming common, to the government's alarm. Authorities have invested in various projects to fight pollution and even empowered courts to mete out the death penalty in serious pollution cases."

165 **stalling levels of happiness**
Richard Easterlin et al., "China's Life Satisfaction, 1990–2010," University of Southern California, Los Angeles, *Proceedings of the National Academy of the Sciences*, May 2012; Richard Easterlin, "When Growth Outpaces Happiness," *New York Times,* September 27, 2012; and Linda Carroll, "Rising Wealth in China Fails to Buy More Happiness," NBC, May 17, 2012.

165 **In China, the experiential luxury sector . . . is growing around 25 percent faster than the personal luxury goods sector**
This is calculated from the following statistics: that, while sales of personal luxury goods in China are rising 22 percent per year, sales of luxury experiences are growing at 28 percent each year. Source: Boston Consulting Group.

166 **It took China around a third of the time to go from the start of its industrialization to overproduction—around sixty years**

I'm taking industrialization to have begun in the late 1950s in the Great Leap Forward. The historian Niall Ferguson believes that China is cramming "a century's worth of industrialisation and urbanisation into about 30 years." Sources: Niall Ferguson, "China Faces Its Own Fiscal Problems," *Newsweek,* August 14, 2011, and Tong Wu, "China's Industrial Revolution Is Happening on a New Planet," Phys.org, September 19, 2013. A report by the McKinsey Global Institute is even more bullish, claiming that China's industrialization has proceeded at ten times the speed of Britain's. Source: *Urban World: Cities and the Rise of the Consuming Class,* McKinsey Global Institute, June 2012.

166 **If [China] continues to follow a similar, accelerated path, it will reach overconsumption by 2037.**

The various factors that are causing Stuffocation over here now are likely to be more, and less, relevant, in China in the future. The environment, for example, is probably going to be a far more pressing problem. In terms of the personal, at-home, clutter crisis aspect of Stuffocation, though, it is unlikely that the average Chinese will reach the same material standard of living as we have in the West for far more years.

Chapter 13. The Gypsy, the Wasp, and the Experience Economy

170 **Punchdrunk**

For more on Punchdrunk, visit www.punchdrunk.com.

171 **Bompas & Parr**

For more on Bompas & Parr, visit www.jellymongers.co.uk.

172 **We live in a cluttered world of too much information and too much stuff**

We consume the equivalent of 174 newspapers' worth of information every day, according to University of Southern California researcher Dr. Martin Hilbert, as reported in Richard Alleyn, "Welcome to the Information Age—174 Newspapers a Day," *Daily Telegraph,* February 11, 2011.

Chapter 14. Can You Be an Experientialist and Still Love Stuff?

174 **consumer spending makes up around 65 percent of the British and 70 percent of the U.S. economy**

Martin Wolf, "Britain Must Fix Its Banks—Not Its Monetary Policy," *Financial Times,* June 6, 2013; Hale Stewart, "Consumer Spending and the Economy," FiveThirtyEight, *New York Times,* September 19, 2010.

175 **the captains of consciousness turned consuming into a patriotic act**
Havas Worldwide Prosumer Report, *The New Consumer and the Shar-ing Economy,* 2014, which reports that 58 percent of respondents believe that "buying products is a patriotic act; it helps my nation's economy."

178 **the experience economy**
This section—and much of the discussion about the experience econ-omy—is inspired and informed by B. Joseph Pine II and James H. Gil-more, *The Experience Economy* (Boston: Harvard Business School Press, 1999); and B. Joseph Pine II and James H. Gilmore, *The Experience Economy Updated Edition* (Boston: Harvard Business School Press, 2011). For a quick introduction to the subject, read B. Joseph Pine II and James H. Gilmore, "Welcome to the Experience Economy," *Harvard Business Review,* July 1998.

180 **Fabien Riggall once boasted about getting people to pay £50 each to see a film**
Nick Curtis, "Secret Cinema: How to Get 25,000 People to Pay £50 for a Film Ticket, Without Knowing What the Film Is," *Evening Standard,* December 7, 2012. For more on Secret Cinema, visit www.secretcinema .org.

180 **Graham Hill**
See Graham Hill's work at TreeHugger.com, his new company Life Edited at www.lifeedited.com, and www.ted.com for his talks.

183 **Colin Wright**
Follow Colin Wright at www.exilelifestyle.com.

183 **"consumer minimalists" are interested in quality**
Consider Emily Sheffield, "How We Shop Now," *British Vogue,* February 2013. Sheffield writes that "a fashion consultant called Anita Borzsyz-kowska says: 'So I am actually spending more per item, but there are fewer buys.'" And Sheffield quotes a report from high-net-worth con-sumer specialist Ledbury Research, which points to "consumers adopt-ing a 'less is more' mentality. So they are focusing more on quality and good experiences than 'look at me' purchases."

188 **"experiential products"**
Darwin Guevarra and Ryan Howell, "To Have in Order to Do: Exploring the Effects of Consuming Experiential Products on Well-being," *Journal of Consumer Psychology,* July 24, 2014.
More on TOMS Shoes: www.toms.com.
Watch Puma's Clever Little Shopper disappear on YouTube.
Stay with Airbnb: www.airbnb.com.

Rent a car from Zipcar: www.zipcar.com.

Get your music from Spotify: www.spotify.com.

More on the Common Threads Partnership between eBay and Patagonia: www.patagonia.com/us/common-threads.

More on OAT Shoes: www.oatshoes.com.

191 **e-readers**

Further reading on the pros and cons of e-readers: Emma Ritch, "The Environmental Impact of Amazon's Kindle," *Cleantech*, 2009; Brian Palmer, "Green Your Notes! Is Taking Notes on a Notepad or an iPad More Environmentally Responsible?," *Slate*, September 6, 2011; Alex Pasternack, "The Environmental Costs (and Benefits) of Our Cell Phones," TreeHugger.com, September 3, 2009; Lucy Siegle, "Should I Stop Buying Paper Books and Use an e-Reader Instead?," *The Observer*, January 6, 2013.

191 **"remanufacturing"**

For more on remanufacuring, read "In Depth—Mobile Phones," Ellen Macarthur Foundation, August 2, 2012; and Steve Statham, "Remanufacturing Towards a More Sustainable Future," Wolfson School of Mechanical and Manufacturing Engineering, Loughborough University, 2006.

192 **every shared car takes up to thirteen others off the road**

The principal reason for this is that one-car households become car-less. Sources: Steven Jones, "Does Carsharing Really Reduce Overall Driving?," *San Francisco Bay Guardian,* May 23, 2014; and Elliot Martin, Susan A. Shaheen, and Jeffrey Lidicker, "Impact of Carsharing on Household Vehicle Holdings," *Transportation Research Record: Journal of the Transportation Research Board*, No. 2143, Transportation Research Board of the National Academies, Washington, DC, 2010, pp. 150–58.

192 **"You feel like you're in the car with a friend"**

Drew Olanoff, "Lyft's Focus on Community and the Story Behind the Pink Mustache," *TechCrunch*, September 17, 2012.

193 **BMW . . . is aiming for more than a million members, in Germany alone, for its DriveNow car share service by 2020**

Tom Phillips, "BMW DriveNow Car Sharing Scheme," *Auto Express*, March 23, 2011.

193 **Airbnb**

Airbnb is having what commentators call "hockey stick growth"—which means it's growing very, very quickly. Launched in 2007, it facilitated three million guest stays in 2012, and six million in 2013. Ryan Lawler, "Airbnb Tops 10 Million Guest Stays Since Launch, Now Has 550,000 Properties Listed Worldwide," *TechCrunch*, December 19, 2013.

193 **Living in an Experiential World**

When reading this forecast, remember what I said before, way back in Chapter 2, about how cultural forecasting works: that you should think of a forecast less as a fact, and more as a road map. So rather than paint an exact picture of what the world will be like, this chapter contains an outline of what is to come. In this sketch, you will no doubt recognize things that are happening today. And so you should: the future, remember, is already here. It is by noting what the innovative few are doing today that we can see what the many in the mainstream will be doing tomorrow. Also bear in mind that I do not expect these changes to happen overnight. Historians may well one day look back and call this a revolution, but to you and me it will feel more like evolution. And while cultural evolution may be far faster than physical evolution, it still takes place over decades, not days.

193 **Madonna was . . . personifying the idea that defined the era: materialism**

Was the song pro-materialism? Madonna has sometimes claimed it was not—although she once admitted that she was "attracted to men who have material things because that's what pays the rent and buys you furs." Source: Christopher Feldman, *Billboard Book of Number 2 Singles* (New York: Watson-Guptill, 2000). That sounds materialistic to me.

194 **"Meaning is the new money"**

Tammy Erickson, "Meaning Is the New Money," *Harvard Business Review Blog Network*, March 23, 2011.

194 **"B corporations"**

Find out more at www.bcorporation.net.

194 **B Team**

Visit www.bteam.org.

194 **work "as an 'experience' rather than merely a place to go to every day"**

Jeanne Meister, "The Death of the Office: What Happens When the Workspace Is Mobile, On-Demand and All About Networking," *Forbes*, November 6, 2013. Also, Leo Mirani, "Inside Google's New 1-Million-Square-Foot London Office—Three Years Before It's Ready," *Quartz*, November 1, 2013; and "It's (Almost) All About Me—Workplace 2030: Built for Us," Deloitte Australia, July 2013.

195 **There has been a significant trend for these Third Place coworking spaces in recent years**

Adam Vaccaro, "Number of Coworking Spaces Has Skyrocketed in the U.S.," *Inc.*, March 3, 2014; and Alex Williams, "Working Alone, Together," *New York Times*, May 3, 2013.

196 **We will not only tidy up every seven years**

On average, people move every seven years. Rachel Rickard Straus, "The Seven-Year Home Itch! We Fall Out of Love with Property and Start House-Hunting After 7 Years and 4 Months," *Daily Mail*, December 9, 2011.

197 **the thriving experiential travel market**

Source: years of working in the travel business and conversations with people in the travel business, e.g., editor of *Family Traveller* Jane Anderson, and Larry Pimentel, president of Azamara Cruises. Also, see a report by Skift Team + Peak Adventure Travel Group called "The Rise of Experiential Travel," June 2014.

197 **Neal Gorenflo**

To find out more about all the sharing economy ideas Neal Gorenflo mentioned, read the publication he founded, *Shareable* (www.shareable .net). For more on tool libraries, read Cat Johnson, "The Tool Library Movement Gains Steam," *Shareable*, January 29, 2014. For more on Seattle's Beacon Food Forest, visit www.beaconfoodforest.org. For more on food forests generally, read Nina Misuraca Ignaczak, "20 Urban Food Forests from Around the World," *Shareable*, July 28, 2014.

Conclusion. Why You Need Experience More Than Ever

My thinking about the good life and attempt to answer the question "How should we live in order to be happy?" have been inspired by, among other texts, Aristotle, *Nicomachean Ethics*, trans. Terence Irwin (Cambridge: Hackett, 1985).

Appendix. The Way of the Experientialist

213 **Bag-and-Box Method**

To see some images from the time Ryan Nicodemus used the bag-and-box method, visit www.theminimalists.com/21days/day3.

213 **The Month of Minimalism Game**

To read about the month of minimalism game, see www.theminimalists .com/game.

214 **100 Thing Challenge**

Dave Bruno doesn't run his 100 Thing Challenge anymore, but you can read about it here: www.guynameddave.com/about-the-100-thing-challenge. You can still do it on your own or, even better, with a friend.

221 **"flow"**

For more on flow, read Mihaly Csikszentmihalyi, *Flow: The Psychology of Optimal Experience* (New York: Harper Perennial Modern Classics, 2008).

221 **Be Your Own Audience**

As Leaf Van Boven once pointed out to me, "It is very difficult to introspect whether your motivation is intrinsic or extrinsic." One reasonable explanation of this is because it is very hard to admit to ourselves when we are doing something more to impress others than for ourselves. This is another reason why Habit 7—Choose Life, Choose Experience—is so important. By choosing an experience over something material, you are more likely to be doing that thing for intrinsic reasons, so you are therefore gaming your own internal system, and more likely to be happier.

222 **intrinsic motivation**

For more on the importance of intrinsic motivation, read Edward L. Deci and Richard M. Ryan, *Intrinsic Motivation and Self-Determination in Human Behavior* (New York: Springer Science & Business Media, 1985); and visit www.selfdeterminationtheory.org.

Index

Adelaide, 28, 184, 186
Adelman, Ken, 49–50, 241*n*–42*n*
advertising, advertising industry, xv,
    23, 37, 40–41, 42, 55, 170, 195,
    201, 229*n*
    consumerist culture and, 37, 41,
        42, 54, 164
    experiential marketing as
        alternative to, 167–73, 179
Affluenza (James), 27, 231*n*, 237*n*
Age Curve, The (Gronbach), 232*n*
aging population, xxiii, xxiv, xxv,
    165, 206, 231*n*–32*n*, 252*n*
agrarian economy, 179
Ahmed, Swarnali, 232*n*–33*n*
Airbnb, 192, 193, 261*n*–62*n*

"allostatic load," 13–14
Andaz hotel chain, 171, 172
Anti-Paparazzi Laws, 49
anxiety:
    experientialism and, 132, 133–34,
        135, 205, 225
    materialism and, xiv, xxi, xxii,
        xxx, 24, 26, 61, 161–62, 204,
        224
    "status," *see* status anxiety
Apple, 110, 190–91
Aristotle, 263*n*
Arlidge, John, 253*n*
Arnold, Jeanne, 3–6, 7, 8, 11,
    234*n*
Austin, Thomas, 51, 52

Australia, 9, 20–21, 51–52, 68, 115, 150, 184, 185, 186, 197
  rabbit colonies in, 51–52
  well-being measures in, 155, 156, 157, 158

Babauta, Leo, 64, 68
bag-and-box experiment, ix–x, xiii, xiv, 63, 67, 68, 71, 213, 263*n*
Bali, 119, 121
Bangkok, 181
Barcelona, 28, 180–81, 182, 197, 220
Beacon Food Forest, 197
Beagle, The (ship), 43
Becker, Joshua, 68
Beijing, xxvi, 160, 161, 162
Belgium, xv, 197
Bellaiche, Jean-Marc, 143
Bellini, James, 242*n*
benefit corporations (B corporations), 194
Bentham, Jeremy, 24–25
Betamax system, 139
Better Life Index, 156
Billings, C. K. G., 249*n*
Blair, Tony, 145, 175, 254*n*
blogs, bloggers, 54, 55, 64, 68, 71, 86, 214, 222, 243*n*
BMW, xxiv, 130, 187, 192
  Drivenow car-sharing service of, 192–93
Bolivia, 118, 156
Bompas, Sam, 169, 171–72, 173
Bompas & Parr, 171–72, 178, 193
  "experiential dinner" event of, 168–69, 170–71, 179
Boomer Consumer (Thornhill), 232*n*

Borzsyzkowska, Anita, 260*n*
Boston Consulting Group, 143
Branson, Richard, 194
Brazil, 24, 161
Brewster's Millions game, 215–16, 227
Bruno, Dave, 64, 214
Burns, Arthur F., 254*n*
Bush, George W., 145, 175, 254*n*

Cage Free Family (blog), 86
California, xxix, 4, 28, 49, 50, 59, 60, 125, 219
California, University of, at Los Angeles (UCLA), 3, 4, 11
California Coastal Records Project, 50
Calkins, Earnest Elmo, 40–42, 240*n*
Canada, 68, 155, 156
Canadian Index of Wellbeing (CIW), 156
Cantwell, Marianne, 113–16, 120, 121, 125, 128, 195, 218, 220, 225
capitalism, xxiv, xxvi, 43, 45, 47, 73–74, 96, 179, 187
  Kitchen Debate (1959) on, 45–47, 241*n*
car-sharing services, 191–93, 197
Carson, Rachel, 23, 24, 235*n*
Carver, Courtney, 67, 68, 71, 213, 214
Casablanca, 177, 178, 180
Center on the Everyday Lives of Families (CELF) project, 3–4, 5–9, 11, 20, 112, 200
  measuring of clutter and stress in, 11–14
Channel Islands, 4–5

Cheryl (Tammy's friend), 59–60, 63
China, 30, 163–66, 258n, 259n
  pollution in, 165, 258n, 259n
  rise of conspicuous consumption
    in, 160–62, 163–65, 259n
  rise of experientialism in,
    165–66, 258n
Chumash tribe, 4–5, 11
Church, 39, 202, 203
cities, move to, xxiii, xxiv, xxv,
    129–30, 138, 143, 165, 233n
Clever Little Shopper, 189
climate change, xxiii, 24, 153
clothes, xvi–xvii, xx, 25, 28, 60, 70,
    103, 113–14, 124, 125, 142, 160,
    161, 186–87, 213, 214, 230n
  growing consumption of, 70–71,
    85, 142
  renting of, 143, 192
clutter, xvi, xvii, xxii, 10–14, 104,
    172, 235n
  CELF project's measuring of
    stress and, 11–14
  experientialism in reducing of,
    137–38, 186, 188, 189, 190,
    191, 192, 205, 206, 207
  as health "crisis," xxiii, 6, 9–11,
    13–14, 231n, 259n
  hoarding and, 15, 17–21, 236n
  mental-health hazards of, 10,
    13–14, 20, 104, 108, 137
  physical dangers of, 15, 17,
    20–21, 236n
collaborative consumption, 143,
    191–93, 196, 197, 206,
    261n–62n, 263n
Collyer, Langley and Homer, 18
Comfort of Things, The (Miller),
    244n

communism, 47
  capitalism vs., 45–47
Conduct of Inquiry, The (Kaplan),
    150
Congress, U.S., 147
conspicuous consumption, 41–42,
    44, 47, 64, 85–86, 89, 109, 125,
    126–28, 129, 130, 132, 193,
    224, 225, 245n
  engineering of, 41–42, 43–44,
    53–54, 70, 85, 95, 164, 165,
    175, 203, 240n
  in experientialism, 128–29, 184,
    250n
  global spread of, 160–63, 164,
    165, 259n
  see also materialism; throwaway
    culture
consumerism, consumerist culture,
    xxiv, xxvi, 9, 10, 24, 25, 47,
    69–71, 73, 97, 109, 119, 127,
    132, 140, 174, 201, 226,
    237n
  advertising role in, 37, 41, 42, 54,
    164
  "captains of consciousness" as
    engineers of, 40, 41–42, 43–44,
    54, 70, 85, 92, 95, 164, 165,
    175, 203, 240n
  continuous growth in, 70–71, 85,
    142
  creation and rise of, 37–44,
    53–54, 70, 85, 95, 163, 164,
    165, 175, 203–4, 206, 240n
  economic arguments in favor of,
    39–40, 47–48, 95, 174–75
  experience economy as
    alternative to, see experience
    economy

consumerism, consumerist culture
(*cont.*)
luxury market in, 143, 164,
165–66, 206, 258*n*
mass-produced goods in, 26, 27,
42, 54, 89, 153, 163, 164, 203
material saturation/"peak stuff"
reached in, 9, 142, 166, 172,
232*n*
overproduction and rise of,
37–40, 41, 53–54, 163, 164,
166, 203, 206
as "patriotic act," 145, 175, 260*n*
rising standards of living in,
xxvi, 44, 47–48, 70, 95, 161,
162, 165, 205, 226
simple living vs., 84, 85–86
"use and discard" mentality in,
41, 42, 43, 44
see also materialism
consumer minimalists, 182–84,
260*n*
cortisol levels, 11, 12–13
Council of Economic Advisers, 147,
157, 254*n*
credit, consumer, 42, 165
Csikszentmihalyi, Mihaly, 135
Cummins, Bob, 150, 155, 158

Darwin, Charles, 43
Davis, James J., 38
de Botton, Alain, xxiii, 131,
231*n*
debt, xii, 14, 25, 27, 61, 98
minimalism and alleviation of,
62, 63, 67, 98
De Pree, Dirk Jan "D. J.," 109
depression, 76
FOMO and, 134

materialism and, xii, xxi, xxx,
12, 13, 14, 24, 26–27, 231*n*
rapid increase in, 26–27
"de-Stuffocation," xvi, 27, 141,
213–15
downsizing in, 61–63, 65, 67,
77–78, 117, 119, 141, 182, 183,
213–14; *see also* minimalism,
minimalists
medium chill approach to,
88–99
simple-living approach to, *see*
simple living
technology in enabling of, xxiv,
xxv, 69, 143, 190–91, 204, 206,
233*n*
"Did you miss it?" game, 67, 71,
213
diffusion of innovations, 31–34,
141, 195
Diffusion of Innovations
(Rogers), 31
Diogenes of Sinope, 80
Dunn, Elizabeth, xxiv, 105

Easterlin, Richard, 24, 103–4, 150,
165, 236–37*n*
eating habits, 76–77
evolutionary psychology and,
xix–xx, xxi, 28
simple living's impact on, 84, 87
eBay, xiii, 124, 189
ebooks, 143, 190, 191, 206, 233*n*
e-commerce, 165, 258*n*
economy, economists, xxv, 24, 142,
143, 149, 164, 232*n*–33*n*, 237*n*,
258*n*, 260*n*
consumer production as goal of,
147, 174, 254*n*

experience, *see* experience economy

experientialism as potentially damaging of, 174–75

experientialism's contributions to, 184, 187, 188, 193, 252*n*

GDP and, xxviii, 143, 145–47, 149–52, 154, 155, 157, 205, 232*n*, 254*n*

growing governmental role of, 146, 147, 157

national income accounts and, 142, 146–47, 155, 157, 158, 159

overproduction and, 37–39, 41, 53–54, 163–64, 166, 206, 257*n*

as predicated on growth, 174, 176

see also consumerism, consumerist culture

Egypt, 5, 55

Elgin, Duane, 80, 84–85

England, 51, 82, 122

environmental degradation, 89, 153, 162, 191, 233*n*

in China, 165, 258*n*, 259*n*

experientialism in reducing of, 137, 188, 190, 191, 197, 207, 225

gadgets in reducing of, 190–91

materialism and, xv, xxiii, xxv, xxvii, xxx, 23–24, 25, 28, 162, 204, 258*n*

minimalism in reducing of, 69

environmentalism, 50

Escape the City, 125

Escape the Room, 197

evolutionary psychology:

eating habits and, xix–xx, xxi, 28

expressing status and "fitness markers" in, 47, 66, 72, 127–28, 241*n*, 244*n*

materialistic impulses and, xx, xxi, xxii, xxiii, 47, 72–73, 127–28, 229*n*, 244*n*

experience economy, 143, 165–66, 167–73, 177–80, 188–93, 194–98, 206, 260*n*

collaborative consumption/ sharing services in, 143, 191–93, 196, 197, 206, 261*n*–62*n*, 263*n*

corporate examples of shifting to, 189–91

corporate workplaces in, 194–96, 197

ecological benefits of, 188, 190–91

free-time changes in, 196–97

marketing in, 167–73, 179, 189

rapid growth of, 179, 206

Secret Cinema events in, 124, 177–78, 180

experiences, xxiv, xxviii, 98–99, 112, 115, 120, 124, 174, 184–87, 201, 207, 225–27, 264*n*

aging population's heightened interest in, 206, 231*n*–32*n*, 252*n*

difficulty in comparing of, 106–7, 108, 135

family time and, 79, 91, 94, 98, 99, 119, 223–24

identity expressed in, xxviii, 107, 108, 135, 144, 204, 217, 226

material goods vs., in fostering happiness, xxvii, xxx, 98, 99, 103, 104–8, 116, 131, 132–33, 134–37, 197, 202, 204, 205, 218, 225, 226, 232*n*, 264*n*

experiences (*cont.*)
  material objects in providing of,
    104, 137, 186–87, 188, 219
  medium-chill and, 91, 93,
    97–98, 99
  minimalism and, 98–99, 182,
    184
  money increasingly spent on,
    125, 252*n*
  "positive reinterpretation" in,
    106, 108, 134, 156
  simple living and, 78–79, 98, 99
  social media as increasing social
    capital value of, 130–32, 140,
    206, 250*n*
  social unity and community
    fostered by, 107–8, 135, 137,
    188, 192, 197, 205, 215, 217
  as status markers, 128, 129–31,
    132, 134, 135, 136–37, 144,
    173, 188–89, 204, 205, 207,
    215, 217, 226, 250*n*
  travel and, 78–79, 115, 117–19,
    122–23, 137, 181–82, 186, 220,
    221–22, 252*n*
"experiential dinner" events,
    168–69, 170–71, 179
experientialism, experientialists,
    xxvii–xxix, xxx, 99, 108,
    112–13, 115–25, 128–44, 176,
    184–98, 200, 201, 205, 212
  Brewster's Millions game in,
    215–16, 227
  China and rise of, 165–66, 258*n*
  city living as conducive of, 138,
    143
  clutter reduction in, 137–38, 186,
    188, 189, 190, 191, 192, 205,
    206, 207
  conspicuous living in, 128–29,
    184, 250*n*
  drawbacks of, 132–34, 135
  ecological benefits of, 137, 188,
    190, 191, 197, 207, 225
  economic contributions of, 184,
    187, 193, 252*n*
  experiential marketing as
    fostering transition to, 173
  in families, 116–19
  FOMO in, 132, 133–34, 135
  forecasting mainstream viability
    of, 140–41
  global benefits of, 137–39
  gradual shift from materialism
    to, xxvii–xxix, 137, 141–44,
    157, 159, 165–66, 173, 188–94,
    195, 196, 206–7, 217,
    231*n*–32*n*, 250*n*, 258*n*
  growing movement in, 124–25,
    141–44
  highly effective, 7 habits of,
    217–27, 264*n*
  hippie culture vs., 120–21
  as "hippies with calculators,"
    121, 124, 125, 137, 219
  luxury market in, 143, 165–66,
    258*n*
  mainstream culture as not
    abandoned in, 115, 120, 121,
    124–25, 187, 195, 219, 220
  material objects as not
    completely rejected in, 115,
    120, 121, 137, 183, 186–87,
    188, 191–93, 219, 224–25
  physical health benefits of, 197,
    205, 221
  potential economic drawbacks
    of, 174–75

principles to live by in, 220–23

quiz on, xxx–xxxiii

redefining success in, xxix, 113, 116, 122, 138, 194, 205, 207, 219

smarter spending shortcuts in, 223–27

status anxiety in, 132, 133–34, 135, 137, 188–89

three steps to, 213–14

tools to analyze your life with, 218–20

see also medium chill; minimalism, minimalists; simple living

experiential products, 188, 219, 224–25

extrinsic motivations, 135–37, 223, 226, 264*n*

Fable of the Bees, The: or, Private Vices, Public Benefits (Mandeville), 39, 175

Facebook, 55, 125, 128, 129, 130, 136, 138, 144, 206, 216

FOMO facilitated by, 132, 133–34, 135

Ferguson, Niall, 259*n*

Ferriss, Tim, 124

fibromyalgia, 76–77, 79, 221

Fifty Shades of Grey (James), 54

fires, 14–17, 20–21, 236*n*

Fisher, Eve, xx, 230*n*

"fitness markers," 66, 72, 127, 128, 207, 244*n*

flashover, 20–21

Florida, Richard, 138

"flow," 135, 137, 205, 221

Fogel, Robert, 142, 143, 146

FOMO (fear of missing out), 132, 133–34, 135, 137, 250*n*

Fontenelle, Bernard Le Bovier de, 152

Forbes, Malcolm, 231*n*–32*n*

Ford, Henry, 44, 109, 240*n*

forecasting, cultural, xxiv, 29–34, 141–42, 233*n*, 262*n*

"diffusion of innovations" model in, 31–34, 141, 195

on evolving Chinese lifestyle, 163–66

gradual shift to experientialism shown in, xxvii–xxix, 141–44, 165–66, 188, 189–94, 195, 196, 206–7, 217

knowledge of past used in, 30–31, 163–64

on medium chill's mainstream viability, 94, 95–97, 247*n*

on minimalism's mainstream viability, 69–74, 97

Fortune, 80–81

4-Hour Workweek, The (Ferriss), 124

France, xv, 9, 68, 94, 126, 142, 154–55, 178, 249*n*

Frederick, Christine, 44, 175

French Polynesia, 122–23

Frost, Randy, 18, 19

Fry, Tam, xviii, 229*n*

Gastro (French bistro), 117, 119, 121, 220, 249*n*

Germany, 9, 28, 147, 155, 253*n*

Gibson, William, 29

Gilmore, James H., 178–79, 188–89, 260*n*

Gilovich, Tom, xxiv, xxvii, 104–5,
     232*n*
Gladwell, Malcolm, 238*n*
Goodall, Chris, 206
Google, 55, 90, 194
Google+, 60, 216
Gorenflo, Neal, 197, 263*n*
Graesch, Anthony P., 234*n*
Grand Budapest Hotel, The,
     180
Great Britain, 9, 26, 51, 142, 145,
     174, 259*n*
  growing consumption in,
     70–71
  National Obesity Forum of,
     xviii
Great Depression, 146, 147
Great Recession (2008), 154
Grist.org (website), 89, 90, 93
gross domestic product (GDP),
     xxviii, 143, 145–47, 149–52,
     154, 156, 157, 159, 205, 232*n*
  and alternative measures of
     progress, 151–52, 155,
     156–59
  as measure of social progress,
     147, 149–52, 154, 155, 157,
     158, 254*n*
  quality of life overlooked in, 151,
     154, 155
  simplicity of, 150–51, 157
  unintended consequences in
     measuring of, 146–47, 149
Gross National Happiness (GNH),
     156

happiness, xxiv, 24–26, 60, 65, 88,
     103–4, 120, 121, 123, 138, 165,
     183, 200, 202–3, 206–7, 215
  experiences vs. material goods in
     fostering of, xxvii, xxx, 98, 99,
     103, 104–8, 116, 131, 132–33,
     134–37, 197, 202, 204, 205,
     218, 225, 226, 232*n*, 264*n*
  "flow" and, 135, 147, 205, 221
  intrinsic vs. extrinsic motivations
     in, 135–37, 205, 222, 226, 264*n*
  materialism's fleeting effect on,
     60, 92, 106, 108
  materialism's negative effect on,
     xii, xxi, xxx, 12, 13, 14, 24,
     26–27, 61, 104, 105, 108, 231*n*
  materialist equation for, xi–xii,
     xiv, xxiv, xxvi, xxvii, 25, 70,
     92, 103–4, 150
  minimalism and, xiii, xiv, 63,
     67, 98
  national well-being measures of,
     151–52, 155–59
  social media's damaging effect
     on, 132, 133–34, 135
Harris, Jeff, 76, 77, 79, 83–84, 86,
     125, 195, 220
Harris, Quinn and Nichola, 77,
     78, 79
Harvard Business Review, 178–79,
     194
Havas Worldwide, 229*n*, 260*n*
health care, xxvi, 142, 143, 154,
     155, 206, 253*n*
hedonic adaptation, 106, 108
Hendrick's gin, 171, 172
Herman Miller (furniture maker),
     109, 110
Highbury Fields (London), 114, 115
Hill, Graham, 180–83, 184, 188,
     196, 220, 225
hippies, 120, 121, 123

hoarders, hoarding, 15, 17–21, 236*n*
  causes of, 18–19
  continuum of, 19–20
Hodges, Cliff, 110–13, 120, 121,
    128, 218, 219, 220, 222, 223,
    225
Hodges, Don, 110–12
Holy Mountain, The (film), 169
home-sharing services, 192, 193,
    196, 261*n*–62*n*
Hoover, Herbert, 37, 39
Howell, Ben, 185–87, 188, 219, 225
Howell, Ryan, xxiv, xxvii, 105, 188
Howell, Sarah, 184–85, 186, 187,
    188, 219

IBM, 200
India, 24, 122, 161, 165, 181
Indicators of Well-being in Canada
    (WIC), 156
Indonesia, 119, 161, 165
Industrial Revolution, xx, 53, 54,
    84, 95, 163, 203, 246*n*, 257*n*
  unintended consequences of,
    53, 54
industrial revolutions, 28, 43, 259*n*
Inglehart, Ronald, xv, xxiii, 141–42,
    165, 206
Instagram, 129, 130, 131, 206
International Monetary Fund
    (IMF), 147, 157, 164, 257*n*
Internet, 33, 54–56, 86, 89, 121,
    154, 181
  minimalist community on,
    55–56, 64, 68, 71, 214, 243*n*
  revolutionary impact of, 54 55
  see also social media
intrinsic motivations, 135, 136, 205,
    223, 226, 264*n*

Iran, 55, 123, 221
Ireland, 68, 124, 143, 165, 252*n*,
    258*n*
"Is This the BRICs [Brazil, Russia,
    India, China] Decade?"
    (Wilson, Kelston, and Ahmed),
    232*n*–33*n*
Italy, xv, 115

James, Oliver, xxiii, 25, 27, 231*n*,
    237*n*
Japan, 9, 47, 111, 186
Johnson, Samuel, 82
Joyless Economy, The
    (Scitovsky), 25
JVC, 139

Kahneman, Daniel, 155, 256*n*
Kaplan, Abraham, 150
Kasser, Tim, xxiv, 139–40
Keeping Up with the Joneses
    (comic strip), 127
Kellogg, W. K., 39
Kelston, Alex L., 232*n*–33*n*
Kennedy, James, 252*n*
Kennedy, Robert, 255*n*
Keynes, John Maynard, 39
Khrushchev, Nikita, xxix, 45–47
Kim, Jim Yong, 48
Kitchen Debate (1959), 45–47, 241*n*
Krispy Kreme, xviii–xix, xxii, 33,
    85, 229*n*, 230*n*
Kuznets, Simon, 146, 157–58, 255*n*

law of unintended consequences,
    50 53, 54 56, 108, 159, 173,
    198, 204
  Australian rabbit colonies and,
    51–52

law of unintended consequences
(*cont.*)
GDP measurements and, 146–47,
149
simple living and, 83–84
Streisand effect and, 49–50,
52, 56
Lenet, Anton, 117, 118, 119
Lenet, Bertrand, 116–19, 120–21,
125, 128, 156, 174, 220, 221,
223–24, 249*n*
Lenet, Jude, 117, 119
Lenet, Solen, 117, 118, 119
Lenet, Sue, 116–19, 120–21, 128,
156, 174, 221, 223
LeVally, Aimée, 75–79, 82–84, 86,
97–98
fibromyalgia of, 76–77, 79, 221
LeVally, Ren, 76, 78
*Life at Home in the Twenty-first
Century* (CELF report), 9
Liu Dandan, 160–61, 166
London, xv, 33, 82, 113, 114, 115,
116, 119, 121, 122, 125, 167,
170, 171, 199, 210, 244*n*, 249*n*
Secret Cinema events in, 177–78,
180
Los Angeles, Calif., xv, xxix, 4, 9,
183
Lothian and Borders police, xviii
Louis Vuitton, 130, 160, 170, 172
Lu, Richard, 161, 166
Luddites, 176
luxury consumers, 143, 164,
165–66, 206, 258*n*
Lyft, 192, 193, 197

Machu Picchu, 117–18
Mad Men (TV show), 22–23

Madonna, 193, 262*n*
Mandeville, Bernard, 39–40, 175
manufacturing economy, 38, 41, 42,
179
marketing, experiential, 167–73,
179, 189
Marrakech, 122, 129
Marwick, Alice, 125, 183, 184
Maryland, 155, 194
Maslow, Abraham, 231*n*
Massachusetts Institute of
Technology (MIT), 110, 112
mass-produced goods, 26, 27, 42,
54, 89, 153, 163, 164, 203 ,
materialism, x, xii, xxiv,
xxvi–xxvii, xxviii, 24–27, 28,
34, 47, 48, 53, 55, 67, 73, 84,
89, 91, 96, 103–4, 113–14, 119,
120, 124, 126–28, 140, 146,
150, 154, 166, 174, 176, 198,
200, 201, 203, 205, 206, 215,
218, 226, 237*n*, 262*n*
anxiety and stress caused by, xii,
xiv, xxi, xxii, xxiii, xxv, xxx,
13–14, 24, 26, 27, 61, 104,
108, 132, 161–62, 204, 224,
231*n*
benefits and upside of, 71–73,
175, 244*n*
CELF research project on, 3–4,
5–9, 11, 20, 200
compromising simple life with,
86–87, 88
ecological impact of, xv, xxiii,
xxv, xxvii, xxx, 23–24, 25, 28,
162, 204, 258*n*
evolutionary psychology of, xx,
xxi, xxii, xxiii, 47, 72–73,
127–28, 229*n*, 244*n*

experiences vs., in fostering happiness, xxvii, xxx, 98, 99, 103, 104–8, 116, 131, 132–33, 134–37, 197, 202, 204, 205, 218, 225, 226, 232n, 264n

experientialism as incomplete rejection of, 115, 120, 121, 137, 183, 186–87, 188, 191–93, 219, 224–25

financial issues caused by, xii, 14, 25, 27, 61, 98

GDP as measuring of, 152, 155, 157, 158, 159

global spread of, 160–63, 164, 165, 198

gradual shift to experientialism from, xxvii–xxix, 141–44, 157, 159, 165–66, 173, 188–94, 195, 196, 197, 206–7, 217, 231n–32n, 250n, 252n, 258n

growing disillusionment with, xv–xvi, xxii–xxvi, xxvii, xxviii–xxix, 80–81, 124, 125, 141–44, 165–66, 172–73, 193–94, 206, 231n–32n, 252n

happiness equation in, xi–xii, xiv, xxiv, xxvi, xxvii, 25, 70, 92, 103–4, 150

happiness negatively affected by, xii, xxi, xxx, 12, 13, 14, 24, 26–27, 61, 104, 105, 108, 231n

"hedonic adaptation" in, 106, 108

identities expressed in, xxvi, xxvii, 25, 72–73, 226

paradox of, 25, 26, 44, 175

post-materialist alternatives to, *see* experientialism, experientialists; medium chill; minimalism, minimalists; simple living

status markers in, xxvi, xxvii, 25, 26, 66, 70, 72, 81, 85, 127, 128, 130, 131, 132–33, 138, 200, 203, 226

unintended consequences of, 25, 53, 108, 204

see also conspicuous consumption; consumerism, consumerist culture; Stuffocation

Measures of Australia's Progress (MAP), 156

medium chill, 88–99, 205

experiences emphasized over materialism in, 91, 93, 97–98, 99

forecasting mainstream viability of, 94, 95–97, 247n

Megachange (Andrews and Franklin), 232n

Mei-Pochtler, Antonella, 143

Melbourne, 20–21

Merton, Robert, 52

middle class, 200

"clutter crisis" in, xxiii, 6, 9–11, 13–14, 259n

global, rise of, xxiii, xxiv, xxv, 137, 161, 162, 165, 232n–33n

Milkman, Ruth, xxiii–xxiv, 138

Millburn, Joshua Fields, xi–xiii, xiv, 14, 20, 65, 68, 71, 92, 98, 214, 218, 228n

Miller, Geoffrey, 94–95

minimalism, minimalists, xiii, 61–74, 89, 96, 98, 185, 204–5

bag-and-box experiment in, ix–x, xiii, xiv, 63, 67, 68, 71, 213, 263n

"consumer," 182–84, 260n

minimalism, minimalists (*cont.*)
  "did you miss it?" game in, 67,
    71, 213
  economic contributions of, 184,
    260*n*
  environmental benefits of, 69
  experiences emphasized over
    materialism in, 98–99, 180,
    184
  experientialism vs., 112–13
  experimental trials in, ix–x, xiii,
    xiv, 62, 63, 64, 67, 68, 71,
    213–14, 263*n*–64*n*
  financial benefits of, 62, 63,
    67, 98
  forecasting mainstream viability
    of, 69–74, 97
  happiness and, xiii, xiv, 63, 67, 98
  materialism vs., xiv, 63, 72, 73
  mental-health benefits of, 62, 67
  obsession with counting in,
    63–65, 66, 67, 71, 80
  100 Things Challenge in, 64, 214,
    264*n*
  online community in, 55–56, 64,
    68, 71, 214, 243*n*
  physical-health benefits of, 62,
    67–68
  rules of counting in, 64–65, 66
  status markers in, 63, 64,
    66–67, 71
*Mismeasuring Our Lives: Why GDP
    Doesn't Add Up* (Fitoussi, Sen,
    and Stiglitz), 155
Momand, Arthur Ragland "Pop,"
    127
Monroe, Marilyn, 193
month of minimalism game,
    213–14, 263*n*

Monty Python's Life of Brian,
    148–49
Morialta Falls, 184, 185
Mourey, Jenna (Jenna Marbles), 54,
    242*n*

national income accounts, 142,
    146–47, 155, 157, 159
  as faulty measure of social
    progress, 147, 158
natural selection, 43
Neighborhood Goods, 192
Nelson, George, 110
Netflix, 143, 192
Netherlands, xv, 68, 190
New Consumer, The (research
    paper), 229*n*, 260*n*
New Mexico, xxix, 75, 78–79,
    82–83, 195, 220
New York, N.Y., xv, 4, 18, 28, 38,
    45, 125, 127, 180, 181, 195, 197
New York Times, 38
Nicodemus, Eric, xi
Nicodemus, Ryan, ix–xiv, xvi,
    xxvii, 14, 20, 68, 92, 112–13,
    214, 228*n*
  bag-and-box experiment of,
    ix–x, xiii, xiv, 63, 67, 68, 71,
    213, 263*n*
  happiness equation of, xi–xii,
    xxvi, 218
Nixon, Richard, xxix, 45–47
nuclear weapons, 45

obesity, xviii, xx–xxii, 28
obsessive compulsive disorder
    (OCD), 18
Occupy movement, xxiv, 55
Ochs, Elinor, 3–4, 5–6, 7, 234*n*

offices, 194–95
  cubicles in, 109–10, 112
Olanoff, Drew, 192
100 Things Challenge, 64, 214,
  264n
organic food, 87
Organisation for Economic
  Co-operation and
  Development (OECD), 156
O'Toole, Garson, 254n
overproduction, 34, 37–39, 41,
  53–54, 163, 203, 206, 257n
  in China, 163–64, 166

Paleolithic tribes, xxix, 94–95
Parr, Harry, 171, 172
Patagonia, 189–90, 191, 193
Peru, 117–18, 221
"Pharma 2020" (PWC report), 253n
Pick-a-Number Challenge, 214
Pine, Joseph, 178–79, 190, 260n
pollution, 153, 165, 204, 258n, 259n
positive reinterpretation, 106, 108,
  134, 156
post-materialism, xv, xxiii,
  xxix–xxx, 28, 34, 65, 115, 165,
  189
  see also experientialism,
    experientialists; medium chill;
    minimalism, minimalists;
    simple living
progress, social, xxviii, 207
  back-and-forth dance of, 152–54,
    198
  GDP as faulty measure of, 147,
    149–52, 154, 155, 157, 158,
    254n
  well-being measures and, 151–52,
    154, 155–59, 205, 206

Proud, Hector, 122
Pryor, Richard, 215
Punchdrunk, 178, 197
  Gypsy event of, 167–68, 170

rabbit colonies, 51–52
rabbit-proof fence, 52
Ranasinghe, Dhara, 164
rarity principle, 130–31
Rent the Runway, 143, 192
Repetti, Rena, 11, 12, 14, 20
retail therapy, xvii, xxxi, 25, 224
reverse-hanger method, 213
Riahi-Belkaoui, Ahmed, 131
Riggall, Fabien, 180
"Rising Middle Class Fuels Global
  Energy Surge" (Wolfram),
  233n
Roberts, David, 89–91, 92–93, 96,
  97–98, 222
Roberts, Jennifer, 89–91, 96, 97–98,
  222
Rogers, Everett, 31–32, 238n
Rolling Stone, 139
Russia, 45–47
Ryan, Richard, 135

Sacramento, Calif., 59, 60
Samuelson, Paul, 147
Sangre de Cristo Mountains,
  xxix, 79
Saporito, Bill, 164
Sarkozy, Nicolas, xxix, 154–55,
  159
Sasplugas, Olga, 180–81, 182, 220
Saulnier, Raymond J., 147, 254n
Saxbe, Darby, xxiii, 10–14, 20, 104
Schwartz, Barry, 157
Scitovsky, Tibor, 25, 26

Scotland, xviii, xix
Seattle, Wash., 89, 197
Secret Cinema, 124, 177–78, 180,
    193
September 11, 2001, terrorist
    attacks of, 145, 175, 254n
service economy, 179
Shareable, 197, 263n
sharing economy, 143, 191–93, 196,
    197, 261n–62n, 263n
Shawshank Redemption, The, 180
Sheen, David, 16
Silent Spring (Carson), 23
Silicon Valley, Calif., 110, 120, 125,
    183–84
Silver, Nate, 238n
simple living, 77–87, 89, 96,
    139–40, 205
  benefits of, 79, 81, 84, 140
  compromised approach to,
    86–87, 88
  consumerist culture vs., 84,
    85–86
  drawbacks in, 81–84, 86, 87
  experiences emphasized over
    materialism in, 78–79, 98, 99
  forecasting mainstream viability
    of, 87, 97
  growing movement in, 80–81
  Thoreau as example of, 80,
    81–82
Sloan, Alfred, 39
Smith, Logan, 60, 61–62, 63,
    67, 68
Smith, Tina, 60, 61
smoking, xxii, 231n
social media, 33, 55, 71, 125, 129,
    136, 138, 140, 153, 183, 184,
    206, 216

experiences as increasing in
    social capital value due to,
    130–32, 140, 206, 250n
  FOMO facilitated by, 132,
    133–34, 135, 137, 250n
  signaling of status on, 129,
    130–32, 133, 136–37, 144
  *see also specific social media sites
    and services*
Social Status Matters (Riahi-
    Belkaoui), 131
Sony, 139
Soviet Union, 45–47
Spotify, 143, 192, 233n
State of the USA (SUSA), 156,
    157
status, status markers, xxix, 97, 99,
    120, 122, 125, 128, 129–32,
    183, 184
  benefits and importance of,
    131–32, 250n
  evolutionary psychology of, 47,
    66, 127–28, 241n, 244n
  experiences as, 128, 129–31, 132,
    134, 135, 136–37, 144, 188–89,
    204, 205, 207, 215, 217, 226,
    250n
  in materialistic culture, xxvi,
    xxvii, 25, 26, 66, 70, 72, 81, 85,
    127, 128, 130, 131, 132–33,
    138, 200, 226
  in minimalist movement, 63, 64,
    66–67, 71
  social media as tool for signaling
    of, 129, 130–32, 133, 136–37,
    144
status anxiety, xxiii, 26, 27, 107,
    132, 161–62, 183, 203, 224,
    231n, 241n

in experientialism, 132, 133–34, 135, 137, 173, 188–89
FOMO as new form of, 132, 133–34, 135, 137, 250n
Status Anxiety (de Botton), 131, 231n
Steketee, Gail, 19, 235n
Stiglitz, Joseph, 155, 159
Story of Stuff, The (online film), xv
streetlight bias, 150
Streisand, Barbra, xxix, 49, 50, 52, 241n–42n
Streisand effect, 50, 52, 56
stress, 62, 91, 137
  CELF study's measuring of clutter and, 11–14
  experientialism as cause of, 132, 133
  materialism as cause of, xii, xxi, xxii, xxiii, xxv, xxx, 13–14, 26, 104, 108, 132, 204
  see also anxiety
Strobel, Tammy, 59–63, 67–68, 98–99, 112, 196, 223, 224
Stuff (Steketee and Frost), 19
Stuffocation, xiv, xvi, xxviii, 25, 27–29, 34, 53, 61, 65, 67, 74, 85, 94, 112, 113, 121–22, 144, 149, 163, 166, 176, 188, 190, 191, 198, 201, 204, 205, 206, 214, 215, 257n
  approaches in combating of, *see* "de-Stuffocation"
  clutter crisis and, xxiii, 6, 9–11, 259n
  demographic factors in, xxiii, xxiv, xxv, 232n, 233n
  economic factors in, xxiv, xxv, 61

mental-health hazards of, xx–xxii, xxiii, xxvii, xxx, 13, 14, 20, 27–28, 61, 108, 224, 231n
  quiz on, xvi–xviii
  reasons for, xxii–xxvi, xxvii, 162, 165, 259n
  and rise of experiential marketing, 172–73
  see also consumerism, consumerist culture; materialism
substitution, 150–51, 155–56
Sweden, 142

Tahiti, 122–23
Taos, N.Mex., 78–79, 82–83
TASS (Soviet news agency), 47
technology, 32, 70, 184, 191, 196
  "de-Stuffocation" enabled by, xxiv, xxv, 69, 143, 190–91, 204, 206, 233n
  experiential workplaces enabled by, 195
TED conferences, 125, 129, 131
Texas, 68, 75, 82, 86, 195
Teyo (Dave Roberts's friend), 90, 91
theater, experiential, 124, 177–78, 180, 193, 197
Theory of the Leisure Class, The (Veblen), 127
Thoreau, Henry David, 80, 81–82
throwaway culture, 41–44, 47, 53, 70, 74, 85–86, 109, 224, 240n
  aesthetic factors in, 42, 44
  evolution of, 43–44
  see also conspicuous consumption
Tickle, Katherine, 114

Time, 81, 164

"To Do or to Have? That Is the Question" (Gilovich and Van Boven), 104–5, 232*n*

Tokyo, 186, 253*n*

Tolle, Eckhart, 135

TOMS (shoe company), 189

Toronto:

St. James Town Community Center in, 14

2010 fire in, 14–17, 20

Toronto Fire Services, 14, 15–17, 21

"Transformer homes," 182

travel, 78–79, 115, 121, 122–23, 130, 137, 180–82, 186, 197, 220, 221–22, 252*n*

negative experiences in, 117–18

see also vacations

TreeHugger.com, 181–82, 220, 225

Tuttle, Mark, 67, 71, 213

Twitter, 55, 129, 130, 131, 133, 138, 144, 206, 216

United Kingdom, xv, xvi, xviii, 18, 24, 68, 115, 143, 150, 229*n*, 252*n*

well-being measures in, 155

United Nations, Human Development Index (HDI) of, 156

United States, 9, 10, 18, 24, 26, 27, 45, 68, 150, 174, 197, 229*n*

creation and rise of consumerist culture in, 37–44, 53–54, 164, 165, 203–4, 206

declining consumption in, 142

declining materialistic values in, xv, xvi, 80–81, 142

growing consumption in, 71, 85

national income accounts adopted in, 146–47, 155, 157, 158, 159

overproduction in, 37–39, 41, 53–54, 163, 164, 203

well-being measures in, 155, 156, 157

vacations, 90, 124, 128–29, 137, 143, 166, 206, 252*n*

Van Boven, Leaf, 104–5, 232*n*, 264*n*

Vassilev, Stephen, 15, 17

Veblen, Thorstein, 126–27

Voluntary Simplicity: Toward a Way of Life That Is Outwardly Simple, Inwardly Rich (Elgin), 80

voluntary simplicity, *see* simple living

Walden; or, Life in the Woods (Thoreau), 81

Walden Pond, 80

Wallman, Alan, 199–201

Wallman, Jack, 199–200, 201–2, 215–16, 227

Wallman, Pam, 199–200, 201

Wansink, Brian "Sherlock," xix, 28

Weissman, Jordan, 253*n*

well-being measures, 151–52, 154, 155–59, 205, 206

benefits of, 158–59, 205

simplicity concerns in, 155–56

Whyte, Jim, 121–24, 128, 174, 221, 225

Wikipedia, 50
Williams, Dee, 62–63
Wilson, Dominic,
    232n–33n
Wolfers, Justin, 237n
Wolfram, Catherine, 233n
World Bank, 48, 164, 229n
World Values Survey, 142
World War I, 38
World War II, 147
Wray, Chris, 68

Wright, Colin, 64, 68, 183
Wright, Robert, 253n

Yau, Nina, 64, 68
YouTube, 242n, 255n

Zappos, 194–95
Zeitz, Jochen, 194
Zhou Zhou, 160–61, 166
Zilok, 192
Zipcar, 143, 191, 233n

About the Author

JAMES WALLMAN is a trend forecaster, journalist, and speaker who has written for *The New York Times, GQ, Fast Company,* and the *Financial Times.* His clients include Absolut, BMW, Burberry, and Nike. He has an MA in classics from Oxford University and an MA in journalism from the University of the Arts London. He has lived in France, Greece, and Palo Alto, California, and currently lives in London with his wife and two children.

stuffocation.org
@JamesWallman

About the Type

This book was set in Sabon, a typeface designed by the well-known German typographer Jan Tschichold (1902–74). Sabon's design is based upon the original letter forms of sixteenth-century French type designer Claude Garamond and was created specifically to be used for three sources: foundry type for hand composition, Linotype, and Monotype. Tschichold named his typeface for the famous Frankfurt typefounder Jacques Sabon (c. 1520–80).